Thomas Haemmerlein
à Kempis

born: Kempen. 1380
died: Swolle. 1471

Thou must be contented for Christ's sake to be esteemed as a fool in this world, if thou desire to lead a religious life

Of the
Imitation of Christ
by Thomas à Kempis

as translated out of Latin by

Richard Whytford

anno mdlvi

Re-edited into modern English with

An Historical Introduction by

Wilfrid Raynal, O.S.B.

Illustrations and designs

by W. Russell Flint

London

Chatto and Windus

mcmviii

The binding of this volume is
adapted from the fine example
of the German style—now No.
I.C. 37028, in the B.M.—dated
Basel, 1475.

A SUMMARY BIBLIOGRAPHICAL NOTE

First Latin Edition *circa* 1486.
First English Version 1503.
First Edition of the present translation 1556.
    Reprinted 1585 and after.
    As re-edited by Dom Raynal 1872.
    New Edition, large crown 8vo, 1908.
    Also a *special edition* in crown 4to, 1908.

Edinburgh : T. and A. CONSTABLE, Printers to His Majesty
The colour-plates engraved in Vienna ; printed by
Henry Stone and Son, Ltd., Banbury

Introduction to the Edition of 1872

RICHARD WHYTFORD's translation of the *Imitatio Christi* is one of the earliest of those published in this country. There can be no doubt that all lovers of archæology would prefer to have the text given exactly as it stands in the original; but as this would have made the book practically useless to many, it has been deemed advisable to modernise the spelling. Though the punctuation has been freely changed, yet the text has been carefully preserved, save where the overcrowding of particles rendered the meaning very obscure.

For the guidance of those who are not well acquainted with the style of the sixteenth century, it may as well be mentioned that certain words were then used in a sense somewhat different from that in which they are at present employed. Thus, *may* is generally used for *can*; *but if* for *unless*; *or* for *before*; and *for* in the sense of *because*. Throughout the book *meekness* invariably expresses *humility*. As these words occur very frequently they are not explained in notes, except where it is necessary to call the reader's attention to them in order to save him the trouble of reading the sentence twice; but some other obsolete words are marked, and the modern meaning is given at the foot of the page.

Introduction to the Edition of 1872

For the sake of those who wish to compare the present edition with the original, several extracts of the edition of 1585 are given in the Appendix, as also portions of Atkynson's translation (1504), and passages from the text of the Countess of Richmond (1503) as it stood before it was corrected by Whytford (1556).

Even if Richard Whytford's work had no literary merit, it would still deserve to be welcomed and adopted by English readers, for none of the many translations published since his day have rendered so forcibly, and yet with such sweet simplicity, the spiritual teachings of the *Imitatio Christi*.

W. RAYNAL.

BELMONT, HEREFORD,
A D 1871.

[*In the present new edition, most of the Biblical
quotations are given in the words of the
Authorised Version.*]

An Historical Introduction

The Following of Christ, more generally, as in the present edition, called *The Imitation of Christ*, was first printed in England in the sixteenth century. The earliest publication consisted merely of the Fourth Book, and was a translation from the French by the mother of Henry VII., Margaret Countess of Richmond and Derby. The work was entrusted to Richard Pynson, the king's printer, and was issued from his press in 1503, and again in 1504.

The title and colophon of the book are given in Lord Orford's *Royal and Noble Authors*,[1] and are not without interest. The title is:

𝔥ere beginethe the forthe boke of the folowinge of 𝔍esu 𝔠ryst, and of the contēpnīge of the world. 𝔍mprinted at the cōmāndement of the most excellent pryncess 𝔐argarete, moder unto our souereyne lorde kinge 𝔥enry the VII. coūtes of 𝔯ichemoūt and 𝔇arby. 𝔄nd by the same pryncess it was translated out of 𝔉renche into 𝔈nglisshe in fourme and maner ensuinge: the yere of our 𝔏ord 𝔊od ml.'d.iiii.

The colophon is as follows:

𝔗hus endeth the forthe boke folowinge 𝔍esu 𝔠ryst, and the contempnynge of the worlde.

[1] Vol i. p 227, *note* Park's edition

An Historical Introduction

That same year a volume came from the press of Wynkyn de Worde, containing the first three books of the *Imitatio Christi*, translated by William Atkynson. As the following title informs us, it was undertaken at the special request of Princess Margaret.

A Devoute and Godely Treatise of ye Imitacion and Folowynge of Cryst, compyld in Laten by John Gerson and translated by Mayster Wyllyam Atkynson, Doctor of Diuynyte: at the speciall Request and Commaundement of ye Pryncesse Margarete, moder of Kynge Henry the VII. and Countesse of Rychemount and Derby.[1]

In 1517 Richard Pynson published the four books in one volume, and later on Thomas Godfray republished it · New examyned, corrected and imprinted. And a lytell deuoute morall Doctryne called the Spirituall Glasse of the Soule.[2]

Before proceeding to speak of Whytford's edition in Queen Mary's time (1556), it will perhaps be interesting to give a short memoir of the pious Countess under whose auspices the *Imitatio Christi* was first given to the people of England in their native tongue.

Margaret was the only child of John Beaufort, Duke of Somerset, and hence was descended from King Edward III. She was thrice married. By her

[1] British Museum, Grenville coll. Also see Lowndes' *Bibliographer's Manual*, art Kempis.
[2] Lowndes, *ibid*.

first marriage with Edmund Tudor, Earl of Richmond, she became the mother of Henry Tudor, who in 1457 succeeded his father in the earldom, and in 1485 became King of England.

The Dowager Countess had for her second husband Sir Henry Stafford, a younger son of Humphrey, Duke of Buckingham. At his death she was united to Thomas Lord Stanley, who on Bosworth Field took the royal crown from the head of the fallen Richard, and, placing it upon the head of his step-son, greeted him as Henry the Seventh. Stanley was soon afterwards made Earl of Derby, and henceforth the royal mother added the name of Derby to that of Richmond.

From her earliest childhood Margaret had been fond of books, and had devoted her time to literary pursuits. The present that most pleased her was some spiritual book or a manual of prayer. Hence the Duchess of Buckingham, her mother-in-law, left her a legacy of pious works, one of which was a beautiful primer, covered with purple velvet, with clasps of silver gilt.[1] Besides the translation of the Fourth Book of the *Imitatio Christi*, the Countess translated and published *The Mirroure of Gold for the sinfull Soule. Emprynted at London, in Flet Strete, at the signe of S. George, by Richard Pynson.* This

---

[1] 'To my daughter of Richmond a book of English called *Legenda Sanctorum*, a book of French called *Lucum*, another book of French of the Epistles and Gospels, and a Primer with clasps of silver gilt, covered with purple velvet'—*Vide* will of Ann Duchess of Buckingham, apud Nicholas's *Testamenta Vetusta*, p. 357.

edition was from a French translation of a work entitled *Speculum aureum Peccatorum*.[1]

The 'Golden Mirror' was also twice published in the year 1522 by Wynkyn de Worde, who informs us in the title that the French translation followed by the Countess had been seen and corrected '*of many clarkis, doctours, and maisters of divinite.*'[2] There can be no doubt that this book was very popular in its day.

Besides her own literary labours, we are indebted to the same noble lady for several spiritual books which were composed or printed at her desire. The best known of the latter is Walter Hilton's *Ladder of Perfection*, which was published in 1494, with a dedication in her honour.

Bishop Fisher, her confessor, has so beautifully drawn her character in the funeral oration he delivered at her death, that we at once recognise in her a humble soul thoroughly imbued with the spirituality of *The Imitation of Christ*.

' She was bounteous and liberal to every person of her knowledge and acquaintance. Avarice and covetise she most hated, and sorrowed it full much in all persons, but specially in any that belonged unto her. She was of singular easiness to be spoken unto, and full-courteous answer she would make to all that came unto her. Of marvellous gentleness she was unto all folks, but specially unto her own, whom she trusted and loved right tenderly. Unkind she

[1] *Royal and Noble Authors*, vol i. p 227. [2] *Ibid*, p. 229.

would not be unto any creature, ne forgetful of any kindness or service done to her before, which is no little part of very nobleness.   She was not vengeable ne cruel, but ready anon to forget and to forgive injuries done unto her, at the least desire or motion made unto her for the same.   Merciful, also piteous, she was unto such as was grieved and wrongfully troubled, and to them that were in poverty or sickness, or any other misery.   She was of singular wisdom, far-passing the common rate of women.   She was good in remembrance, and of holding memory; a ready wit she had also to conceive all things, albeit they were right dark.   Right studious she was in books, which she had in great number, both in English, and in Latin, and in French; and for her exercise and for the profit of others, she did translate divers matters of devotion out of the French into English. In favours, in words, in gesture, in every demeanour of herself, so great nobleness did appear, that what she spake or did it marvellously became her.   She had in a manner all that was praiseable in a woman, either in soul or body.'[1]

In her declining years she spent her days amongst her royal grandchildren, to whom she appears to have been devoted.   'Blessed be God,' she writes from Sheen to the Earl of Ormond, 'the king, the queen, and all our sweet children be in good health.'[2] She lived to see one of these crowned as Henry VIII., but was spared by death (1509) from witnessing the

---

[1] *Royal Authors,* p. 231   [2] *Excerpta Historica,* p 285.

later life of that monarch, and his attacks upon the Church.

Richard Whytford was, in all probability, chaplain to Fox, Bishop of Winchester, when the Countess Margaret departed this life. His birth-place is not known, but as it was the general custom at that time to take the surname from the place of birth, he may be considered a native of Whytford in Flintshire. Richard Whytford his uncle is known to have possessed property in that locality; a fact which shows that the family must have originally come thence. Anthony à Wood tells us that our author was for a short period at Oxford, though there is no record that he took his degree in that university. Nothing save this fact is known of his early history till we find him occupying the post spoken of above. It was in that position that he became acquainted with Sir Thomas More, then a young man, with whom he contracted a truly Christian friendship. As the event that first brought them together not only serves to illustrate the personal character of Whytford, but affords us an insight of his times, it will perhaps repay us to give it at length.

King Henry the Seventh, in the last years of whose reign many private persons were almost ruined by the levy of unjust and exorbitant fines, petitioned Parliament for an impost of a subsidy and three-fifteenths on the occasion of the marriage of his daughter Margaret with James IV. King of Scotland (1501). Owing to the opposition headed by Sir

Thomas More, the motion was rejected by the Commons. This unusual spirit greatly angered the King, whose revengeful nature was doubly stirred when he was told by a courtier that the prime mover of the opposition was but a beardless boy. It would not have served the King's purpose to do violence to the personal liberty of the young burgess, for in those days as in these Englishmen kept strict watch over their parliamentary freedom. Means, however, were speedily discovered to satisfy the royal displeasure. Sir John More, the father of Sir Thomas, was unjustly sentenced to pay a heavy fine, and in default was cast into prison. His son was naturally much grieved at the affliction endured for his sake by an aged father to whom he was deeply attached. He asked the advice of several influential and friendly persons, as to what he had better do to obtain the release of his father. Amongst others he consulted Bishop Fox, who, true to the courtly policy of the English episcopate of that day, advised the youth to acknowledge his fault and beg the King's pardon. This Sir Thomas would gladly have done had not such an act implied a sacrifice of principle, and an avowal of a wrong of which he knew he had never been guilty. His noble heart and delicate conscience instinctively shrank from a line of conduct so contrary to honour and duty. Yet, being unwilling to trust the inexperience of his youthful years, he betook himself to Richard Whytford, the bishop's chaplain. He soon saw that in him he had to deal with a real

An Historical Introduction

spiritual counsellor, and not with an ecclesiastical courtier. Whytford knew too well the weakness of the bishop's mind in all matters that related to the royal power or will, and he perceived at once how ill-advised he had sent away from him the sorrowing youth. Therefore, with all the earnestness of his soul he besought Sir Thomas, for the love of the Passion of Christ, not to follow his lord's advice. This fervent appeal spoke to the heart of the young man; at once all wavering ceased, and he made up his mind to be true to duty. At first he resolved to go over to the Continent in order to avoid further persecution, but afterwards thought it better to conceal himself for a time. During this practical imprisonment he devoted himself to the study of languages and of science, and when at times he felt wearied in mind he used to take up his fiddle, and thus, as his biographer says, '*would recreate his tyred spiritis.*'[1]

The same author, his great-grandson, speaks most reverently of Richard Whytford as '*a verie holie and grave man,*'[2] and says that he afterwards became a Father of Syon, and was the same that translated the *Imitatio Christi.*

This monastery of Saint Saviour of Syon, or, as it was usually called, Syon House, was founded by Henry v. in A.D. 1414, in the manor of Isleworth, in the county of Middlesex, at the special request of his

---

[1] More's *Life of Sir Thomas More*, chap ii.
[2] *Ibid*, p 37.

xiv

chamberlain, Lord Henry Fitzhugh.[1]   The members, as we learn from the charter of foundation,[2] followed the Rule of St. Austin, according to the reform of St. Bridget.   Unlike any other community of that period, Syon House contained a double monastery, one of nuns and another of Regular Canons. The two were entirely separate as regards both jurisdiction and enclosure.   The convent was built and endowed for sixty nuns.   The canons who served the church were seventeen in number, thirteen of whom were priests, and the rest deacons: there were besides eight lay brethren.   The duties of the canons consisted chiefly of the services of the sanctuary, the spiritual direction of the nuns, and a daily solemn Mass for the Founder's intention.   The title of father confessor was borne by their superior, who, though independent of the abbess, was expected to consult the convenience of the sisterhood in the regulation of the services.

'These two convents,' says Weever,[3] 'had but one church in common; the nuns had their church aloft in the roof, and the brethren beneath upon the ground; each convent severally enclosed and never allowed to come out, except by the Pope's special licence.   Upon whom this godly and glorious king (Henry v.) had bestowed sufficient living (taken from the Priors Aliens, all which he utterly sup-

---

[1] *Archæologia*, vol. xvii. p. 326.

[2] Dugdale's *Monasticon Angl.*, Bohn's ed., vol. vi. p. 542.

[3] *Funereal Monuments*, p. 297, ed. 1767, which incorrectly attributes the foundation to Henry I.

pressed), he provided by a law that, contenting themselves therewith, they should take no more of any man,
but what surplus soever remained of their yearly in-
come, they should bestow it upon the poor.'

Such a regulation as this was calculated to sustain
a spirit of holy poverty amongst the members, and
as the community was still in the days of its fervour
when the monasteries were dissolved, we need not be
surprised that Cardinal Pole enumerates the Brigit-
tines amongst those who at the period of the Re-
formation were noted for regular observance.[1] This
commendation of the great Cardinal is in truth a
eulogium on Syon House,[2] since it was the only monastery of that order in England.   Besides, it is a
voucher to us of the singleness of purpose that ani-
mated Richard Whytford, when, having to make a
choice amongst the many monasteries then existing,
he selected one in which there was a spirit of fervour
and strict discipline.   It is not known when he left
the episcopal palace of Winchester, but in all probability it was before the year 1513, for we find that
at that date Thomas Wolsey, afterwards the cele-
brated Cardinal, held the post of chaplain to Bishop
Fox. Two years before the date just given an event
occurred at Syon House which in all likelihood
made Whytford visit that monastery, and may have
led to the step he afterwards took.   This was the

[1] See Lingard, vol. v p 37, *note*, ed 1849

[2] The archæologist will find interesting information connected
with Syon House in vol 1. of *Collectanea Topographica*, as also in *Excerpta Historica*

burial of his uncle, the wealthy clerk, of whom mention was made at the outset, and who in his last days became a Brigittine. It is possible that the nephew had become a member of that order even in the uncle's lifetime, for in 1507, at the request of Dame Elizabeth Gybs, who was lady abbess of the nuns of Syon from 1487 to 1521, he published his first known work, entitled *A daily exercise and experience of Death*. In any case, he must have joined before 1520, as in that year he supplied a conventual need that shows he was no stranger to the wants of his brethren. This was the publication of the Sarum Martyrology *'as it is read at Syon, with additions.'* [1]

The cloistral life of Whytford, from the time of the publication of the Syon Martyrology till the memorable year 1534, when Henry's commissioners came to tender to him and his brethren the oath of supremacy, was one of constant application to the composition or translation of spiritual works, needed either by the sisters or by those who in a secular estate required the help of ascetical teaching. A list of these books was first made by Anthony à Wood, in his *Athenæ Oxonienses*; but as it was imperfect,

[1] Dr Milner mentions a fact regarding this book which is worth noticing, namely, that when, in the early part of this century, some of the nuns of Syon House at Lisbon returned to England, they brought back, among other precious relics, the very copy of this Martyrology which their predecessors had used in the choir in the days of Whytford In this precious volume the chief events of their remarkable history had been recorded, and thus saved from oblivion (*Archæologia*, vol. xvii, ap. i. p. 328). Unfortunately, this and other relics have been lost.

Bliss has added several more. Since these two writers paid no attention to the chronological order of publication, it has been thought more in keeping with a biographical sketch to follow the date of each book, and to enumerate it as the history of the author proceeds.

1. 𝔄 𝔡𝔞𝔦𝔩𝔶 𝔢𝔵𝔢𝔯𝔠𝔦𝔰𝔢 𝔞𝔫𝔡 𝔢𝔵𝔭𝔢𝔯𝔦𝔢𝔫𝔠𝔢 𝔬𝔣 𝔇𝔢𝔞𝔱𝔥. 1507.

2. 𝔗𝔥𝔢 𝔖𝔞𝔯𝔲𝔪 𝔐𝔞𝔯𝔱𝔶𝔯𝔬𝔩𝔬𝔤𝔶, 𝔞𝔰 𝔲𝔰𝔢𝔡 𝔞𝔱 𝔖𝔶𝔬𝔫, 𝔴𝔦𝔱𝔥 𝔞𝔡𝔡𝔦𝔱𝔦𝔬𝔫𝔰. 1520. Printed by Wynkyn de Worde.

3. 𝔖. 𝔄𝔲𝔰𝔱𝔦𝔫'𝔰 𝔎𝔲𝔩𝔢.

This Rule had been previously translated, and, under the title of *The Reule of S. Austyne*, is found in a MS. folio of the middle of the fifteenth century given to the library of S. Paul's by Robert Hare.[1] The nuns not being satisfied with this first translation, they requested Whytford to give them another, and, that it might be more serviceable to both communities, had it printed by Wynkyn de Worde. It was thrice published. The first edition appeared in 1525, and bore for its title :

𝔗𝔥𝔢 𝔎𝔲𝔩𝔢 𝔬𝔣 𝔖. 𝔄𝔲𝔤𝔲𝔰𝔱𝔦𝔫𝔢, 𝔱𝔯𝔞𝔫𝔰𝔩𝔞𝔱𝔢𝔡 𝔬𝔲𝔱 𝔬𝔣 𝔏𝔞𝔱𝔦𝔫 𝔦𝔫𝔱𝔬 𝔈𝔫𝔤𝔩𝔦𝔰𝔥, 𝔦𝔫𝔡𝔦𝔣𝔣𝔢𝔯𝔢𝔫𝔱𝔩𝔶 𝔲𝔫𝔱𝔬 𝔟𝔬𝔱𝔥 𝔰𝔢𝔵𝔢𝔰, 𝔱𝔥𝔞𝔱 𝔦𝔰 𝔱𝔬 𝔰𝔞𝔶, 𝔲𝔫𝔱𝔬 𝔱𝔥𝔢 𝔅𝔯𝔬𝔱𝔥𝔢𝔯𝔰 𝔞𝔫𝔡 𝔖𝔦𝔰𝔱𝔢𝔯𝔰 𝔬𝔣 𝔱𝔥𝔞𝔱 𝔭𝔯𝔬𝔣𝔢𝔰𝔰𝔦𝔬𝔫.

The second edition contained the Latin copy of the Rule as well as the translation, and also two ex-

---

[1] Vide *Excerpta Historica*, p 414   There also will be found the form of the religious profession made by the fathers of the monastery of Syon, as it is given in the twelfth chapter of the above Rule.

positions of the text. In the British Museum there is a MS.[1] which once belonged to Syon House, and was, in all probability, written soon after its foundation (1414). In this volume there are two expositions of S. Austin's Rule, one by Hugh of S. Victor, and the other by Nicholas Trevet, who is thought to have been a Father of the monastery.[2] Whytford in all likelihood prepared his book from this very manuscript.

The third time the Rule appeared it contained merely the English translation, without either of the two expositions. The colophon of the second edition contains the title which the humble religious always loved to assume, viz. *The wretch of Syon.*

Here endeth this poor labour of the rule of S. Augustine, both in Latin and in English, with our simple notes, and the profitable exposition of the holy saint Hugh de Sancto Victore, by the wretch of Syon, Richard Whytford.

4. The four Revelations of St. Bridget. 1531.

5. The Golden Epistle of S. Bernard. 1531.

This letter was republished A.D. 1585, and appended to the second edition of the author's translation of the *Imitatio Christi*. At the head of it we find these words :

Here beginneth a godly treatise, and it is called a notable lesson, otherwise it is called the Golden Epistle.

[1] No 5028 Add MSS.

[2] See *Collectanea Topographica*, vol. 1. p. 29.

An Historical Introduction

Under this stands a sixteenth century etching of our Blessed Lady and Child. On a label are the words:

'*Jesu Fili David, miserere mei*'
'*O Mater Dei, memento mei.*'

Before commencing the text of the letter itself, Whytford gives '*The exposition of the name of this lytle Booke.*'

'A right good and wholesome lesson,' he says, 'profitable unto all Christians, ascribed unto S. Bernard, and put among his works, I think by some virtuous man that would it should thereby have the more authority and the rather be read, and better be borne away; for doubtless it is a good matter and edificative unto all them that have zeal and care unto soul-health, and desire of salvation. It is called in the title *Notabile documentum*, that is to say, *A notable lesson.* And some do call it *The Golden Epistle.* It followeth immediately after a little work called *Formula honestæ vitæ*, the form and manner of an honest life, or of honest living.'

The letter occupies twelve 12mo pages, and at its conclusion the translator gives us a brief narrative of his labour and concludes by asking the prayers of his readers for his own soul.

This lesson was brought unto me in Englishe, of an old translation, rough and rude, with request to amende it. I thought lesse labour to write new the whole, which I have done accordinge to the meaning of the authour, though not worde for worde: and in divers places added some things

xx

followinge upon the same, to make the matter more sentetious and full. I beseeche you take all unto the best, and pray for the old wretched brother of Sion, Richard Whytford.

6. A Werke for Householders, and for them that have the Gydyng or Gouernaunce of any Company. Printed by W. de Worde. 1530.

In 1538 it was newely corrected and prynted agayne with an addicion of Polici for Housholding. By Robert Redman.

7. S. Bonaventure his lessons. 1532.

8. The Pomander of Prayer. 1532.

This ascetical treatise closes the long list of devotional works edited between 1520 and 1534. To estimate the amount of labour that the author went through we must not forget that some of them were printed more than once even during so short a period; nor must we overlook the difficulties that must have beset publishers and authors who laboured to produce a correct and perfect text in days when printing was in its infancy. We must remember, besides, that this was not his only occupation, for he had the usual duties of his holy state to attend to, namely, the Divine Office, preaching, and hearing confessions. That the latter was at times exercised in behalf of the laity is certain from a passage in a letter of the commissioner Bedyll to Cromwell. 'We think it best,' he says, 'that the place where these friars have been wont to hear outward confessions of all comers at certain times of the year be walled up, and that use[1] to be foredone for ever; for that hearing of outward confessions hath been the cause of much evil and of much treason, which has been sowed abroad in this matter of the king's title, and also in the king's grace's matter of his succession and marriage.'[2]

It may have been in the discharge of the duty of the confessional that the fathers of Syon first became acquainted with the Holy Maid of Kent, who was spoken to by Sir Thomas More in one of the chapels of their church, and was warmly supported by Father Reynolds, their martyred *confrère*.

Certainly, from the day that the Holy Maid visited Syon, its inmates began to be suspected at court of hostility to the measures to which Henry VIII. had resolved to make all his subjects assent, namely, his shameless divorce and uncanonical supremacy.

When the oath of adhesion to the latter was first tendered to the English clergy, the members of Syon were loyal to the Holy See; it was their good counsel, in fact, which directed the monks of the Charterhouse, and their holy influence which encouraged them to suffer death for the faith.[3] When these holy

---

[1] *i e.* custom.

[2] *Letters relating to the Suppression of the Monasteries*, p. 49

[3] Vide *Commentariol de Martyrio xviii Cartusian Angl a Maur Chancæo* Gandavi, 1608, editus Arnoldo Havensio The Father Confessor of Syon on his deathbed thus speaks of Prior Houghton of the Charterhouse 'Ego illi animum addidi, ut in sententia constanter persistens intrepidus mortem occumberet, pro ea causa, propter quam et ipse vita privatus supplicium gravissimum pertulit, et ob quam vos huc adducti estis' (p 95)

men were being drawn to the place of martyrdom,
Father Reynolds of Syon was in their company, and
with them endured the sufferings of a cruel death
rather than seem to betray the cause of Christ. Many
of those that they had left behind soon began to give
way to human considerations, and to waver in their
duty to the Church of God. At the Charterhouse the
defaulters were rather in the minority, but at Syon,
amongst the fathers at least, the faithful ones were at
last few in number.

Maurice Chancey, who was at that time living at
Sheen, has left us an account of what befell his Car-
thusian brethren during the evil days that interven-
ed between the death of Prior Houghton (May 4,
1535) and the dissolution of the monastery (Nov.
15, 1539). He tells us that though for two years
after the martyrdom of the prior none of the brethren
were cast into prison, yet during the whole of that
time they were harassed with unceasing persecution.
They were placed under the care of lay administra-
tors, who so carefully looked after themselves that
the poor monks were left almost to starve. Rude and
drunken men would push their way into the cloister,
and shamefully ill-treat the members of the community. Another troublesome kind of visitor was
the Royal Commissioner, who, former priest as he
generally was, came to act the part of pious counsellor amongst them. We have from the pen of one of
these very men a letter that gives an account of one
of his own visits, from which a rather long extract

must be taken, even at the risk of indulging in un-
necessary digression.

'Please it you to understand,' writes Bedyll to
Cromwell on Ascension-day 1535, 'that on Tuesday,
forthwith upon my departure from you, I repaired
to the Charter-house, and had with me divers books
and annotations, both of mine own and others, against
the primacy of the Bishop of Rome, and also Saint
Peter, declaring evidently the equality of the apostles
by the law of God. And after long communication,
more than one hour and a half, with the vicar and
procurator of the house, I left these books and annotations with them, that they should see the Holy
Scriptures and doctors thereupon concerning the said
matters, and thereupon reform themselves accord-
ingly. And yesterday they sent me the said books
and annotations again home to my house by a servant
of theirs, without any word or writing. Wherefore
I sent to the procurator to come and speak with me,
seeing I kept my bed by reason of sickness, and could
not come to him. At his coming I demanded of him
whether he and the vicar and other of the seniors
had seen or heard the said annotations, or perused
the titles of the books making most for the said
matters. And he answered that the vicar, and he, and
Nudigat, had spent the time upon them till ix. or x.
of the clock at night, and that they saw nothing in
them whereby they were moved to alter their
opinion.'

This unwished-for outcome of his polemical efforts

somewhat angered the poor commissioner, who at once laid aside arguments and took to browbeating and intimidation. But he was forced to confess that this method did not answer with these patient and detached souls.

'I then declared to him,' continues Bedyll, 'the danger of his opinion, which was like to be the destruction of them and their house for ever: and as far as I could perceive by my communication with the vicar and procurator on Tuesday, and with the procurator yesterday, they be obstinately determined to suffer all extremities rather than alter their opinion, regarding no more the death of their father in word or countenance than he were living and conversant among them. I also demanded of the procurator whether the residue of his brethren were of like opinion, and he answered he was not sure, but he thought that they were all of one mind.'[1]

This happy unity truly existed in that holy house, but the commissioners spared no trouble and left no means untried to crush this opposition, or at least to win over the majority of the members. To gain their end they were wont to repair to the Charterhouse at all times, and, after summoning the brethren to the chapter, to keep them discussing for hours the theological point at issue. Another expedient to which they had recourse in order to wear out their patience was to fill their friends with alarm, and then to send them to the monastery to entreat the monks

---

[1] *Letters relat Sup of Monast*, pp 40, 41

with tears to yield to the wishes of the king. Find-
ing at length that neither of these measures prevailed
in the least, they resolved to sequester those who
were suspected to be the leaders of the rest. As, in the
summer of 1536, eight of these faithful men were
sent to Syon House, we must now go back to that
community, and see what led the commissioners to
hope that the Carthusians would be likely to yield,
if they were kept for a time in the society of the Syon
fathers. The mere fact of their entertaining such a
hope shews that a great change must have come over
Syon House since Father Reynolds left it to go to
his prison cell. A change had certainly taken place,
but seemingly not till great pressure had been put
upon the community. Fortunately, there are yet
existing two letters from Bedyll which give us some
insight into the doings of Henry's agents.

On the 28th day of July 1535, he writes to Cromwell thus : ' I have also been to Syon sith your departing with my lord of London, where we have
found the lady abbess and sisters as conformable in
everything as might be devised. And as touching
the Father Confessor and Father Curson (which be
the saddest men there and the best learned) they shewed themselves like honest men ; and I think the confessor will now on Sunday next in his sermon make
due mention of the king's title of supreme head, according as he is commanded. What towardness or
intowardness we have seen in some other of the
brethren there, I will inform you at your return to

London, and omit it now because I have hope that by the wisdom of the father confessor and Father Curson the residue shall shortly be brought to good conformity. And if not, there be two of the brethren must be weeded out, which be somewhat seditious, and have laboured busily to infect their fellows with obstinacy against the king's said title.'[1]

We learn from this letter that for some months at least all the fathers of Syon refused to take the oath of supremacy. It seems nevertheless that the visits of Cromwell and his commissioners had at last told upon the father confessor and Father Curson, and that not only was their submission expected, but their influence was looked upon as likely to lead to the conformity of the rest, though Bedyll could not conceal his misgivings on that point. One fact deserves special attention, viz. the loyalty to the Holy See which was found in the two who are spoken of as the leaders of their brethren. In a letter written by Bedyll on December 17th of the same year we have express mention made of the two '*whiche be somwhat sediciose.*' Meanwhile we learn from a letter to Cromwell from his '*assurede poore Preste,*' Richard Layton, who writes from Syon '*this Sonday xii. Decembris,*' that on that day a long-wished-for event had taken place. 'Hit may please your goodness to understonde that Bisshope this day prechede and declarede the kinges title verawell, and hade a gret audience, the churche full of people. One of the

---

[1] *Letters*, etc., p. 45.

focares [1] in his saide declaration openly callede hym fals knave with other foolisshe wordes. Hit was that folishe felowe with curlede hede that knelyde in your way whan ye came forthe of the confessors chambre. I cannolesse do but set hym in prison, *ut pena ejus sit metus aliorum*.[2]

A second letter may be given almost *in extenso*, as it throws some light on Richard Whytford's history at this period.

'Right worshipful, after most hearty commendations, please it you to understand that Master Leighton [3] and I have had much business with this house sythens your departing hence ; and as for the brethren, they stand stiff in their obstinacy as you left them. Copynger and Lacke were sent to my lord of London on Monday. Here were on Tuesday doctor Butts and the Queen's almoner to convert Whytford and Little ; and on Wednesday here were doctor Aldrigg, doctor Curven, doctor Bawghe, and doctor Morgan, sent by the king's grace for that purpose, but they nothing profited. I handled Whytford after that in the garden, both with fair words and with foul, and showed him that through his obstinacy he should be brought to the great shame of the world for his irreligious life. . . . Whereby (I said) he might be the occasion that shrift shall be laid down through England ; but he hath a brazen fore-

---

[1] *Vide* Du Cange, verb *Focarius*, here applied to the fathers who were true to the Holy See

[2] *Letters*, etc., p 47   [3] or *Layton*, as above

head which shameth at nothing. One Matthew, a lay-brother, upon hope of liberty is reformed. We would fain know your advice what we shall do with Whytford and Little, and a lay-brother, one Turnyngton, which is very sturdy against the king's title. We have sequestered Whytford and Little from hearing of the ladies' confessions; and we think it best that the place where these friars have been wont to hear outward confessions of all comers at certain times of the year be walled up, and that use to be foredone for ever; for that hearing of outward confessions hath been the cause of much evil and of much treason which hath been sowed abroad in this matter of the king's title, and also in the king's grace's matter of his succession and marriage.'

This statement proves that Whytford was one of the two faithful men alluded to in Bedyll's first letter as the cause of their brethren's steadfastness to duty. The king, it appears, was unwilling to proceed to violent measures, and hoped that disputation would bring them to conformity. Hence the visit of doctor Butts and the Queen's almoner on the Tuesday, and on the next day the coming of the four doctors of divinity in company with the commissioners. Bedyll's account of his '*handling*' Whytford in the garden '*with faire wordes and with foule*,' shews what good men had then to endure from these fellows, and the incident would be almost amusing if we could only lose sight of the shamefulness of the whole proceeding. Whytford was evidently a man of holy patience, and as he seemed so entirely unmoved either by fair or by foul words, his accuser quite lost his temper, and had not found it again even when, two days after, he was sending to Cromwell an account of his interview. The suspension of Whytford and Little was all that the commissioners had in their power to do, but they apparently hoped to be allowed afterwards to deal more sternly both with them and the sturdy lay-brother Turnyngton.

All this while they had not lost sight of the nuns. That the expectation of perfect conformity expressed by Bedyll in his July letter was not realised is clear from the December correspondence. As several interesting facts connected with the noble resistance of the abbess and convent are stated in the official document, it will now be continued.

' On Wednesday my lord Wyndsor came hither, sent for by Master Leighton and me, and laboured much that day for the converting of his sister [1] and some other of his kinswomen here ; and yesterday we had my lord of London here in the chapter-house of women, and the confessor also, which both took it upon their conscience and upon the peril of their souls, that the ladies ought by God's law to consent to the king's title, wherewith they were much comforted ;

[1] She was the prioress. Mention is made of her in the will of Lord Windsor dated 26th March 1543, and proved 31st July 1543 ' To my sister Margaret Windsor, late prioress of the late monastery of Sion, an annuity lxxx*l* vi*s* viii*d*. out of my manor of Crainford, in com. Middlesex, to pray for my soul, my father and mother's souls '—Vide *Testamenta Vetusta*, p. 699.

and when we willed all such as would not consent
thereunto to depart out of the chapter-house there
was found none among them which departed. Albeit
I was informed this night that one Agnes Smyth, a
sturdy dame and a wilful, hath laboured divers of her
sisters to stop that we should not have their convent
seal ; but we trust we shall have it this morning, with
the subscription of the abbess for herself and all her
sisters, which is the best fashion that we can bring
it to.' [1]

This proves that the father confessor's '*wisdom*'
had not succeeded in persuading the nuns to betray
their faith. Moreover, it shows the amount of influence from outside which was brought to bear upon
the convent. First of all we have Lord Windsor's
visit, who at the request of the commissioners comes
to persuade his sister and other relatives to yield.
When we know that this nobleman owed almost all
his position to the favour of Henry VIII., and that he
was one of the temporal lords who in 1530 had signed
a letter to Clement VII. intimating to him that unless he complied with the petition of divorce they
should seek their end by other means,[2] it is not hard
to guess that he would prove a very earnest advocate
in behalf of the Crown.

After being thus prepared on Wednesday, we have
the poor nuns brought face to face on the Thursday

[1] *Letters,* etc , pp 49, 50.
[2] Rymer's *Fœdera,* vol xiv. p. 405, ap , Collins's *Peerage,* v. 3,
art. Earl of Plymouth

with the Bishop of London, the father confessor, and the commissioners, in their chapter-house. We can form some idea of the painfulness of the situation in which these sisters found themselves when we hear Bedyll say that they were '*much comforted*' by the assurances of their bishop and the father confessor. The commissioners no doubt thought that they had at last prevailed, as the community sat motionless when all dissentients were bidden to rise and depart. The fact was that the opposition had too much sense to comply with the request, for they perceived the snare which had been prepared for them, one which, if successful, would have shewn who were their leaders.

The commissioners had not even left the convent before they found out their mistake, and fearing total failure they resolved to accept the signature of the abbess, and to rest satisfied with this as a submission in the name of the whole convent. Bedyll, almost wearied out by the resistance of the sisters, deemed this '*the best fashion*' that the affair could be brought to.

Whether the signature was obtained cannot be positively ascertained, but even if the abbess proved faithless,[1] it is clear from the compromise to which

[1] The abbess at this time (1535) was Agnes Jordan, who at the dissolution received a pension of £200 She was buried in the church at Denham in Buckinghamshire The inscription on her monument ran thus. '*Of your charity pray for the sowle of Dame Agnes Jordan, sometyme Abbesse of the Monastery of Syon, which departed this Lyfe the 29 of Januarye in the yere of our Lord 15 . . . On whose Soule Jesu have mercye Amen*'—*Vide* Bohn's edition of *Dugdale*, vol. vi. p. 541, *note k*.

the Commissioners had recourse, and from the after-history of the nuns, that the body of the sisterhood always remained faithful to the Holy See.

The opposition that arose against the delivery of the convent seal manifests the real feeling of the community, even after the Bishop of London had soothed and much comforted them by counselling perfect submission.[1] It is remarkable that throughout their career of misfortune the good nuns of Syon never gave up the possession of the seal, which they had received from Henry v. at their foundation. It was among those precious heirlooms of the convent which were brought over to this country from Portugal by the nuns who came to England early in the present century. The preservation of this relic proves that Agnes Smith, '*the sturdy dame and the wilful*,' carried the day against the Commissioners, who no doubt wanted to get hold of the seal in order to make use of it to ruin the convent. Dr. Milner has given an impression of it in the appendix of vol. xvii. of *Archæologia*.

Richard Whytford, as we see, proved himself staunch to Catholic unity, and a powerful influence without, as well as within, his convent. In all probability he was, as Bedyll above expressed it, '*weeded*

[1] The Bishop of London at this time was John Stokesly, who in 1530 had succeeded Cuthbert Tunstall on his translation to Durham. 'In John Stokesly,' says Storer, 'Henry viii had a ready instrument, who lent himself to further the king's wishes with regard to his criminal divorces and marriages.'—*Hist. and Antiq. of the Cathedral Churches of Great Britain*, vol iii, art 'S Paul, London.'

An Historical Introduction

out.' Dodd says that he was received into the house
of William Blount Lord Mountjoy, who is known
to have been extremely charitable to all who then
suffered for the Faith.[1] As this good man's death
occurred in 1535, it is very evident that Whytford
must have been driven from his cloister before the
suppression of the monastery in 1539.

During the twenty-two years that elapsed between
his departure from Syon and the accession of the
Catholic Queen Mary, he devoted himself to writing
and publishing books, working as if he were still at
peace in his monastic cell. It was in his retirement,
and when acting as chaplain to the Mountjoy family,
that he published the following useful works:[2]

9. 𝔄 𝔇ialogue or Communication between the
Curate or Ghostly Father, and the Parocheine or
Ghostly Chyld, for a due Preparacion unto the
Houselyng. 1537.

10. 𝔄 Treatise of Patience. 1541.

11. 𝔄n Instruction to aboid and eschew bices.
Translated from the lessons of St. Isidore, with some
few additions. 1541.

12. 𝔒f derraction. Translated from St. John
Chrysostom. 1541.

13. Solitary Meditations.

[1] *Church Hist of Eng*, part 1. b. 2, art. vi p 245, ed 1742   Lord
Mountjoy was the father-in-law of Lord Windsor, and therefore well
acquainted with some of the inmates of Syon House
[2] Whytford published in 1532 *The Pype or Tonne of the Life of
Perfection* a work on the three vows of religion, written against
the Lutherans

14. Finally, Psalterium Jesu, both in Latin and English. This prayer is that which is known amongst English Catholics as the *Jesus Psalter*.

The very titles of these books bespeak the troubles that had befallen him, and also the truly apostolic vigour with which he patiently laboured at the sanctification of those who like himself needed the strength of grace to keep steadfast in the holy faith. His beautiful *Jesus Psalter* became widely spread amongst the Catholics of England during the persecution which they suffered for the Unity of the Catholic Church, and was to many a favourite daily devotion. Though many manuals of piety have been published within the last sixty years, still it is difficult to find in them devout aspirations so soul-stirring as those contained in Whytford's Psalter. Had he done nothing more for English Catholics than compose this prayer, his name would still deserve to be held in benediction.

Even during the dark days of Edward vi. Whytford's heart failed not. He was reading and meditating and retranslating the *Imitatio Christi*. When at length in Queen Mary's reign England was reunited to the Holy See, he had the unspeakable joy of welcoming back to Syon House those holy nuns who, by the help of the Spanish ambassador, had crossed the sea and settled on the Continent in 1539. As the community of the Canons was never restored, it is not known whether Whytford returned to Syon as one

An Historical Introduction

of the conventual chaplains, or remained in the family
which had sheltered him for well-nigh twenty years.
In any case, his influence made itself felt amongst
Catholics by the publication in 1556 of his translation
of the *Imitatio Christi*, which was printed by Cawood,
the Queen's printer.

This had been to him a work of love, for he tells
us in his Preface that he had read the Book of the
Imitation very many times, that the more he read it
the more he liked it, and that he ever found therein
profit to his soul's health. His short but pithy Preface
will be found at pp. xliii, xliv of this volume; and few
will peruse it without feeling an earnest desire to adopt
Whytford's advice, and daily read a portion of this
most devout book. As he tersely but beautifully says:
It teacheth the true mortification of the flesh to the spirit.
And this not so much in theory as in practice. In
each of the first three Treatises or Books, we have no
system of spirituality, it is true, but the great truths
which belong to the three different states of a ghostly
life are set before us, and so forcibly do they appeal
to the understanding that the will is almost imper-
ceptibly drawn to the love of God, and the mind
stored with those golden principles which in the day
of trial ensure perseverance and fortitude.

The teaching of the First Book may be summed
up in this short word: That to become spiritual men
we must needs first mortify our many passions, and
that of these passions none is more dangerous or
more subtle than pride of intellect, or, as Whytford

styles it, '*vain cunning*.' The knowledge of our end
and of ourselves, compunction of heart, the remembrance of the four last things, all belong to the pur-
gative way of the spiritual life, and hence find their
place in that First Book which bids us follow Christ's
steps and study His life.

As the second stage of the spiritual life is that in
which we become more thoroughly severed from
created things, and inwardly illumined to know our
nothingness; in which also by the light of God's holy
grace we are given to see the beauty of virtue, and are
filled with a desire to love Jesus and Jesus only; so
the Second Book invites us to the inward life, to the
joys of a good conscience, and to the sweet friendship
of Jesus crucified. It is now that the soul begins to
realise what spirituality truly means, and becomes so
far mortified inwardly that it no longer seeks human
comfort in tribulation, but lovingly follows Jesus
bearing the cross.

In the heart of such a man there is but one desire,
the peace of God's love. Hence in the Third Book
the soul is taught the path that leads to peace, is prepared for the dangers which beset its course, and is
mightily stirred to long for the heavenly union of love
that shall never pass away. The inward speakings of
Christ to the soul, and the outpourings of the soul's
love to her Divine Lord, as given in that treatise of
the contemplative state, have never been excelled in
any book that has not been blessed with inspiration.

The special merit of *The Imitation of Christ* is, that

An Historical Introduction

it has the wonderful power of reflecting every soul
that beholds itself in its mirror, and of giving at the
same time to thoughtful minds a deeper insight into
the things of God. Hence it is the most widespread
and the most popular spiritual book in the Catholic
Church.

Of the Fourth Book we must needs speak specially,
though it be but briefly. There the Catholic will find
both a light for his mind and a fire of devotion for his
heart. To know the love of Jesus for us poor sinners
in the great Sacrament of the altar, and to be filled
with loving faith and trust in our Blessed Lord, is
the spiritual fruit gotten by the frequent perusal and
continual meditation of that holy treatise. The be-
ginner and the proficient all nestle in the tabernacle
of divine love, and in that holy resting-place regain
strength to follow Jesus and to carry His cross even
unto the end. To the contemplative the foot of the
altar is a paradise on earth, for there it is sometimes
given to his soul to have a foretaste of the heavenly
union of never-ending blessedness.

That Richard Whytford had thus been perfected
in the love of contemplation, no one can reasonably
doubt who can appreciate the full fervour with which
his soul seems to break forth in the rendering of the
many beautiful prayers that occur throughout the
Third Book. How long it pleased God to prolong
his earthly pilgrimage we know not, but as at the accession of Queen Mary he must have been at least
eighty years of age, he had in all probability sung

his *Nunc dimittis* ere Elizabeth ruled the land. He
was thus happily spared the affliction of seeing the
nuns of Syon again driven out of their cloister-
home, and exiled once more from the land of their
birth. It was during the stay of this persecuted community at Rouen in 1585 that the second edition of
Whytford's translation of the *Imitatio Christi* appeared. This small book is in black-letter, but bears
no name either of printer or place of publication.
From certain mistakes which occur in the English
text, and from the substitution of V for W in the
ornamental letters which begin each chapter, it seems
highly probable that the book was printed abroad,
and if so, most likely at Rouen, where several
English works had previously been published. This
edition is very rare. It is to be found in the Bodleian,
but not in the British Museum. The present reprint
is from a copy in Downside Abbey library, the kind
gift of Miss Morrice of Bath.

Besides the Introduction and Preface given below,
this edition also contains the Spiritual Glass, the
Golden Epistle of St. Bernard, and the Rules of a
Christian Life by John Picus the elder, Earl of
Mirandula. The last-mentioned and the Spiritual
Glass have been reprinted, but as it seemed unneces-
sary to reproduce the Golden Epistle, it has been
omitted.

A Biographical Note
on Dom Raynal

PAUL RAYNAL was born on 30th November 1830, at Port Louis, in the Island of Mauritius. His family was of French origin, and was closely connected with the well-known Abbé Raynal, author of the once famous *Histoire philosophique*.

When only eleven years old, he was sent to England to be educated by the English Benedictine community of St. Gregory, at Downside, near Bath : and in 1848 he took the religious habit in that monastery, assuming in religion the name of Wilfrid. This act was strongly opposed by his family, and his guardian absolutely refused to give his consent to it. As Dom Wilfrid, however, was just as certain that he was doing right, matters remained at a deadlock until he attained the age of twenty-one, when he at once took the vows of religion.

After some twelve uneventful years of hard work at Downside, Dom Raynal was transferred, in 1862, to the monastery of Belmont, near Hereford, which had been founded a few years previously as a common noviciate house for all the English Black Monks of St. Benedict. Here he filled the professorship of Church History until, in the year 1872, he became Superior of the house, with the rank of Prior.

This latter post he retained for no less a time than

xl

twenty-eight years, during which period he came into close personal touch with all those aspiring to join the English Benedictine Congregation who spent the first four years of their life as monks under his care.

It was just before his appointment as Prior of Belmont that Dom Raynal published his edition of the *Imitation of Christ*. His text is the old English translation made by Richard Whytford, a Brigittine Canon of Syon House, and was published in 1556 during the brief restoration of that community under Queen Mary. Dom Raynal modernised the spelling so as to make the book of real practical use, and brought the punctuation into line with current practice; but, apart from this, he kept the text as nearly as possible what Whytford had made it. His edition was for long out of print, which is to be regretted the more as it offers what is beyond doubt the finest English version of the great spiritual masterpiece.

During his long period of office as Prior of Belmont, Dom Raynal found scant opportunity for literary work; what he did in this direction consisting almost wholly in editions of various liturgical works, especially the monastic Breviary and Missal.

In 1901 Dom Raynal retired from the post he had held so long, and was appointed *Procurator in Curia Romana*, or Roman representative of the English Benedictine monks, with titular rank as Abbot of St. Alban's. He died in Rome on 9th June 1904, after a brief illness, and was buried there. His edition of the *Imitation of Christ* is perhaps his best and most appropriate monument, for it may be doubted whether, amongst the numberless editors of Thomas à Kempis, there has been any more wholly united to him in spirit than was Paul Wilfrid Raynal.

G ROGER HUDLESTON, O S B.

DOWNSIDE ABBEY,
BATH.

The Introduction of 1556

Hereafter foloweth a booke called in Latin 'Imitatio Christi,' that is in Englishe, the folowing of Christe, wherein be conteyned foure litle bookes. Which booke, as some men affirme,[1] was firste made and compyled in Latin by the famous Clerke master John Gerson, Chauncellour of Paris. And the sayed foure bookes be nowe of late newly translated into English in such maner as hereafter appeareth. And though three of the first bookes of the sayd foure bookes have bene before this time right well and devoutlie translated into Englishe by a famous Clerke called master William Atkinson which was a doctour of divinitie. Yet for as muche as the sayde translatour (for some cause him movinge) in divers places left out muche parte of some of the Chapters, and sometime varied from the letter, as in the thirde chapter, and in the 18 and 19 chapters of the first booke, and also in divers other chapiters of the sayde three books will appeare to them that will examine the Latin and the sayd first translation together: Therefore the sayed 3 bookes be eftsones translated into English, in such manner as hereafter foloweth, to the intent that they that list maye at their pleasure be occupied with the one or the other, after as their devotion shall

[1] These words shew that even in the days of Richard Whytford the authorship of the *Imitatio Christi* was contested. The editor has carefully avoided a topic which might give rise to useless discussion.

xliii

stirre them when they have seene them both.
And after the sayde three bookes foloweth the
fourth booke, which was first translated out of
Frenche into Englishe by the right noble and excellent Princes Margaret late Countesse of Rich-
monde and Darbye, mother unto the noble Prince
of blessed memorie Kynge Henry the 7, father
unto our late soueraine Lord Kinge Henry the 8.
And for as much as it was translated by the sayed
noble Princes out of Frenche, it coulde not folowe
the Latin so nigh nor so directlie as if it had been
translated out of Latin. And therefore it is nowe
translated out of Latin, and yet neuertheless it
keepeth the substaunce and the effect of the first
translation out of Frenche, though sometime it
varie in wordes, as to the Reader will appeare.
And in the latter end, after the fourth booke, is a
short morall doctrine, which is called The spirituall glasse of the soule. And it is right good and
profitable to every person ofte tymes to looke upon
it.

A Preface
to the Booke folowinge

Amonge manye Treatises, which have bene put
out both in Latin and Englishe, in this perillous
worlde, to seduce the simple people and to bring
them from the unitie of the Catholike Churche
into pervers and abhominable errours, there hath
bene also in tyme past before made by divers
learned and vertuous men many good Treatises,
which yf men woulde be so diligent to looke upon,
as they are curious to looke on the other, they
shoulde not so soone fall from the true know:
ledge of Christes doctrine and the right sense
of holie Scripture, whiche ever hath bene taught
by continuall succession in this holie Churche,
of the holie ghost, the spirit of truth, who shall
ever remayne with it.   And amonge many of
these good Treatises, there is one called the
Imitation or folowinge of Christe, whiche in
my judgement is excellent: and the more it is
seriouslye and advisedlie reade and looked upon,
the more it shall like every Christian reader, who
will set his minde earnestlie to folow Christ his
steppes.   Let them prove by reading every day a
chapter when they have best leasure, and I doubt
not, but they shall finde my sayinges true.   I
have reade it over very many times, and the more
I reade, the more I like it and finde profite to my

xlv

A Preface to the Booke folowinge

soule health. It teacheth the true mortification of the fleshe to the spirite, accordinge to the right sense of holie Scripture, and the doctrine of S. Paul. Which J consideringe desired the Queenes highnes printer[1] to take the paynes eftsones to imprint it, seeinge the other[2] is worne awaye whiche was verie faultie in many places. And in this he hath done his diligence in correction thereof, as you shall well perceyve in conferring them together. Thus fare you well in Christ and praye for them that have taken paynes in this behalfe.

[1] Cawood, Queen Mary's printer.
[2] Dr Wm Atkynson's translation, printed in 1504

Contents

The First Book

Admonitions useful for a spiritual life

xlvii

Contents

The Second Book

Admonitions tending to things internal

The Third Book

Of internal consolation

Thomas à Kempis

Contents

1

Thomas à Kempis

The Fourth Book

Concerning the Sacrament

li

Contents

Illustrations

[*The inscriptions to the plates, having been chosen
from a different version, do not agree verbally
with the text of the present volume.*]

Let all peoples · nations
and languages praise
Thee, and magnify Thy
holy and most delicious
Name with highest exult-
ation and ardent devotion.
·Amen·

Of the Imitation of Christ

four books by

Thomas à Kempis

The first book

Amonitions useful for a spiritual life

A

The First Book
Admonitions useful for a spiritual life

The First Chapter: Of the Imitation or Following of Christ, and of the despising of all vanities of the world.

'E *that followeth me,*' saith Christ our Saviour, '*shall not walk in darkness, but shall have the light of life.*'[1] These be the words of our Lord Jesus Christ, whereby we be admonished and warned, that we shall follow His teachings and His manner of living, if we will truly be illumined and be delivered from all blindness of heart. Let all the study of our heart be, therefore, from henceforth to have our meditation wholly fixed in the life and in the holy teachings of Jesus Christ: for His teachings are of more virtue and of more ghostly strength than are the teachings of all Angels and Saints.

And he that through grace might have the inner eye of his soul opened into soothfast beholding of the Gospels of Christ, should find in them Manna,

[1] John viii. 12.

3

that is to say, spiritual food of the soul : but it is oftentimes seen that some persons, who often hear the
Gospels of Christ, have little sweetness therein : and
that is, for that they have not the spirit of Christ.
Wherefore, if we will have the true understanding
of Christ's Gospels, we must study to conform our
life to His life as nigh as we can.

What availeth it a man to reason high secret mysteries of the Trinity, if he lack meekness, whereby he
displeaseth the Trinity ? Truly nothing. For high
curious reasons make not a man holy nor rightwise,
but a good life maketh him beloved with God. I had
rather feel compunction of heart for my sins, than
only to know the definition of compunction. If thou
couldst all the Bible without the book, and also the
sayings of all philosophers by heart, what should it
profit thee without grace and charity ? All that is in
this world is vanity, but to love God and only to serve
Him. This is the most noble and the most excellent
wisdom that may be in any creature—by despising
of this world to draw daily nearer and nearer to the
kingdom of heaven.

It is therefore a great vanity to labour inordinately
for worldly riches, which shortly shall perish, and to
covet honour, or any other inordinate pleasures or
fleshly delights in this life, whereby a man after this
life shall be sore and grievously punished. How
great a vanity is it also to desire a long life, and little
to care for a good life : to heed things present, and
not to provide for things that are to come : to love

things that shortly shall pass away, and not to haste thither where is joy everlasting.

Also have this common proverb oft in thy mind : '*That the eye is not satisfied nor fully pleased with the sight of any bodily thing, nor the ear with hearing*' :[1] and therefore study to withdraw the love of thy soul from all things that be visible, and turn it to things that be invisible. For they that follow their sensuality hurt their own conscience, and lose the grace of God.

The Second Chapter : Against vain secular cunning, and of a meek knowing of ourself. ¶ Every man naturally desireth to know but what availeth knowledge without the dread of God ? A meek husbandman that serveth God is much more acceptable to Him than is a curious philosopher who considering the course of heaven wilfully forgetteth himself · he that well knoweth himself is vile and abject in his own sight, and hath no delight in the vain praisings of man. If I knew all things that be in this world without charity, what would it avail me before God, that judgeth every man after his deeds?

Let us therefore cease from the desire of such vain knowledge : for oftentimes is found therein great distraction and deceit of the enemy, whereby the soul is much hindered and let from the perfect and true love of God. They that have great cunning desire commonly to be seen and to be holden wise in the world. But there be many things, the knowledge of

[1] See Eccles i. 8

which bring but little profit and fruit to the soul, and he is very unwise that taketh heed to any other thing, than to that which shall profit him to the health of his soul. Words feed not the soul ; but a good life refresheth the mind, and a clean conscience bringeth a man to a firm and stable trust in God.

The more cunning thou hast, if thou live not thereafter, the more grievously shalt thou be judged for the misusing thereof. Therefore, raise not thyself into pride for any craft or cunning that is given unto thee, but have the more fear and dread in thy heart ; for certain it is that thou must hereafter yield the straiter account. If thou think that thou knowest many things and hast great cunning, yet know that there be many more things that thou knowest not : and so thou mayest not right wisely think thyself cunning, but oughtest rather to confess thine ignorance. Why wilt thou prefer thyself before another, sith there be many others more excellent and more cunning than thou, and better learned in the law? If thou wilt anything learn and know profitably to the health of thy soul, learn to be unknown and be glad to be holden vile and nought.

The most high and the most profitable cunning is this, that a man have a soothfast knowledge and a full despising of himself. Also not to presume of himself, but always to judge and think well and blessedly of another, is a sign and a token of great wisdom, and of great perfection, and singular grace If thou see any person sin or commit any great crime openly before thee, yet judge not thyself to be better than he, for thou knowest not how long thou shalt persevere in goodness. We be all frail: but thou shalt judge no man more frail than thyself.

The Third Chapter: Of the teaching of truth. ¶ Happy and blessed is that person whom truth teacheth and informeth, not by figures and deceitful voices, but as the truth is: our opinion and our wit many times deceive us, for we see not the truth. What availeth us the knowledge of such things as shall neither help us at the day of judgment if we know them, nor hurt us if we know them not! It is therefore great folly to be negligent in such things as be profitable and necessary to us, and to labour for such things that be but curious and damnable. Truly, if we do so, we have eyes but we see not.

And what availeth us the knowledge of the kind and working of creatures? Truly nothing. He to whom the Everlasting Word (that is, Jesus) speaketh is discharged of many vain opinions. Of that Word all things proceed, and all things openly shew and cry that He is God. No man without Him understandeth the truth, nor rightly judgeth. But he to whom all things are one, and he that all things draweth into one, and all things setteth in one, and desireth nothing but one, may quickly be established in heart, and be fully pacified in God.

O Truth, that God art, make me one with Thee in perfect charity; for all that I read, hear, or see without Thee is grievous to me: for in Thee is all that I

will or may desire! Let all doctors be still in Thy
presence, and let all creatures keep themselves in
silence, and do Thou only Lord speak to my soul.
The more that a man is joined to Thee and the more
that he is gathered together in Thee, the more he
understandeth without labour high secret mysteries,
for he hath received from above the light of understanding.

A clean, pure, and a stable heart is not broken nor
lightly overcome with ghostly labours, for he doeth
all things to the honour of God : and for that he is
clearly mortified to himself, therefore he coveteth to
be free from following his own will. What hindereth
thee more than thy affections, not fully mortified to
the will of the spirit ? Truly nothing more.

A good devout man so ordereth his outward business that it draweth him not to the love of it ; but that
he compel it to be obedient to the will of the spirit,
and to the right judgment of reason. Who hath a
stronger battle than he that laboureth to overcome
himself? And this should be our daily labour and
our daily desire to overcome ourself, that we may be
made stronger in spirit, and increase daily from better
to better. Every perfection in this life hath some im-
perfection annexed unto it ; and there is no knowledge in this world, but that is mixed with some blindness of ignorance. And therefore a meek knowing
of ourself is a surer way to God than is the searching
for highness of cunning.

Cunning well-ordered is not to be blamed, for it is

good and cometh of God : but a clean conscience and
a virtuous life is much better and more to be desired.
Because some men study to have cunning rather than
to live well, therefore they err many times and bring
forth little good fruit, or none. O if they would be
as busy to avoid sin and to plant virtues in their souls
as they be to move questions, there should not be so
many evil things seen in the world, nor so much evil
example given to the people, nor yet so much dissolute
living in religion ! At the day of judgment it shall
not be asked of us what we have read, but what we
have done : nor how well we have said, but how re-
ligiously we have lived.

Tell me now, where be all the great Clerks and
famous Doctors, whom thou hast well known? When
they lived they flourished greatly in their learning,
and now other men occupy their prebends and promo-
tions, and I cannot tell whether they think any thing
of them : in their life they were holden great in the
world, and now is little speaking of them. O how
shortly passeth away the glory of this world with all
the false deceivable pleasures of it ! Would to God
their life had accorded well with their learning, for
then had they well studied and read ! How many
perish daily in this world by vain cunning, that care
little for a good life nor for the service of God. And
because they desire rather to be great in the world
than to be meek, therefore they vanish away in their
learnings as smoke in the air.

Truly he is great that hath great charity ; and he is

great that is little in his own sight, and that setteth at nought all worldly honour.

He is very wise that accounteth all worldly pleasures as vile dung, so that he may win Christ. And that person is very well taught who forsaketh his own will and followeth the will of God.

𝕮𝖍𝖊 𝕱𝖔𝖚𝖗𝖙𝖍 𝕮𝖍𝖆𝖕𝖙𝖊𝖗 : 𝕮𝖍𝖆𝖙 𝖑𝖎𝖌𝖍𝖙 𝖈𝖗𝖊𝖉𝖊𝖓𝖈𝖊 𝖎𝖘 𝖓𝖔𝖙 𝖙𝖔 𝖇𝖊 𝖌𝖎𝖛𝖊𝖓 𝖙𝖔 𝖜𝖔𝖗𝖉𝖘. ¶ It is not good lightly to believe every word or instinct that cometh, but the thing is advisedly and leisurely to be considered and pondered, that Almighty God be not offended through our lightness. But alas for sorrow! We be so frail, that we anon believe of another evil sooner than good. Nevertheless perfect men be not so light of credence, for they know well that the frailty of man is more prone to evil than to good, and that it is in words very unstable. It is therefore great wisdom not to be hasty in our deeds ; nor to trust much in our own wits ; nor lightly to believe every tale ; nor to shew anon to others all that we hear or believe.

Take always counsel of a wise man, and covet rather to be instructed and ordered by another, than to follow thine own invention. A good life maketh a man wise to God, and instructeth him in many things, that a sinful man shall never feel nor know. The more meek that a man is in himself, and the more obedient that he is to God, the more wise and the more peaceful shall he be in every thing that he shall have to do.

Of the Imitation of Christ

The Fifth Chapter: Of the reading of Holy Scripture. ¶ Charity is to be sought in Holy Scripture and not eloquence. And it should be read with the same spirit that it was first made. We ought also to seek in Holy Scripture ghostly profit rather than curiosity of style, and as gladly shall we read simple and devout books as books of high learning and cunning. Let not the authority of thine author mislike thee, whether he were of great cunning or little : but let the love of the very pure truth stir thee to read. Ask not who said this, but take heed what is said. Men pass lightly away, but ' *the truth of the Lord endureth for ever.*'[1]

Almighty God speaketh to us in His Scripture in divers manners without accepting of persons . but our curiosity oft letteth us in reading of Scripture, when we will reason and argue things that we should meekly and simply pass over. If thou wilt profit by reading of Scripture, read meekly, simply, and faithfully, and never desire to have thereby the name of cunning. Ask gladly and hear meekly the sayings of Saints, and mislike not the parables of ancient Fathers, for they were not spoken without great cause.

The Sixth Chapter: Of inordinate affections. ¶ When a man desireth any thing inordinately, forthwith he is unquiet in himself. The proud man and the covetous man never have rest: but the meek man and the poor in spirit live in great abundance of rest and

---

[1] Ps cxvii. 2.

peace. A man that is not yet mortified to himself, is lightly tempted and overcome in little and small temptations. And he that is weak in spirit and is yet somewhat carnal and inclined to sensible things, may hardly withdraw himself from worldly desires. Therefore he hath oft great grief and heaviness of heart, when he withdraweth himself from them ; and he disdaineth anon, if any man resist him.

If he obtain that he desireth, yet is he unquieted with grudge of conscience, for he hath followed his passion which nothing helpeth to the getting of that peace he desired. By resisting of passions, then, is gotten the very true peace of heart, and not by following of them. There is, therefore, no peace in the heart of a carnal man, nor in the heart of a man that giveth himself all to outward things : but in the heart of a ghostly man, who hath his delight in God, is found great peace and inward quietness.

The Seventh Chapter : That vain hope and elation of mind are to be fled and avoided. ¶ He is vain that putteth his trust in man, or in any creature. Be not ashamed to serve others for the love of Jesus Christ, and to be poor in this world for His sake : trust not thyself, but all thy trust set in God : do what is in thee to please Him, and He shall well help forth thy good will. Trust not in thine own cunning, neither in the cunning or policy of any creature living, but rather in the grace of God, which helpeth meek persons ; and those that presume of themselves, He suffereth to fall till they be meek.

Of the Imitation of Christ

Glorify not thyself in thy riches, nor in thy worldly friends, for that they be mighty ; but let all thy glory be in God only, that giveth all things, and that desireth to give Himself above all things. Exalt not thyself for the largeness or fairness of body, for with a little sickness it may be soon defouled. Joy not in thyself for thy ability or readiness of wit, lest thou displease God, of whose gift it is all that thou hast.

Hold not thyself better than another, lest haply thou be thereby impaired in the sight of God, Who knoweth all that is in man. Be not proud of thy good deeds, for the judgments of God be other than the judgments of man, to Whom it displeaseth oft times that which pleaseth man. If thou have any goodness or virtue in thee, believe yet that there is much more goodness and virtue in others, so that thou mayest always keep thee in meekness. It hurteth not though thou hold thyself worse than any other, though it be not so indeed; but it hurteth much if thou prefer thyself above any other, be he never so great a sinner. Great peace is with the meek man, but in the heart of the proud man is always envy and indignation.

The Eighth Chapter: That much familiarity is to be avoided. ¶ Open not thy heart to every person, but to him that is wise, secret, and dreading God. Be seldom with young folks and strangers ; flatter not rich men, and afore great men do not lightly appear. Accompany thyself with meek persons and simple in heart, who be devout and of good governance, and treat with them of things that may edify and strengthen the soul. Be not familiar to any woman, but all good women commend to God. Covet to be familiar only with God and with His Angels : but the familiarity of man, as much as thou mayest, look thou eschew. Charity is to be had to all : but familiarity is not expedient. Sometimes it happeneth that a person unknown through his good fame is much commendable, whose presence afterwards liketh us not so much. We ween sometimes with our presence to please others, when we rather displease them, through the evil manners and evil conditions that they see and will consider in us.

The Ninth Chapter: Of meek subjection and obedience, and that we should gladly follow the counsel of others. ¶ It is a great thing to be obedient, to live under a prelate, and in nothing to seek our own liberty. It is a much surer way to stand in the state of obedience, than in the state of prelacy. Many be under obedience more of necessity than of charity, and they have great pain, and lightly murmur and grudge : and they shall never have liberty and freedom of spirit, till they wholly submit themselves unto their superior. Go here and there where thou wilt, and thou shalt never find perfect rest ; but in meek obedience under the governance of thy prelate. The imagining and changing of place hath deceived many a religious person. Truth it is, that every man is disposed to do after his own will, and best can agree with them that follow his ways. But if we will that God

be amongst us, we may sometimes leave our own will,
(though it seem good), that we may have love and
peace with others. Who is so wise that he can fully
know all things? Truly no one. Therefore trust not
too much to thine own wit, but hear gladly the counsel of others. And if percase the thing which thou
wouldst have done be good and profitable, and yet
nevertheless thou leavest thine own will therein, and
followest another, thou shalt find much profit thereby. I have oftentimes heard say, that it is the surer
way to hear and take counsel than it is to give it. It
is good to hear every man's counsel; but not to agree,
when reason requireth, is a sign of a great singularity
of mind, and of much inward pride.

**The Tenth Chapter: That we should avoid
superfluity of words, and the company of worldly-living
people.** ¶ Flee the company of worldly-living people
as much as thou mayest: for the treating of worldly
matters letteth greatly the fervour of spirit: though
it be done with a good intent, we be anon deceived
with vanity of the world, and in manner are made as
thrall unto it, if we take not good heed. I would I
had held my peace many times when I have spoken,
and that I had not been so much amongst worldly
company as I have been. But why are we so glad to
speak and commune together, sith we so seldom depart without some hurt of conscience? This is the
cause. By our communing together we think to comfort each other, and to refresh our hearts when we be
troubled with vain imaginations, and we speak most

gladly of such things as we most love, or else of things that be most contrarious unto us.

But alas for sorrow! All is vain that we do ; for this outward comfort is no little hindrance of the true inward comfort that cometh of God. Therefore it is necessary that we watch and pray, that the time pass not away from us in idleness. If it be lawful and expedient to speak, speak then of God and of such things as are to the edifying of thy soul or of thy neighbours. An evil use and a negligence of our ghostly profit maketh us oftentimes to take little heed how we should speak. Nevertheless, sometimes it helpeth right much to the health of the soul, a devout communing of spiritual things, specially when men of one mind and spirit in God do meet and speak and commune together.

The Eleventh Chapter : The means to get peace, and of desire to profit in virtues. ¶ We might have much peace, if we would not meddle with other men's sayings and doings, that belong not unto us. How may he long live in peace, that wilfully will meddle with other men's business, and that seeketh occasions abroad in the world, and seldom or never gathereth himself together in God? Blessed be the true simple, and meek persons, for they shall have great plenty of peace. Why have many Saints been so perfectly contemplative, for they always studied to mortify themselves from worldly desires, that they might freely with all the power of their heart tend to our Lord! But we be occupied with our passions, and

16

be much busied with transitory things, and it is very seldom that we may fully overcome any one vice. And we be nothing quick to our duties, wherefore we remain cold and slow to devotion. If we were perfectly mortified to the world and to the flesh, and were inwardly purified in soul, we should anon savour heavenly things, and somewhat should we have experience of heavenly contemplation. The greatest hindrance of the heavenly contemplation is, that we are not yet clearly delivered from all passions and concupiscence, and we enforce not ourself to follow the way that holy Saints have gone before us : but when any little adversity cometh to us, we be anon cast down therein, and turn us over-soon to seek man's comfort. But if we would as strong men and as mighty champions fight strongly in this ghostly battle, we should undoubtedly see the help of God come in our need. for He is always ready to help all them that trust in Him, and He procureth occasions of such battle, to the end that we should overcome and have the victory, and in the end to have the greater reward therefor.

If we set the end and perfection of our religion in these outward observances, our devotion shall soon be ended. Wherefore we must set our axe deep to the root of the tree, that we (purged from all passions) may have a quiet mind. If we would every year overcome one vice, we should anon come to perfection. But I fear rather, that contrariwise we were better and more pure in the beginning of our conversion, than we be many years after we were converted. Our fervour and desire to virtue should daily increase in us, as we increase in age. But it is now thought a great thing, if we may hold a little sparkle of the fervour that we had first. If we would at the beginning break the evil inclination we have to ourself and to our own will, we should after do virtuous works easily, and with great gladness of heart.

It is a hard thing to leave evil customs, but is harder to break our own will, but it is most hard, evermore to lie in pain and endlessly to lose the joys of heaven. If thou overcome not small things and light, how shalt thou then overcome the greater ? Resist therefore quickly in the beginning thy evil inclinations, and leave off wholly all thine evil customs, lest haply by little and little they bring thee after to greater difficulty. O if thou wouldst consider how great inward peace thou shouldst have thyself, and how great gladness thou shouldst cause in others, in behaving of thyself well, I suppose verily thou wouldst be much more diligent to profit in virtue than thou hast been before this time !

The Twelfth Chapter: Of the profit of adversity. ¶ It is good that we have sometime griefs and adversities, for they drive a man to behold himself, and to see that he is here but as in an exile, and be learned thereby to know that he ought not to put his trust in any worldly thing. It is good also that we suffer sometime contradiction, and that we be holden of others as evil, and wretched, and sinful, though we do well and intend well : for such things help us to meekness and mightily defend us from vain-glory and pride. We take God the better to be our judge and witness, when we be outwardly despised in the world, and the world judgeth not well of us.

Therefore, a man ought to settle himself so fully in God, that what adversity soever befall unto him, he shall not need to seek any outward comfort. When a good man is troubled or tempted, or is inquieted with evil thoughts, then he understandeth and knoweth that God is most necessary to him, and he may nothing do that is good without Him. Then he sorroweth, waileth, and prayeth for the miseries that he rightfully suffereth. Then it irketh him also the wretchedness of this life, and he coveteth to be dissolved from this body of death, and to be with Christ. Then also he seeth well, that there may be no full peace nor perfect quietness here in this world.

The Thirteenth Chapter: Of temptations to be resisted. ¶ As long as we live in this world we may not be fully without temptation. For, as Job saith, '*The life of man upon earth is a warfare*';[1] therefore every man should beware well against his temptations, and watch in prayers that the ghostly enemy find not time and place to deceive him, which never sleepeth, but always '*walketh about, seeking whom he may devour.*'[2] There is no man so perfect nor so holy in this world, that he sometime hath not temptations. And we may not fully be without them, for though they be for the time very grievous and painful, yet if

---

[1] See Job vii. 1.   [2] 1 Peter v. 8.

Thomas à Kempis

they be resisted they be very profitable; for a man
by experience of such temptations is made more
meek, and is also purged, and informed in diverse
manner, which he would never have known, but by
experience of such temptations.

All blessed Saints, that now be crowned in heaven,
grew and profited by temptations and tribulations,
and those that could not well bear temptations, but
were finally overcome, be taken perpetual prisoners
in hell. There is no order so holy, no place so secret,
that is fully without temptation, and there is no man
that is fully free from it here in this life: for in
our corrupt body we bear the matter whereby we
be tempted, that is, our inordinate concupiscence,
wherein we were born.

As one temptation goeth another cometh, and so
we shall always have somewhat to suffer: and the
cause is, for we have lost our innocence. Many folk
seek to flee temptation, and they fall the more grievously into it: for by only fleeing we may not have
victory, but by meekness and patience we be made
stronger than all our enemies.

He that only flieth the outward occasions and cut-
teth not away the inordinate desires hid inwardly in
the heart shall little profit: yea temptations shall
lightly come to him again, and grieve him more than
they did first. By little and little, with patience and
sufferance, and with the help of God, thou shalt sooner
overcome temptations than with thine own strength
and importunity. In thy temptation it is good that

thou oft ask counsel, and that thou be not rigorous to a person that is tempted ; but be glad to comfort him as thou wouldest be comforted.

The beginning of all evil temptations is inconstancy of mind, and too little a trust in God. For as a ship without guide is driven hither and thither with every storm, so an unstable man, that anon leaveth his good purpose in God, is diversely tempted. The fire proveth gold, and temptation proveth the righteous man. We know not many times what we can suffer, but temptation sheweth plainly what we are, and what virtue is in us. It is necessary, in the beginning of every temptation, to be well wary, for then the enemy is soon overcome, if he be not suffered to enter into the heart; but that he be resisted and shut out as soon as he proffereth to enter. For as bodily medicine is very late ministered, when the sickness has been suffered to increase by long continuance; so is it with temptation. First cometh to the mind an unclean thought, and after followeth a strong imagination, and then delectation and diverse evil motions, and in the end followeth a full assent, and so by little and little the enemy hath full entry, for he was not wisely resisted in the beginning.

Some persons have their greatest temptations in the beginning of their conversion, some in the end, and some in a manner all their life time be troubled therewith, and there be many that be but lightly tempted: all this cometh of the great wisdom and righteousness of God, which knoweth the state and merit of every person, and ordaineth all things for the best, and to the everlasting health and salvation of His elect and chosen people.

Therefore we shall not despair when we be tempted, but shall the more fervently pray unto God, that He of His infinite goodness and fatherly pity vouchsafe to help us in every need, and that He, according to the saying of St. Paul, so prevent us with His grace in every temptation, that we *'may be able to bear it.'*[1] *'Let us humble ourselves therefore under the mighty hand of God,'*[2] for He will save all them and exalt all them that be here meek and lowly in spirit.

In temptations and tribulations a man is proved how much he hath profited, and his merit is thereby the greater before God, and his virtues are the more openly shewed. It is no great marvel if a man be fervent and devout when he feeleth no grief: but if he can suffer patiently in time of temptation or other adversity, and therewithal can also stir himself to fervour of spirit, it is a token that he shall greatly profit hereafter in virtue and grace. Some persons be kept from many great temptations, and yet daily they be overcome through little and small occasions, and that is of the great goodness and sufferance of God to keep them in meekness, that they shall not trust nor presume of themselves, that see themselves so lightly, and in so little things daily overcome.

[1] 1 Cor. x 13.   [2] 1 Peter v. 6.

Of the Imitation of Christ

The Fourteenth Chapter: That we shall not judge lightly other men's deeds, nor cleave much to our own will. ¶ Have always a good eye to thyself, and beware thou judge not lightly other men. In judging other men a man oft laboureth in vain, oft erreth, and lightly offendeth God: but in judging himself and his own deeds, he always laboureth fruitfully and to his ghostly profit. We judge oftentimes after our own heart and affections, and not after the truth: for we oft lose the true judgment through our private love. But if God were always the whole intent of our desire, we should not so lightly err in our judgments, nor so lightly be troubled, for that we be resisted of our will.

But commonly there be in us some inward inclination, or some outward affection, that draweth our heart with them from the true judgment. Many persons through a secret love that they have to their self, work indiscreetly after their own will, and not after the will of God, and yet they ween not so: they seem to stand in great inward peace when things follow after their mind, but if it follow otherwise than they would, anon they be moved with impatience, and be right heavy and pensive. By diversities of opinions be sprung many times dissensions between friends and neighbours, and also between religious and devout persons.

An old custom is hardly broken, and no man will lightly be removed from his own will: but if thou cleave more to thine own will, or to thine own reason, than to the meek obedience of Jesus Christ, it will be long or thou be a man illumined with grace. For Almighty God wills that we be perfectly subject and obedient to Him, and that we ascend and rise high above our own will, and above our own reason, by a great burning love and a whole desire to Him.

The Fifteenth Chapter: Of works done in charity.

¶ For nothing in the world, nor for the love of any creature, is evil to be done, but sometimes for the need and comfort of our neighbour a good deed may be deferred, or be turned into another good deed, for thereby it is not destroyed, but is changed into better. Without charity the outward deed is little to be praised : but whatsoever is done of charity, be it never so little, or never so despicable in sight of the world, it is right profitable before God, Who judgeth all things after the intent of the doer, and not after the greatness or worthiness of the deed.

He doth much that much loveth God, and he doth much that doeth his deed well, and he doeth his deed well, that doth it rather for the commonalty than for his own will. A deed sometimes seemeth to be done of charity and love of God, when it is rather done of carnality, and of a fleshly love, than of a charitable love: for commonly some carnal inclination to our friends, or some inordinate love to ourself, or some hope of a temporal reward, or the desire of some other profit, moveth us to do the deed, and not the pure love of charity.

Charity seeketh not himself in that he doth, but

he desireth to do only that which shall be honour and
praising to God. He envieth no man, for he loveth
no private love, neither will he joy in himself, but he
coveteth above all things to be blessed in God He
knoweth well that no goodness beginneth originally of
man, and therefore he referreth all goodness to God,
of whom all things proceed, and in whom all blessed
Saints do rest in everlasting fruition. Oh, he that had
but a little sparkle of this perfect charity, should feel
soothfastly in his soul that all earthly things be full of
vanity!

**The Sixteenth Chapter: Of the suffering of
other men's defaults.** ¶ Such defaults as we cannot
amend in ourselves nor in others, we must patiently
suffer, till our Lord of His goodness will otherwise
dispose. And we shall think that haply it so is best
to be for proving of our patience, without which our
merits are but little to be pondered. Nevertheless
thou shalt pray heartily for such impediments, that
our Lord of His great mercy and goodness vouchsafe
to help thee, that thou mayest patiently bear them.

If thou admonish any person once or twice, and he
will not take it, strive not over much with him, but
commit all to God, that His will be done, and His
honour in all His servants, for He can well by His
goodness turn evil into good. Study always that thou
mayest be patient in suffering of other men's defaults,
for thou hast many things in thee that others do suffer
of thee: and if thou canst not make thyself to be as
thou wouldst, how mayest thou then look to have

another to be ordered in all things after thy will? We would gladly have others perfect, but will not amend our own defaults.

We would that others should be straitly corrected for their offences, but we will not be corrected. It misliketh us that others have liberty, but we will not be denied of that we ask. We would also that others should be restrained according to the statutes, but we in nowise will be restrained. Thus it appeareth evidently that we seldom ponder our neighbour, as we do ourselves. If all men were perfect, what had we then to suffer of our neighbours for God?

Therefore God hath so ordained that each one of us shall learn to bear another's burden: for in this world no man is without default, no man without burden, no man sufficient to himself, nor no man wise enough of himself. Wherefore it behoveth each one of us to bear the burden of others, to comfort others, to help others, to inform others, and to instruct and admonish others in all charity. Who is of most virtue appeareth best in time of adversity. Occasions make not a man frail, but they shew openly what he is.

The Seventeenth Chapter: What should be the life of a true religious person. ¶ It behoveth thee to break thine own will in many things, if thou wilt have peace and concord with others. It is no little thing to be in monasteries or in congregations, and to continue there without complaining or missaying, and faithfully to persevere there unto the end: blessed are they that there live well and make a good end. If thou wilt stand surely in grace, and much profit in virtue, hold thyself as an outlaw and as a pilgrim here in this life, and be glad for the love of God to be holden as a fool, and as a vile person, as thou art.

The habit and the tonsure help little, but the changing of life and the mortifying of the passions make a person a perfect and true religious. He that seeketh any other thing in religion than purely God and the health of his soul, shall find nothing there but trouble and sorrow, and he may not long stand there in peace and quietness that laboureth not to be least and subject to all.

It is good, therefore, that thou remember oft, that thou comest to religion to serve and not to be served, and that thou art called thither to suffer and to labour, and not to be idle or tell vain tales. In religion a man shall be proved as gold in a furnace, and no man may stand long there in grace and virtue, but he will with all his heart meek himself for the love of God.

The Eighteenth Chapter: Of the examples of holy Fathers. ¶ Behold the lively examples of holy Fathers and blessed Saints, in whom flourished and shined all true perfection of life and perfect religion, and thou shalt see how little it is, and well nigh as nothing, that we do now in these days, in comparison of them. O what is our life, if it be to them compared! They served our Lord in hunger and thirst, in heat and in cold, in nakedness, in labour and weariness, in vigils and fastings, in prayers and in holy meditations, in persecutions and in many reproofs.

27

Thomas à Kempis

O how many and how grievous tribulations suffered the Apostles, Martyrs, Confessors, Virgins,
and other holy Saints, that would follow the steps of
Christ! They refused honours and all bodily pleasures here in this life, that they might always have the
everlasting life. O how strait and abject a life led the
holy Fathers in wilderness! How grievous temptations suffered they! How fiercely were they with
their ghostly enemies assailed, and how fervent prayer
offered they daily to God! What rigorous abstinence used they, how great zeal and fervour had they
to spiritual profit! How strong battle held they
against all sin, and how pure and whole intent had
they to God in all their deeds!

In the day they laboured, and in the night they
prayed. And though they laboured in the day bodily, yet they prayed in mind, and so they spent their
time always fruitfully, and thought every hour short
for the service of God: and for the great sweetness
that they had in heavenly contemplation they forgot
ofttimes their bodily refection. All riches, honour,
dignities, kinsmen, and friends they renounced for
the love of God. They coveted to have nothing in
the world, and scarcely they would take what was
necessary for the bodily kind. They were poor in
worldly goods, but they were rich in grace and virtue.
They were needy outwardly, but inwardly in their
souls they were replenished with grace and ghostly
comforts.

To the world they were aliens and strangers, but

to God they were right dear and familiar friends. In the sight of the world and in their own sight they were vile and abject, but in the sight of God and His Saints they were precious and singularly elect. In them shined all perfection of virtue, true meekness, simple obedience, charity, and patience, with other like virtues and gracious gifts of God. Wherefore they profited daily in spirit, and obtained great grace of God. They be left as an example to all religious persons: and more ought their examples to stir them to devotion, and to profit more and more in virtue and grace, than the great multitude of dissolute and idle persons should anything draw them aback.

O what fervour was in religious persons at the beginning of their religion! What devotion in prayers! What zeal to virtue! What love to ghostly discipline! And what reverence and meek obedience flourished in them under the rule of their superior! Truly their deeds yet bear witness that they were holy and perfect, and so mightily subdued the world and thrust it underfoot. Nowadays he is accounted virtuous that is no offender, and that may with patience keep some little sparkle of that virtue and fervour that he had first.

But alas for sorrow! It is through our own sloth and negligence, and through losing of time, that we be so soon fallen from our first fervour into such a ghostly weakness and dulness of spirit, that in manner it is too tedious to us for to live. But would to God that the desire to profit in virtue slept not so utterly in thee, that so oft hast seen the holy examples of blessed Saints!

The Nineteenth Chapter: Of the exercises of a good religious person. ¶ The life of a good religious man should shine in all virtue, and be inward as it appeareth outward. And that much more inward, for Almighty God beholdeth the heart, Whom we should always honour and reverence as if we were ever in His bodily presence, and appear before Him as Angels clean and pure, shining in all virtue We ought every day to renew our purpose in God, and to stir our heart to fervour and devotion, as though it were the first day of our conversion, and daily we shall pray and say thus: Help me, my Lord Jesu, that I may persevere in good purpose, and in Thy holy service unto my death, and that I may now this present day perfectly begin, for it is nothing that I have done in time past.

After our purpose, and after our intent shall be our reward. And though our intent be never so good, yet it is necessary that we put thereto a good will and a great diligence. For if he that oftentimes purposeth to do well and to profit in virtue, yet faileth in his doing, what shall he do then, who seldom or never taketh such purpose? Let us intend to do the best we can, and yet our good purpose may happen to be hindered and letted in divers manners. And our special hindrance is this, that we so lightly leave off our good exercises that we have used to do before time · for it is seldom seen that a good purpose wilfully broken may be recovered again without great spiritual hindrance. The purpose of righteous men dependeth in the grace of God more than in themselves, or in their own wisdom : for man purposeth, but God disposeth: nay, the way that man shall walk in this world is not in himself but in the grace of God.

If a good custom be sometimes left off for help of our neighbour, it may soon be recovered : but if it be left off through sloth, or through our own negligence, it will greatly hinder us, and hardly will it be recovered again. Thus it appeareth that though we encourage ourselves all that we can to do well, yet it is good that we always take such good purpose, especially against such things as hinder us most. We must also make diligent search both within us and without us, that we leave nothing inordinate unreformed in us, as nigh as our frailty may suffer.

And if thou cannot for frailty of thyself do thus continually, yet at the least, that thou do it once in the day, evening or morning. In the morning thou shalt take a good purpose for that day following, and at night thou shalt discuss diligently how thou hast behaved thee the day before, in word, in deed, and in thought: for in them we do often offend God and our neighbour. Arm thee as Christ's true knight with meekness and charity, against all the malice of the enemy. Refrain gluttony, and thou shalt more lightly refrain all carnal desires. Let not the ghostly enemy find thee all idle, but that thou be reading, writing, praying devoutly, thinking, or some other good labour doing for the commonalty. Bodily exercises are to be done discreetly: for that which is profitable to one is sometimes hurtful to another: and also spiritual labours done of devotion are more sure done in private than in open place.

And thou must beware that thou be not more ready to private devotions than to them that thou art bound to by duty of thy religion. But when thy duty is fulfilled, then add thereto, after as thy devotion giveth. All may not use one manner of exercise, but one in one manner, another in another manner, as they shall feel to be most profitable to them. Also, as the time requireth, so divers exercises are to be used, for one manner of exercise is necessary on the holy day, another on the ferial day: one in the time of temptation, another in the time of peace and consolation: one when we have sweetness in devotion, another when devotion withdraweth.

. Also against principal feasts we ought to be more diligent in good works and devoutly to call for help to the blessed Saints, that then be worshipped in the Church of God, than at other times, and to dispose ourselves in like manner, as if we should then be taken out of the world, and be brought into the everlasting feast in heaven.

And sith that bliss is yet deferred from us for a time, we may well think that we be not yet ready, nor worthy to come thereto And therefore we ought to prepare ourselves to be more ready another

Of the Imitation of Christ

time. For, as St. Luke saith: '*Blessea is that servant, whom his Lord when he cometh*'—at the hour of death—'*shall find ready*':[1] for He shall take him, and lift him up high above all earthly things, into the everlasting joy and bliss in the kingdom of heaven. Amen.

The Twentieth Chapter: Of the love of loneliness and silence. ¶ Seek for a convenient time to search thine own conscience, and think oft on the benefits of God. Leave off all curious things, and read such matters as shall stir thee to compunction of heart for thy sins, rather than read only for occupying of the time. If thou wilt withdraw thyself from superfluous words, and from unprofitable runnings about, and from the hearing of rumours and vain tales, thou shalt find time convenient to be occupied in holy meditations. The most holy men and women that ever were fled the company of worldly-living men with all their power, and chose to serve God in secret of their heart.

One holy man said: '*As oft as I have been among worldly company, I have departed with less fervour of spirit than I came.*' And this we know well when we talk long: for it is not so hard to keep always silence, as it is not to exceed in words when we speak much. It is also more light to be always solitary at home, than to go forth into the world and not offend. Therefore he that intendeth to come to inward setting of his heart to God and to have the grace of devotion,

[1] Luke xii. 43

must with our Saviour Christ withdraw him from the
people. No man may surely appear among the people,
but he that would gladly be solitary, if he might: nor
no man is sure in prelacy, but he that would gladly
be a subject: no, none may surely command, but he
that hath learned gladly to obey: and none joyeth
truly, but he whose heart witnesseth that he hath a
clean conscience: yea, none speaketh surely, but he
that would gladly keep silence if he might.

The surety of good men and blessed men hath
always been in meekness and dread of God. And
though such blessed men shined in all virtue, yet they
were not therefore lifted up into pride, but were therefore the more diligent in the service of God, and the
more meek in all their doings. On the contrarywise,
the surety of evil men riseth of pride and of presumption, and in the end it deceiveth them. Therefore
think thyself never sure in this life, whether thou be
religious or secular: for ofttimes, they that have been
holden in the sight of the people most perfect, have
been suffered to fall more grievously for their presumption.

Also, it is much more profitable to many persons
that they have sometimes temptations (lest haply
they think themselves overmuch safe, and be thereby lift up into pride, or run to seeking outward consolation,) than that they be always without temptations. O how pure a conscience should he have that
would despise all transitory joy, and never would
meddle with worldly business! And what peace and

inward quietness should he have, that would cut away
from him all business of mind, and only think on
heavenly things!

No man is worthy to have ghostly comforts, unless
he have first been well exercised in holy compunction.
And if thou wilt have compunction, go into a secret
place, and put from thee all the clamorous noise of
the world: for the Prophet David saith: '*Stand in
awe, and sin not: commune with your own heart upon
your bed, and be still.*'[1] In thy cell thou shalt find great
grace, which thou mayest lightly lose without. Thy
cell well continued shall wear sweet and pleasant to
thee, and shall be to thee hereafter a right dear friend;
and if it be but ill kept, it shall grow very tedious and
irksome to thee. But if in the beginning thou be oft
therein, and keep it well in good prayers and holy
meditations, it shall be after to thee a special friend,
and one of thy most special comforts.

In silence and quietness of heart a devout soul profiteth much and learneth the hidden sentences of
Scripture, and findeth therein also many sweet tears
in devotion, wherewith every night she washeth her
mightily from all filth of sin, that she may be so much
the more familiar with God, as she is dissevered from
the clamorous noise of worldly business. Therefore
they that for the love of virtue withdraw them from
their acquaintance and friends, our Lord with His
Angels shall draw nigh to them, and shall abide with
them. It is better that a man be solitary, and well

[1] Ps. iv 4

take heed of himself, than that he do miracles in the world, forgetting himself. It is also a laudable thing in a religious person seldom to go forth, seldom to see others, and seldom to be seen of others.

Why wilt thou see that which it is not lawful for thee to have ? The world passeth away, with all his concupiscence and deceitful pleasures. Thy sensual appetite moveth thee to go abroad, but when the time is past, what bearest thou home again but remorse of conscience and unquietness of heart? It is often seen that after a merry going forth followeth a heavy returning; and that a glad eventide causeth a heavy morning : and so all fleshly joy entereth pleasantly, but in the end it biteth and slayeth. What mayest thou see without thy cell that thou mayest not see within? Lo, heaven and earth, and all the elements, whereof all earthly things be made! What mayest thou elsewhere see under the sun that may long endure ?

And if thou might see all earthly things, and also have all bodily pleasure present at once before thee, what were it but a vain sight? Lift up thine eyes, therefore, to God in heaven, and pray heartily that thou mayest have forgiveness of thine offences. Leave vain things to them that will be vain, and take thou heed only to those things that our Lord commandeth thee. Shut fast the door of thy soul, that is to say, thy imagination, and keep it warily from beholding of any bodily thing, as much as thou mayest : and then lift up thy mind to the Lord Jesu,

and open thy heart faithfully to Him, and abide with
Him in thy cell, for thou shalt not find so much peace
without. If thou hadst not gone forth so much as
thou hast done, nor hadst given hearing to vain tales,
thou shouldst have been in much more inward peace
than thou art: but for as much as it delighteth thee
to hear new things, it behoveth thee therefore to
suffer sometimes both trouble of heart and unquietness of mind.

**The Twenty-first Chapter: Of compunc-
tion of the heart.** ❡ If thou wilt anything profit to the
health of thy soul keep thee always in the dread of
God, and never desire to be fully at liberty, but
keep thee always under some wholesome discipline.
Never give thyself to indiscreet mirth, for any manner of thing, as nigh as thou mayest. Have perfect
compunction and sorrow for thy sins, and thou shalt
find thereby great inward devotion. Compunction
openeth to the sight of the soul many good things,
which lightness of heart and vain mirth soon driveth
away. It is marvel that any man can be merry in this
life, if he consider well how far he is exiled out of his
country, and how great peril his soul daily standeth
in: but through lightness of heart and negligence of
our defaults we feel not the sorrow of our own soul:
but oftentimes we laugh when we ought rather to
weep and mourn, for there is no perfect liberty, nor
true joy, but in the dread of God and in a good conscience.

That person is right happy, that hath grace to

avoid all things that let him from beholding of his own sins, and that can turn himself to God by inward compunction : and he is happy also that avoideth all things that may offend, or grieve his conscience. Fight strongly therefore against all sins, and dread not overmuch, although thou be encumbered by an evil custom, for that evil custom may be overcome with a good custom. And excuse thee not that thou art let by other men ; for if thou wilt leave thy familiarity with others, they will suffer thee to do thy deeds without impediment.

Meddle thee not with other men's goods, neither busy thee in great men's causes : have always an eye to thyself ; and diligently inform and admonish thyself before all others. If thou have not the favour of worldly-living people, sorrow not therefor : but let this be thy daily sorrow, that thou behavest not thyself in thy conversation, as it beseemeth a good religious person to do. It is more expedient and more profitable that a man sometimes lack consolations in this life, than that he have them always after his own will, namely, fleshly consolations. Nevertheless, that we have not sometimes heavenly consolations, or that we so seldom feel them as we do, is through our own default : for we seek not to have true compunction of heart, nor do we cast fully away from us false outward consolations.

Hold thyself therefore unworthy to have any consolation, and worthy to have much tribulation. When a man sorroweth perfectly for his sins, then

all worldly comforts be painful to him. A good man
findeth always matter enough why he ought justly
to sorrow and to weep: for if he behold himself, or
if he think on his neighbour, he seeth well that no
one liveth here without great misery, and the more
thoroughly he considereth himself, the more sorrow
he hath. And always the matter of true sorrow, and
of true inward compunction, is the remembrance of
our sins, wherein we be so wrapt on every side that
we seldom behold any ghostly things.

But if we would oftener think of our death than
we do on a long life, no doubt but we should more
fervently apply ourselves to amendment: and I believe also, that if we would heartily remember the
pains of hell and of purgatory, we should more gladly
sustain all labours and sorrows, and we should not
dread any pain in this world, whereby we might avoid
the pains that are to come.

But, forasmuch as these things go not to the heart,
and we yet love the flattering and false pleasures of
this world, therefore we remain cold and void of
devotion, and oft it is through the weakness of the
spirit that the wretched body so lightly complaineth.
Pray, therefore, meekly to our Lord, that He of His
great goodness will give thee the spirit of compunction, and say with the Prophet: ' *How long, Lord?
wilt thou be angry for ever? shall thy jealousy burn
like fire?* '[1]

[1] Ps. lxxix. 5

The Twenty-second Chapter: Of the considering of the misery of mankind, and wherein the felicity of man standeth. ¶ A wretch thou art, whosoever thou be, whithersoever thou turn thee, but if thou turn to God. Why art thou so lightly troubled for that it falleth not to thee as thou wouldst and desirest? Who is he that hath all things after his will? Neither thou, nor I, nor any living man · for none liveth here without some trouble or anguish, be he King or Pope.[1]

Who, thinkest thou, is in most favour with God? Truly, he that suffereth gladly most for God. But many persons, weak and feeble in spirit, say thus in their hearts: Lo, how good a life that man leadeth, how rich he is, how mighty he is, how high in authority, how great in sight of the people, how fair and beautiful in his bodily kind . but if thou take heed to the goodness everlasting, thou shalt well see that these worldly goods and worldly likings are but little worth, and that they be rather more grievous than pleasant, for they may not be had nor kept but by great labour and business of mind. The felicity of man standeth not in abundance of worldly goods, for the mean is best. And, verily, to live in this world is but misery: and the more ghostly that a man would be, the more painful it is to him to live, for he feeleth more plainly the defaults of man's corruption. For to eat, to drink, to sleep, to wake, to rest, to labour, and to serve all other necessities of the

[1] These two words are omitted by Atkinson and by Whytforde

40

body is great misery and great affliction to a devout soul, which would gladly be free from the bondage of sin, that it might without let serve our Lord in purity of conscience and in cleanness of heart.

The inward man is greatly grieved through the bodily necessities in this world. Wherefore the Prophet David desired that he might be delivered from such necessities.[1] But woe be to them that know not their own misery, and greater woe be to them that love this wretched and corruptible life: for some love it so much, that if they might ever live here, though they might get their living with labour and begging, yet they would never care for the kingdom of heaven.

O mad and unfaithful creatures are they that so deeply set their love in earthly things, that they have no feeling, nor taste, but in fleshly pleasures! Truly in the hour of death they shall know how vile, and how naughty it was, that they so much loved. But holy Saints and devout followers of Christ, did not what pleased the flesh, nor what was pleasant in the sight of the world, but they held their whole intent and desire to things invisible, and feared lest by sight of things visible they might be drawn down to the love of them.

My well-beloved brother, lose not the desire to profit in spiritual things, for thou hast yet good time and space. Why wilt thou any longer defer the time? Arise, and now this same instant begin, and

[1] 'O bring thou me out of my distresses.'—Ps. xxv. 17.

say thus: Now is the time to labour in good works,
now is the time to fight in ghostly battle, and now
is the time for making amends for trespass that is
passed. When thou art troubled, then is the best
time to merit and get rewards of God. It behoveth
thee to go through fire and water before thou come
to the place of recreation, and if thou can but fully
have the mastery over thyself thou shalt never overcome sin, nor live without great tediousness and
sorrow. We would gladly be delivered from all
misery and sin · but because through sin we have
lost our innocency, we have lost also the very joy
and felicity. Wherefore we must hold us in patience,
and with good hope abide the mercy of God, till
wretchedness and misery be overpassed, and this
bodily life be changed into the life everlasting.

O how great is the frailty of man, that he is ever
ready and prone to sin! This day thou art confessed,
and to-morrow thou fallest again. Now thou pur-
posest to beware, and intendest to go forth strongly
in good works, and shortly after thou dost, as if thou
never hadst taken such purpose. Rightfully therefore we ought to meek ourselves, and never to think
in us any virtue or goodness, for that we be so frail
and unstable. Soon may that be lost through negligence, which with much labour and special grace was
hardly gotten.

But what shall become of us in the end, when we
so soon wax dull and slow? Soothly sorrow and woe
shall be to us, if we fall to bodily rest now, as though

we were in ghostly sickerness,[1] when yet there appeareth not either sign or token of virtue, or of good living, in our conversation. Wherefore it were expedient to us, that we were yet again instructed as novices to learn good manners, if haply there might by that means be found hereafter any trust of amendment and spiritual profit in our conversation.

The Twenty-third Chapter: Of the remembrance of death. ¶ The hour of death will shortly come, and therefore take heed how thou orderest thyself; for the common proverb is true · *To-day a man, to-morrow none.* And when thou art taken out of sight, thou art anon out of mind, and soon shalt thou be forgotten. O the great dulness and hardness of man's heart, that only thinketh on things present, and little provideth for the life to come ! If thou didst well, thou shouldst so behave thyself in every deed and in every thought, as though thou shouldst in this instant die. If thou hadst a good conscience, thou wouldst not much fear death. It were better for thee to leave sin than fear death. O my dear brother, if thou be not ready this day, how shalt thou be ready to-morrow? To-morrow is a day uncertain, and thou canst not tell whether thou shalt live so long.

What profit is it to us to live long, when we thereby so little amend our life ? Long life does not always bring us to amendment, but ofttimes increaseth sin. Would to God that we might be one day well conversant in this world ! Many reckon their years of

---

[1] security

43

conversion, and yet there is but little fruit of amendment, or of any good example, seen in their conversation. If it be fearful to die, peradventure it is more perilous to live long. Blessed be those persons that ever have the hour of death before their eyes, and that every day dispose themselves to die. If thou ever sawest a man die, remember that thou must needs go the same way.

In the morning doubt whether thou shalt live till night, and at night think not thyself sure to live till to-morrow. Be always ready, and live in such manner that death find thee not unprovided. Remember how many have died suddenly and unprovided, for our Lord hath called them in such an hour as they least thought. And when that last hour shall come, thou shalt begin to feel all otherwise of thy life past, than thou hast done before. And thou shalt then sorrow greatly that thou hast been so slow and negligent in the service of God as thou hast been.

O how happy and wise therefore is he that laboureth now to stand in such state in this life, as he would be found in at his death! Truly a perfect despising of the world and a fervent desire to profit in virtue, a love to be taught, a fruitful labour in works of penance, a ready will to obey, a forsaking of ourself, and a willing suffering of all adversities for the love of God, shall give us a great trust that we shall die well. Now, whilst thou art in health, thou mayest do many good deeds, but if thou be sick, I cannot tell what thou mayest do. For why? Few be amended through sickness. And likewise, they that go much on pilgrimage, be seldom thereby made perfect and holy.

Put not thy trust in thy friends and thy neighbours, neither defer thy good deeds till after thy death ; for thou shalt sooner be forgotten than thou weenest. Better it is to provide for thyself betime, and to send some good deeds before thee, than to trust to others who peradventure will lightly forget thee. If thou be not now busy for thyself, and for thine own soul's health, who shall be busy for thee after thy death? Now is the time very precious, but alas for sorrow, that thou spendest the time so unprofitably, in the which thou shouldst win the life everlasting! The time shall come, when thou shalt desire one day or one hour to amend thee, but I wot not whether it shall be granted unto thee.

O my dear brother, from how great peril and dread mightest thou now deliver thyself, if thou wouldst always in this life dread to offend God, and always have the coming of death suspect! Therefore study now to live so, that at the hour of death thou mayest rather joy than dread. Learn now to die to the world, that thou mayest then live with Christ. Learn also to despise all worldly things that thou mayest then freely go to Christ. Chastise now thy body with penance, that thou mayest then have a sure and steadfast hope of salvation.

Thou art a fool, if thou think to live long, sith thou art not sure to live one day to the end. How many have been deceived through trust of long life, and suddenly have been taken out of this world or they had thought. How oft hast thou heard say that such a man was slain, and such a man was drowned, and such a man fell and broke his neck? This man as he ate his meat was strangled, and this man as he played took his death ; one with fire, another with iron, another with sickness, and some by theft have suddenly perished ! And so the end of all men is death, for the life of man as a shadow suddenly fleeth and passeth away.

Think oft, who shall remember thee after thy death, and who shall pray for thee? Do now for thyself all thou canst, for thou wottest not when thou shalt die, nor what shall follow after thy death. Whilst thou hast time gather thee riches immortal, think of nothing abidingly but on thy ghostly health. Set thy study only on things that be of God, and that belong to His honour. Make thee friends against that time, worship the Saints and follow their steps, that when thou shalt go out of this world they may receive thee into the everlasting tabernacles.

Keep thee as a pilgrim and as a stranger here in this world to whom nothing belongeth of worldly business. Keep thy heart always free and lifted up to God, for thou hast here no city long abiding. Send thy desires and thy daily prayers always upward to God, and pray perseverantly, that thy soul at the hour of death may blessedly depart out of this world and go to Christ.

Of the Imitation of Christ

The Twenty-fourth Chapter: Of the Last
Judgment, and of the pain that is ordained for sin. ¶ In
all things behold the end, and oft remember how
thou shalt stand before the high Judge, to Whom
nothing is hidden ; who will not be pleased with rewards, nor receive any manner of excuses, but in all
things will judge what is righteous and true. O most
unwise and wretched sinner, what shalt thou then answer to God, Who knoweth all thy sins and wretchedness, sith thou sometimes dreadest here the face of
a mortal man ?

Why dost thou not now provide for thyself
against that day, sith thou mayest not then be
excused nor defended by another; but every man
shall then have enough to do to answer for himself? Now thy labour is fruitful, and thy weeping
is acceptable; thy mourning is worthy to be heard,
and thy sorrow also is satisfactory and purgeth of
sins.

The patient man, who suffereth injuries and
wrongs of others, and yet nevertheless sorroweth
more for their malice than for the wrong done to
himself, hath a wholesome and blessed purgatory in
this world : so have they that gladly can pray for
their enemies, and for them that be contrarious unto
them ; or that in their heart can forgive those that
offend them, and tarry not long to ask forgiveness.
And so also, they that be more lightly stirred to
mercy than to vengeance, and that can as it were by
violence break down their own will, strongly resist

sin, and labour always to subdue their body to the spirit. It is better now to purge sin and to put away vice, than to reserve it to be purged hereafter. But verily we deceive ourselves by the inordinate love that we have to our bodily kind.

What shall the fire of purgatory devour but thy sins? Truly nothing. Therefore the more thou sparest thyself now and the more thou followest thy fleshly liking, the more grievously shalt thou wail hereafter, and the more matter thou reservest for the fire of purgatory. In such things as a man most has offended, shall he most be punished. The slothful person shall be there pricked with burning pricks of iron, and gluttons shall be tormented with great hunger and thirst. Luxurious persons and lovers of voluptuous pleasures, shall be filled full with burning pitch and brimstone: and envious persons shall wail and howl, as mad dogs do.

There no sin shall be without its proper torment. The proud man shall be filled with all shame and confusion, and the covetous man shall pine with penury and need. One hour there in pain shall be more grievous than here a hundred years in sharpest penance. There shall be no rest nor comfort to the damned souls: but here sometimes we feel relief of our pains, and have sometimes consolation of our friends. Be now sorrowful for thy sins, that at the day of judgment thou mayest be saved with blessed Saints. ' *Then shall the just stand with great constancy against those that have afflicted them, and taken away their labours* '[1] Then shall He stand as a Judge that here submitted Himself meekly to the judgment of men. Then shall the meek poor man have great confidence and trust in God, and the obstinate proud man shall quake and dread.

Then shall it appear that he was wise in this world, that for the love of God was content to be taken as a fool, and to be despised, and set at nought. Then shall it also please him much the tribulation that he suffereth patiently in this world, for '*all iniquity shall stop her mouth.*'[2] Then every devout person shall be joyful and glad, and the irreligious shall wail and dread. Then shall the flesh, that hath been with discretion chastised, joy more than if it had been nourished with all delectation and pleasure. Then shall the vile habit shine clear in the sight of God, and the precious garments shall wax foul and loathsome to behold. Then the poor cottage shall be more hallowed than the palace over-gilded with gold. Then shall a constant patience more help than all worldly power and riches. Then shall meek obedience be exalted higher than all worldly wisdom and policy, and then shall a good clean conscience make us more gladsome and merry than the cunning of all philosophy.

Then the despising of worldly goods shall be more of value than all worldly riches and treasures. Then shalt thou have more comfort for thy devout praying than for all thy delicate feeding. Then shalt thou also joy more for thy silence keeping, than for thy long

[1] Wisd. v. 1   [2] Ps. cvii. 42.

talking and jangling. Then good deeds shall plenteously be rewarded, and fair words shall little be regarded. Then shall it please more a strait life and hard penance here, than all worldly delectation and pleasure. Learn now therefore to suffer small tribulations in this world, that thou mayest then be delivered from the greater ones there ordained for sin. First prove here what thou mayest suffer hereafter. And if thou canst not now suffer so little a pain, how shalt thou then suffer the everlasting torments? And if now so little a passion[1] make thee impatient, what shall then do the intolerable fire of purgatory or of hell?

Thou mayest not have two heavens; that is to say, to joy here and to have delectation here, and after to joy also with Christ in heaven. Moreover, if thou hadst lived always unto this day in honours and fleshly delectations, what should it profit thee now, if thou shouldst this present instant depart the world? Therefore all things are vanity, but to love God and to serve Him. He that loveth God with all his heart, dreadeth neither death, nor torment, nor judgment, nor hell; for perfect love maketh a sure passage to God: but if a man yet delight in sin, it is no marvel though he dread both death and hell. And though such a dread be but a thrall-dread, yet nevertheless it is good, that if the love of God withdraw us not from sin, that the dread of hell constrain us thereto. He that setteth apart the dread of God, may not

[1] suffering.

long stand in the state of grace, but soon shall he run
into the snare of the devil, and lightly shall he therewith be deceived.

**The Twenty-fifth Chapter: Of the fervent
amending of all our life, and that we shall specially
take heed of our own soul's health, before all others.**
¶ My son, be waking and diligent in the service of
God, and think oft wherefore thou art come, and
why thou hast forsaken the world. Was it not that
thou shouldst live to God, and be made a spiritual
man? Yes, truly. Therefore stir thyself to perfection, for in a short time thou shalt receive the full
reward of all thy labours, and from thenceforth shall
never come to thee either sorrow or dread. Thy
labour shall be little and short, and thou shalt receive
therefore everlasting rest and comfort. If thou abide
faithful and fervent in good deeds, without doubt
our Lord will be faithful and liberal to thee in His
rewards. Thou shalt always have a good trust that
thou shalt come to the palm of victory, but thou shalt
not set thee in a full surety thereof, lest haply thou
wax dull and proud in heart.

A certain person, who oftentimes doubted whether
he were in a state of grace or not, on a time fell prostrate in the church, and said thus: ' *O that I might
know whether I should persevere in virtue to the end of
my life !* ' And anon he heard inwardly in his soul
the answer of our Lord, saying: ' *What wouldst thou
do if thou knewest thou shouldst persevere? Do now as
thou wouldst do then, and thou shalt be safe.*' And anon

he was comforted, and committed himself wholly to
the will of God, and all his doubtfulness ceased, and
never after would he curiously search to know what
should become of him, but rather he studied to know
what was the will of God against him, and how he
might begin and end all his deeds to the pleasure of
God and His honour.

'*Trust in the Lord, and do good*,' saith the Prophet
David; '*so shalt thou dwell in the land, and verily thou
shalt be fed.*'[1] But one thing withdraweth many from
profiting in virtue, and from amendment of life, that
is, a horror and a false worldly dread that they may
not abide the pain and labour that is needful for the
getting thereof. Therefore they shall most profit
in virtue before all others, that enforce themselves
mightily to overcome those things that be most grievous and contrarious to them. For a man profiteth
most, and there winneth most grace, where he most
overcometh himself and mortifieth his body to the
soul.

But all men have not in like to mortify and overcome, for some have more passions than others.
Nevertheless, a fervent lover of God, though he have
greater passions than others, yet shall he be stronger to
profit in virtue than another that is better-mannered,
and that hath fewer passions, but is less fervent to
virtue. Two things help a man much to amendment
of life; that is, a mighty withdrawing of himself
from those things that the body most inclineth him

[1] Ps. xxxvii. 3.

to, and a fervent labour for such virtues as he hath most need of.

Study also to overcome in thyself those things that most mislike thee in other men, and take always some special profit in every place wheresoever thou come; as, if thou see any good example, enforce thee to follow it; and if thou see any evil example, look thou eschew it. As thy eye considereth the works of others, right so and in the same wise be thy works considered by others. O how joyous and how delectable is it to see religious men devout and fervent in the love of God, well-mannered, and well taught in ghostly learning: and, on the contrary part, how heavy and sorrowful it is to see them live inordinately, not using those things that they have chosen and taken themselves to! Also, how inconvenient a thing is it, for a man to be negligent in the purpose of his first calling, and to set his mind to things that be not committed to him!

Think oft therefore on the purpose that thou hast taken, and set before the eye of thy soul the memory of Christ's Passion; and if thou behold well and diligently His blessed Life, thou mayest well be ashamed that thou hast not conformed thyself to Him more than thou hast done. He that will inwardly and devoutly exercise himself in the most blessed Life and Passion of our Lord Jesus Christ shall find therein plenteously all that is necessary for him, so that he shall not need to seek anything without Him. O if Jesu Crucified were oft in our hearts and in our remembrance, we should soon be learned in all things necessary for us!

A good religious man that is fervent in his religion taketh all things well, and doth gladly all that he is commanded to do: but a religious person that is negligent and slothful hath trouble upon trouble, and suffereth great anguish and pain on every side, for he lacketh the true inward comfort; and to seek the outward comfort he is prohibited. Therefore a religious person that liveth without discipline is like to fall in great ruin. Also he that in religion seeketh to have liberty and releasing of his duty shall always be in anguish and sorrow, for one thing or other shall ever displease him.

Therefore take heed how other religious persons do, that be right straitly kept under the rule of their religion. They go seldom forth, they live hardly, they eat poorly, and be clothed grossly: they labour much, speak little, watch long, rise early, make long prayers, read often, and keep themselves always in some wholesome doctrine. Behold the Carthusians, the Cistercians, and many other monks and nuns of divers religions, how they rise every night to serve our Lord! And therefore it were great shame to thee, that thou shouldst wax slow and dull in so holy a work, when so many begin to laud and praise our Lord.

O how joyous a life were it, if we should nothing else do, but with heart and mouth continually praise our Lord! Truly if we should never need to eat, drink, nor sleep, but that we might always laud Him, and only take heed to spiritual studies, then were we much more happy and blessed than we are now, when we are bound of necessity to serve the body. O would to God that these bodily meats were turned to spiritual refections, which (alas for sorrow!) we take but seldom!

When man is come to that perfection that he seeketh not his consolation in any creature, then beginneth God first to savour sweet unto him, and then also he shall be contented with everything that cometh, be it in liking or misliking. Then shall he be glad for no worldly profit, be it ever so great; nor shall he be sorry for the wanting of it, for he hath set and established himself wholly in God, Who is unto him all in all; to Whom nothing perisheth nor dieth, but all things live to Him, and after His bidding serve Him without ceasing.

In everything remember the end, and that time lost cannot be called again. Without labour and diligence thou shalt never get virtue. If thou begin to be negligent thou beginnest to be feeble and weak; but if thou apply thee to fervour thou shalt find great help of God, and for the love of virtue thou shalt find less pain in all thy labours than thou didst first. He that is fervent and loving is always quick and ready to all things that be of God and to His honour. It is more labour to resist vices and passions, than it is to toil and sweat in bodily labours. He that will not flee small sins, shall by little and little fall into greater.

Thomas à Kempis

Thou shalt always be glad at night, when thou hast spent the day fruitfully. Take heed to thyself, and always stir thyself to devotion. Admonish thyself, and howsoever thou rememberest others, forget not thyself: and as thou canst break thine own will and follow the will of God, so much shalt thou profit in virtue.

The second book

Admonitions tending to things internal

The Second Book
Admonitions tending to things internal

The First Chapter: Of inward conversation.

'THE *kingdom of God is within you,*'[1] saith Christ our Saviour. Turn thee therefore with all thy heart to God, and forsake this wretched world, and thy soul shall find great inward rest. Learn to despise outward things, and give thyself to inward things, and thou shalt see the kingdom of God come into thyself. The kingdom of God is peace and joy in the Holy Ghost, that is not given to wicked people. Our Lord Jesus Christ will come to thee and will show to thee His consolations. If thou wilt make ready for Him in thy heart a dwelling-place, that is all He desireth to have in thee, and there it is His pleasure to be. Betwixt Almighty God and a devout soul there are many ghostly visitings, sweet inward speaking, great gifts of grace, many consolations, much heavenly peace, and wondrous familiarity of the blessed presence of God.

[1] Luke xvii. 21.

Therefore, thou faithful soul, prepare thy heart to Christ thy Spouse, that He may come to thee and dwell in thee: for He saith Himself: '*If a man love me, he will keep my words: and my Father will love him, and we will come unto him, and make our abode with him.*'[1] Give, therefore, to Christ free entry into thy heart, and keep out all things that may let His entry: and when thou hast Him thou art rich enough, and He only shall suffice to thee. He shall be thy provider and defender, and thy faithful helper in every necessity: so that thou shalt not need to put thy trust in any other without Him. Man is soon changed, and lightly falleth away, but Christ abideth for ever, and standeth strongly with His lover unto the end.

There is no great trust to be put in man, that is but mortal and frail, though he be right much profitable, and also much beloved unto thee: nor is any great heaviness to be taken, though he sometime turn and be against thee; for they that this day be with thee, to-morrow may happen to be against thee, and may oft turn, as doth the wind. Put thy full trust therefore in God, and let Him be thy love and dread above all things. He will answer for thee, and will do for thee in all things as shall be most needful and expedient for thee. Thou hast here no place of long abiding, for wheresoever thou be, thou art but a stranger and a pilgrim, and never shalt thou find perfect rest till thou be fully united to God.

[1] John xiv. 23.

Of the Imitation of Christ

Why dost thou look to have rest here, sith this is not thy resting-place? Thy full rest must be in heavenly things, and all earthly things thou must behold as things transitory and shortly passing away: be well wary thou cleave not overmuch to them, lest thou be taken with love of them, and in the end perish thereby. Let thy thoughts be always upward to God, and direct thy prayers to Christ continually: and if thou may not for frailty always occupy thy mind in contemplation of the Godhead, be then occupied with mind of His Passion, and in His blessed Wounds make thee a dwelling place. And if thou fly devoutly to the wound of Christ's Side, and to the marks of His Passion, thou shalt feel great comfort in every trouble. Thou shalt little force[1] though thou be openly despised in the world, and what evil words soever be spoken of thee, they shall little grieve thee.

Our Master Christ was despised in the world by all men, and in His most need was forsaken of His acquaintance and friends, and left among shames and rebukes. He would suffer wrongs, and be nought set by in the world, and we will not that any man do us wrong, or dispraise our deeds. Christ had many adversaries and backbiters, and we would have all to be our friends and lovers. How shall thy patience be crowned in heaven, if no adversity befall thee on earth? If thou wilt suffer no adversity, how mayest thou be the friend of Christ? It behoveth thee to

[1] be little troubled.

suffer with Christ, and for Christ, if thou wilt reign with Christ.

Truly, if thou hadst once entered into the bloody wounds of Jesus, and hadst there tasted a little of His love, thou wouldst little care for likings and mislikings of the world, but wouldst rather have great joy when wrongs and reproofs were done unto thee : for perfect love of God maketh a man perfectly to despise himself. The true inward lover of God, that is free from all inordinate affections, may anon turn himself freely to God, and lift himself up in spirit by contemplation, and fruitfully rest in Christ.

Also he to whom all things be esteemed as they be, and not as they be taken and thought to be by worldly people, is very wise, and is rather taught of God than of man. And he that can inwardly lift his mind upward to God, and little regard outward things, needeth not to seek for time and place to go to prayers, or to do other good deeds, or virtuous occupations. For the ghostly man may soon gather himself together and fix his mind in God, for he never suffereth it to be fully occupied in outward things. Therefore his outward labours, and his worldly occupations necessary for the time, hinder him but little ; for as they come, so he applieth himself to them, and referreth them always to the will of God. Moreover, a man that is well ordered in his soul, forceth little the unkind demeanour of worldly people, nor yet their proud behaviour. As much as a man loveth any worldly thing more than it should be loved, so much his mind is hindered and letted from the true ordinate love that he should have to God.

If thou wert well purged from all inordinate affections, then, whatsoever should befall thee would go to thy ghostly profit, and to the great increasing of grace and virtue in thy soul. But the cause why so many things displease thee and trouble thee, is that thou art not yet perfectly dead to the world, nor art thou yet fully severed from the love of earthly things. Nothing so much defileth the soul as an unclean love to creatures. If thou forsake to be outwardly comforted by worldly things, thou mayest behold more perfectly heavenly things, and thou shalt then continually sing lauds and praisings to Him with great joy and inward gladness of heart.

The which grant thee and me the Blessed Trinity. Amen.

The Second Chapter: Of the meek knowing of our own defaults. ¶ Regard not much who is with thee, nor who is against thee, but be this thy greatest study, that God may be with thee. In everything that thou dost have a good conscience, and He shall well defend thee. And whomsoever He will help and defend, him no malice may hinder or grieve. If thou can be still and suffer awhile, thou shalt without doubt see the help of God come in thy need. He knoweth the time and place how to deliver thee, and therefore thou must resign thyself wholly to Him. It pertaineth to Him to help and to deliver from all confusion. Nevertheless it is oftentimes much profitable to us, for the surer keeping of meekness, that other men know our defaults and reprove us for them.

When a man meeketh himself for his offences, he lightly pleaseth others, and reconcileth himself to them whom he hath offended. The meek man Almighty God defendeth and comforteth; to him He inclineth Himself and sendeth him great plenty of His grace. To him also He showeth His secrets and lovingly draweth him to Himself, and after his oppressions He lifteth him up to glory. The meek man, when he hath suffered confusion and reproof, is in good peace, for he trusteth in God, and not in the world. Moreover, if thou wilt come to the highness of perfection, think not thyself to have profited anything in virtue, till thou canst feel meekly in thy heart that thou hast less meekness and less virtue than hath any other.

The Third Chapter: How good it is for a man to be peaceful. ¶ First put thyself in peace, and then mayest thou the better pacify others. A peaceful and patient man profiteth more to himself and others also, than a man learned, who is unpeaceful. A man that is passionate turneth oftentimes good into evil, and lightly believeth the worst part: but a good peaceful man turneth all things to the best, and hath suspicion of no man. But he that is not content is oft troubled with many suspicions, and neither is he quiet himself, nor yet suffereth he others to be quiet. He

speaketh oftentimes that he should not speak, and he
omitteth to speak that which it were more expedient
to be spoken. He considereth greatly what others
be bound to do, but to do that whereunto he himself
is bounden, he is full negligent. Have therefore first
a zeal and a respect to thyself and to thine own soul,
and then mayest thou, the more righteously and with
the more due order of charity, have zeal upon thy
neighbours.

Thou art anon ready to excuse thine own defaults,
but thou wilt not hear the excuses of thy brethren.
Truly it were more charitable and more profitable to
thee that thou shouldst accuse thyself and excuse thy
brother ; for if thou wilt be borne, bear another.
Behold how far thou art yet from perfect charity and
meekness, which cannot be angry with any one but
with themselves. It is no great thing to be well conversant with good and tractable men, for this naturally pleaseth all, and every man gladly hath peace and
most loveth them that are of his way of thinking : but
to live peaceably with evil men, or with froward men
that lack good manners and be untaught, or with those
that be also contrarious unto us, is a great grace and
a manly deed, and is much to be praised : for it cannot
be done but through great ghostly strength.

Some persons can be quiet themselves, and can also
live quietly with others ; and some can neither be
quiet themselves, nor yet suffer others to be quiet.
They be grievous to others, but they be more grievous
to themselves. Some can keep themselves in good

peace, and can bring others to live in peace. Never-theless, all our peace, while we be in this mortal life, standeth more in meek suffering of troubles, and of things that be contrarious unto us, than in the not feeling of them · for no man may live here without some trouble. Therefore, he that can best suffer shall have most peace. He it is who truly overcometh himself, and thus is a lord of the world, a friend of Christ, and the true inheritor of the kingdom of heaven.

The Fourth Chapter: Of a pure mind and a simple intent. ¶ Man is borne up from earthly things with two wings, that is to say, with plainness and cleanness : plainness is in the intent, and cleanness is in the love. The good, true, and plain intent looketh toward God, but the clean love taketh assay, and tasteth His sweetness. If thou be free from all inordinate love, no good deed shall hinder thee, but thou shalt therewith increase in the way of perfection. If thou intend well, and if thou seek nothing but God and the profit of thine own soul, and that of thy neighbour, thou shalt have great inward liberty of mind. And if thy heart be straight with God, then every creature shall be to thee a mirror of life and a book of holy doctrine, for there is no creature so little or so vile, but that sheweth and representeth the goodness of God.

If thou wert inwardly in thy soul pure and clean, thou wouldst then without letting take all things to the best. A clean heart pierceth both heaven and hell. Such as a man is in his conscience inwardly, such he sheweth himself to be in his outward conversation. If there be any true joy in this world, that hath a man of a clean conscience. And if there be anywhere tribulation or anguish, an evil conscience knoweth it best. Also, as iron put into the fire is cleansed from rust, and is made all clean and pure, right so a man turning himself wholly to God, is purged from all slothfulness, and is suddenly changed into a new man.

When a man beginneth to wax dull and slow to ghostly business, then a little labour feareth him greatly, and then he gladly taketh outward comforts of the world and of the flesh : but when he beginneth perfectly to overcome himself, and to walk strongly in the way of God, then he regardeth those labours but little, that he thought before to be right grievous and importable to him.

The Fifth Chapter : Of the knowing of ourself. ¶ We may not trust much in ourselves, or in our own wit, for ofttimes through our presumption we lack grace, and right little light of understanding is in us : and what we have, many times we lose through our own negligence. Yet we do not see, neither will we see, how blind we are. Ofttimes we do evil, and in defence thereof we do much worse. Sometimes we be moved with passion, and we ween it to be of a zeal to God. We can anon reprove small defaults in our neighbours, but our own defaults, that be much greater, we will not see. We feel anon and ponder greatly what we suffer of others, but what others suffer of us we will not consider. But he that would well and righteously judge his own defaults should not so rigorously judge the defaults of his neighbours.

A man that is inwardly turned to God taketh heed of himself before all others; and he that can well take heed of himself can lightly be still of other men's deeds. Thou shalt never be an inward man and a devout follower of Christ, unless thou canst keep thyself from meddling with other men's deeds, and canst especially take heed of thine own. If thou take heed wholly to God and to thyself, the defaults which thou seest in others shall little move thee. Where art thou when thou art not present to thyself? And when thou hast run over all things, and hast considered much other men's works, what hast thou profited thereby, if thou have forgotten thyself? If thou wilt therefore have peace in thy soul, and be perfectly united to God in blessed love, set apart all other men's deeds, and only set thyself and thine own deeds before the eye of thy soul, and what thou seest amiss in thee, shortly reform it.

Thou shalt much profit in grace if thou keep thee free from all temporal cares, but it shall hinder thee greatly if thou set price by any temporal things. Therefore let nothing be in thy sight high, nothing great, nothing liking or acceptable to thee, but it be purely God, or of God. Think all comforts vain that come to thee by any creature. He that loveth God, and his own soul for God, despiseth all other love : for he seeth well that God alone, Who is eternal, incomprehensible, and that fulfilleth all things with His goodness, is the whole solace and comfort of the soul, and that He is the very gladness of heart, and none other but only He.

The Sixth Chapter : Of the gladness of a clean conscience. ¶ The glory of a good man is the witness of God that he hath a good conscience.[1] Have therefore a good conscience, and thou shalt always have gladness. A good conscience may bear many wrongs, and is ever merry and glad in adversities ; but an evil conscience is always fearful and unquiet. Be never glad but when thou hast done well. Evil men never have perfect gladness, and feel not inward peace, for ' *There is no peace, saith the Lord, unto the wicked.*'[2] And though they say · We be in good peace, there shall no evil come to us ; lo ! who may grieve us or hurt us ?—believe them not, for suddenly the wrath of God shall fall upon them unless they amend, and all that they have done shall turn to nought, and what they would have done shall be undone.

It is no grievous thing for a fervent lover of God to joy in tribulation, for all his joy and glory is to joy in the cross of our Lord Jesus Christ. It is a short glory that is given by man, and commonly some heaviness followeth after. The glory of good men is in their own conscience. The joy of righteous men is in God and of God, and their gladness is in virtue and in a good life. He that desireth the very

[1] See 2 Cor. 1 12   [2] Isaiah xlviii. 22

perfect joy that is everlasting, setteth little price by
temporal joy ; and he that seeketh any worldly joy,
or doth not in his heart fully despise it, showeth himself openly to love but little the joy of heaven.   He
hath great tranquillity and peace of heart, that neither
regardeth praises nor dispraises ; and he shall soon
be pacified and content that hath a good conscience.

Thou art not the better because thou art praised,
nor worse if thou be dispraised, for as thou art, thou
art ; and whatsoever be said of thee, thou art no
better than Almighty God (Who is the searcher of
man's heart) will witness thee to be.   If thou behold
what thou art inwardly, thou shalt not care much
what the world speaketh of thee outwardly.   Man
seeth the face, but God beholdeth the heart.   Man
beholdeth the deed, but God beholdeth the intent of
the deed.   It is a great token of a meek heart for a
man ever to do well, and yet to think himself to have
done but little.   And it is a great sign of cleanness
of life, and of inward trust in God, when a man taketh
not his comfort of any creature.

When a man seeketh no outward witness for himself, it appeareth that he hath wholly committed himself to God.   Also after the words of St. Paul, '*not
he that commendeth himself is approved, but whom the
Lord commendeth*' ;[1] and he that hath his mind always
lifted up to God, and is not bound with any inordinate affection outwardly, is in the degree and in the
state of a holy and blessed man.

[1] 2 Cor x. 18.

Of the Imitation of Christ

The Seventh Chapter: Of the love of Jesus above all things.

¶ Blessed is he that knoweth how good it is to love Jesus, and for His sake to despise himself. It behoveth the lover of Jesus to forsake all other love beside Him, for He will be loved only above all other. The love of creatures is deceivable and failing, but the love of Jesus is faithful and always abiding. He that cleaveth to any creature must of necessity fail, as doth the creature ; but he that cleaveth abidingly to Jesus shall be made stable in Him for ever. Love Him, therefore, and hold Him thy friend ; for when all others forsake thee, He will not forsake thee, nor suffer thee finally to perish.

Thou must of necessity be departed from thy friends, and from all man's company, whether thou wilt or not. Therefore, living and dying, keep thyself with thy Lord Jesus, and commit thee to His fidelity, for He will be with thee and help thee when all others forsake thee. Thy Beloved is of such nature that He will not admit any other love, for He will have alonely the love of thy heart, and will sit therein as a king in his proper throne. If thou couldst well avoid from thee the love of creatures, He would always abide with thee, and never would forsake thee. Whatsoever trust thou hast put in anything beside Jesus, thou shalt find in a manner all as lost. Put not thy trust, therefore, in any such thing that is but as a quill full of wind, or as a hollow stick, which is not able to sustain thee or help thee, but in thy most need will deceive thee; for man is but as hay, and all his glory is as a flower in the field, which suddenly vanisheth and slideth away.

If thou take heed only to the outward appearance thou shalt soon be deceived; and if thou seek thy comfort in anything but in Jesus, thou shalt feel thereby great spiritual loss. If thou seek in all things thy Lord Jesus, thou shalt truly find thy Lord Jesus; and if thou seek thyself, thou shalt find thyself, but it shall be to thine own great loss. Truly a man is more grievous and more hurtful to himself, if he seek not his Lord Jesus, than all the world and all his adversaries may be.

The Eighth Chapter: Of the familiar friendship of Jesus.

¶ When our Lord Jesus is present all things are liking, and nothing seemeth hard to do for His love; but when He is absent, all things that are done for His love are painful and hard. When Jesus speaketh not to the soul, there is no faithful consolation: but if He speak one word only, the soul feeleth great inward comfort. Did not Mary Magdalen rise soon from weeping, when Martha shewed her that her Master Christ was nigh and called her? Yes, truly. O that is a happy hour when Jesus calleth us from weeping to joy of spirit! Remember how dry and how indevout thou art without Jesus, and how unwise, how vain, and how uncunning thou art when thou desirest anything beside Jesus; truly that desire is more hurtful to thee than if thou hadst lost all the world.

Of the Imitation of Christ

What may this world give thee but through the help of Jesus? To be without Jesus is a pain of hell, and to be with Jesus is a pleasant paradise. If Jesus be with thee there may no enemy grieve thee, and he that findeth Jesus findeth a great treasure, that is best above all other treasures; but he that loseth Jesus loseth very much, and more than all the world. He is most poor that liveth without Jesus; and he is most rich that is with Jesus.

It is great cunning to be well conversant with Jesus, and to keep Him is right great wisdom. Be meek and peaceful, and Jesus shall be with thee; be devout and quiet, and Jesus will abide with thee. Thou mayest anon drive away thy Lord Jesus and lose His grace, if thou apply thyself to outward things; and if through negligence thou lose Him, what friend shalt thou then have? Without a friend thou mayest not long endure, and if Jesus be not thy friend before all others, thou shalt be very heavy and desolate. Therefore thou dost not wisely, if thou trust or joy in any other thing beside Him. We should rather choose to have all the world against us, than to offend God. Of all therefore that be to thee lief[1] and dear, let thy Lord Jesus be to thee most lief and dear. Let all others be beloved for Him, and He only for Himself.

Jesus only is to be beloved for Himself, for He only is proved good and faithful before all other friends. In Him and for Him both enemies and

[1] beloved

73

Thomas à Kempis

friends are to be beloved, and for them all we ought
meekly to pray to Him, that so He may be beloved
and honoured of all His creatures.   Never desire to
be singularly loved or commended, for that belongeth only to God, Who hath none like unto Him.
Desire not that any one be occupied with thee in his
heart, nor be thou occupied with love of any creature;
but let thy Lord Jesus be in thee, and in every good
man and woman.

Be pure and clean inwardly, without letting[1] of any
creature, for it behoveth thee to have a right clean
and pure heart to Jesus, if thou wilt know and feel
how sweet He is.   And verily thou mayest not come
to that purity unless thou be prevented and drawn
through His grace, and, having set apart all other
things, thou be inwardly knit and united to Him.
When the grace of God cometh to a man, then is he
made mighty and strong to do everything that belongeth to virtue; and when grace withdraweth, then
is he made weak and feeble to do any good deed, and
left as it were only to punishment and pain.   If it
happen so with thee, yet despair not overmuch, nor
leave thy good deeds undone ; but always stand
strongly after the will of God, and turn all things
that shall come to thee to the laud and praisings of
His Name.   For after winter cometh summer ; after
the night cometh the day ; and after a great tempest
sheweth again right clear and pleasant weather.

[1] hindrance

74

Of the Imitation of Christ

The Ninth Chapter : Of the wanting of all solace and comfort.

¶ It is no great thing to despise man's comfort when the comfort of God is present; but it is a great thing, and that a right great thing, for a man to be so strong in spirit that he may bear the wanting of them both, and for the love of God, and to His honour, to have a ready will to bear desolation of spirit, and yet in nothing to seek himself, or his own merits. What proof of virtue is it if a man be merry and devout in God when grace cometh and visiteth the soul? for that hour is desired of every creature. He rideth safely whom the grace of God beareth and supporteth; and what marvel is it if he feel no burden who is borne up by Him Who is Almighty, and is led by the sovereign guide, God Himself.

We be always glad to have solace and consolation, but we would have no tribulation, and we do not lightly cast from us the false love of ourself. The blessed martyr St. Laurence, through the love of God, mightily overcame the love of the world and of himself, for he despised all that was liking and delectable in the world; and Sixtus the Pope, whom he most loved, he meekly suffered for the love of Christ to be taken from him. So through the love of the Creator he overcame the love of man; and instead of man's comfort he chose rather to follow the will of God. Do thou in like wise, and learn to forsake some necessary and well-beloved friend for the love of God. Take it not grievously when thou art left or forsaken of thy friend, for of necessity it behoveth worldly friends to be dissevered.

It behoveth a man to fight long and to strive mightily with himself, before he shall learn fully to overcome himself, or be able freely and readily to set all his desires in God. When a man loveth himself, and trusteth much to himself, he falleth anon to man's comforts; but the very true lover of Christ, and the diligent follower of virtue, falleth not so lightly to them, and seeketh not sensible sweetness, but rather is glad to suffer great labours and hard pain for the love of Christ.

Nevertheless, when ghostly comfort is sent to thee of God, take it meekly, and give humble thanks for it; but know for certain that it is of the great goodness of God that sendeth it to thee, and not of thy deserving. Look thou be not therefore lifted up into pride, or that thou joy much thereof; presume not vainly therein, but be rather the more meek for so noble a gift, and more wary and fearful in all thy works; for that time will pass away, and the time of temptation will shortly follow after. When comfort is withdrawn, despair not, but patiently abide the visitation of God; for He is able and of power to give thee more grace and more ghostly comfort than thou hadst first. Such alteration of grace is no new or strange thing to them that have had experience in the way of God, for the like alteration was many times found in great Saints and holy Prophets.

Wherefore the Prophet David saith: '*Ego dixi in*

abundantia mea, non movebor in æternum.[1] That is to say: When David had abundance of ghostly comfort, he said to our Lord, that he trusted he should never be removed from such comfort. But after, when grace withdrew, he said: '*Avertisti faciem tuam a me, et factus sum conturbatus.*'[1] That is: O Lord! Thou hast withdrawn Thy ghostly comforts from me, and I am left in great trouble and heaviness. Yet nevertheless he despaireth not, but prayed heartily unto our Lord, and said: '*Ad te, Domine, clamabo, et ad Deum meum deprecabor.*'[1] That is to say: I shall busily cry to Thee, O Lord, and I shall meekly pray to Thee for grace and comfort. Anon, he had the effect of his prayer, as he himself witnesseth, saying thus: '*Audivit Dominus et misertus est mei, Dominus factus est adjutor meus.*'[1] That is: The Lord hath heard my prayer, and hath had mercy on me ; He hath again sent me His help and ghostly comfort. Therefore he saith afterwards: '*Thou hast turned for me my mourning into dancing ; thou hast put off my sackcloth, and girded me with gladness.*'[1] If Almighty God hath thus done with holy Saints, it is not for us weak and feeble persons to despair, though we sometimes have fervour of spirit, and sometimes be left cold and void of devotion. The Holy Ghost goeth and cometh after His pleasure, and therefore the holy man Job saith : '*What is man, that thou shouldest magnify him ? . . . and that thou shouldest visit him every morning,*' that is to say, in the time of com-

[1] Ps. xxx 6, 7, 8, 10, 11

fort, '*and try him every moment*,'[1] by withdrawing such comforts from him.

Wherein then may I trust, or in whom may I have any confidence, but only in the great grace and endless mercy of God? For neither the company of good men, nor the fellowship of devout brethren and faithful friends : neither the having of holy books or devout treatises, nor the hearing of sweet songs or of devout hymns, may little avail, and bring forth but little comfort to the soul, when we are left to our own frailty and poverty. When we be so left, there is no better remedy but patience, with a whole resigning of our own will to the will of God.

I never yet found any religious person so perfect, but that he had sometimes absenting of grace, or some minishing of fervour : and there was never yet any Saint so highly ravished but that he first or last had some temptation. He is not worthy to have the high gift of contemplation, that hath not suffered for God some tribulation. The temptations going before were wont to be a soothfast token of heavenly comfort shortly coming after. For to them that be found stable in their temptations is promised by our Lord great consolation. And therefore He saith thus : ' *To him that overcometh will I give to eat of the tree of life.*'[2]

Heavenly comfort is sometimes given to a man, that he may after be more strong to suffer adversities : but temptation followeth that he be not lifted

---

[1] Job vii. 17, 18.   [2] Rev ii 7.

up into pride, and think himself worthy of such consolation. The ghostly enemy sleepeth not, neither
is the flesh yet fully mortified: therefore thou shalt
never cease to prepare thyself to ghostly battle, for
thou hast enemies on every side, that will ever be
ready to assail thee, and hinder thy good purpose all
that they can.

**The Tenth Chapter: Of yielding thanks to
God for His manifold graces.** ¶ Why seekest thou
rest here sith thou art born to labour? Dispose thyself to patience rather than to comforts, to bear the
cross of penance rather than to have gladness. What
temporal man would not gladly have spiritual comforts if he might always keep them? For spiritual
comforts exceed far all worldly delights and all bodily
pleasures; since all worldly delights be either foul
or vain, but ghostly delights are alone jocund and
honest, brought forth by virtues and sent of God
into a clean soul. Such comforts no man may have
when he would, for the time of temptation tarrieth
not long.

The false liberty of will, and the overmuch trust
that we have in ourself, be much contrary to the
heavenly visitations. Our Lord doth well in sending
such comforts, but we do not well when we yield no
thanks to Him again. The greatest cause why the
gifts of grace may not lightly come to us, is that we
be unkind to the Giver and yield not thanks to Him
from whom all goodness comes. Grace is always
given to them that be ready to yield thanks. And

therefore that shall be taken from the proud man which is wont to be given to the meek man.

I would none of that consolation that should take from me compunction, nor any of that contemplation that should lift my soul into presumption. Every high thing in the sight of man is not holy, nor every desire clean and pure · every sweet thing is not good, nor is every thing dear to man always pleasant to God. We shall therefore gladly take such gifts whereby we shall be the more ready to forsake ourself and our own will. He that knoweth the comforts that come through the gift of grace, and knoweth also how sharp and painful is the absenting of grace, will not dare to think that any goodness cometh of himself, but he will openly confess that of himself he is right poor and naked of all virtue · yield therefore to God that which is His, and to thyself that which is thine : that is to say, thank God for His manifold graces, and blame thyself for thine offences.

Hold in thee always a sure foundation of meekness, and then the highness of virtue shall shortly be given unto thee : for the high tower of virtue may not long stand, but if it be borne up with the low foundations of meekness. They that be greatest in heaven, be least in their own sight : and the more glorious they be, the meeker they are in themselves, full of truth and heavenly joy, not desirous of vain-glory and praising of men. They also that be fully stabled and confirmed in God may in nowise be lifted up into pride. And they that ascribe all goodness to God seek no vain-glory or vain praisings in the world, but they desire only to joy and to be glorified in God, and desire in heart that He may be honoured, lauded, and praised above all things, both in Himself and in all His Saints: and that is always the thing that perfect men most covet, and most desire to bring about. Be thou loving and thankful to God for the least benefit that He giveth thee, and then shalt thou be the more apt and worthy to receive of Him greater benefits. Think the least gift that He giveth is great, and the most despisable things accept as special gifts and great tokens of love: for if the dignity of the Giver be well considered, no gift that He giveth will seem little. It is no little thing that is given of God· for though He send pain and sorrow we should take them gladly and thankfully, for it is for our ghostly health all that He suffereth to come unto us. If a man desire to hold the grace of God let him be thankful for such grace as he hath received, patient when it is withdrawn, and pray devoutly that it may shortly come again. Let him be meek and low in spirit, that he lose it not again through his presumption and pride of heart.

The Eleventh Chapter: Of the small number of the lovers of the Cross. ¶ Jesus hath many lovers of His kingdom of heaven, but He hath few bearers of His cross. Many desire His consolation, but few desire His tribulation. He findeth many fellows at eating and drinking, but He findeth few

that will be with Him in His abstinence and fasting.
All men would joy with Him, but few would anything suffer for Christ. Many follow Him to the
breaking of His bread for their bodily refection, but
few will follow Him to drink a draught of the chalice of His Passion. Many marvel and honour His
miracles, but few will follow the shame of His cross.
Many love Jesus so long as no adversity befalleth
them, and can praise Him and bless Him when they
receive any benefit of Him : but if Jesus a little withdraw Himself from them, and a little forsake them,
anon they fall to some great grudging, or to over-
great dejection.

They that love Jesus purely for Himself, and not
for their own profit and commodity bless Him as
heartily in temptation, tribulation, and all other adversities as they do in the time of consolation. And
if He never sent them consolation, yet would they
always laud Him and praise Him.

O how much may the love of Jesus do to the help
of a soul, if it be pure and clean, not mixed with any
inordinate love to self ! May not they then that ever
look for worldly comforts, and for worldly consolations, be called worldly merchants and worldly lovers,
rather than lovers of God ? Do they not openly
shew by their deeds that they rather love themselves
than God ?

O where may be found any that will serve God
freely and purely, without looking for some reward
for it again ' And where may be found any one so

spiritual that he is clearly delivered and bereft of love of himself, that is truly poor in spirit, and wholly avoided from love of creatures? I trow none such can be found but it be far hence and in far countries. If a man gave all his substance for God, yet it is nought: and if he do great penance for his sins, yet it is but little: and if he have great cunning and knowledge, yet he is far from virtue: and if he have great virtue and burning devotion, yet much wanteth in him: and that is specially *'one thing needful'*[1] to him. What is that? That all things forsaken, and himself also forsaken, he go clearly from himself, and keep nothing to himself of any private love. And when he hath done all that he ought to do, that he feel in himself as he had nothing done.

Also that he think not that great which others might think great, but that he think himself truly, as he is, an unprofitable servant: for the Author of Truth our Saviour Christ saith : *'When ye shall have done all those things which are commanded you, say, We are unprofitable servants.'*[2] Then he that can thus do may well be called poor in spirit, and naked of private love: and he may well say with the Prophet David: *'I am desolate and afflicted.'*[3] There is none more rich, none more free, nor any of more power than he that can forsake himself and all passing things, and that truly can hold himself to be lowest and vilest of all others.

[1] Luke x 42   [2] Luke xvii. 10   [3] Ps xxv 16.

Thomas à Kempis

The Twelfth Chapter: Of the way of the Cross, and how profitable patience is in adversity.

¶ The words of our Saviour be thought very hard and grievous when He saith thus: '*If any man will come after me, let him deny himself, and take up his cross, and follow me.*'[1]   But much more grievous shall it be to hear these words at the last day: '*Depart from me, ye cursed, into everlasting fire.*'[2]   But those that now gladly hear and follow the words of Christ, whereby He counselleth them to follow Him, shall not then need to dread for hearing those words of everlasting damnation.   The sign of the cross shall appear in heaven when our Lord shall come to judge the world, and the servants of the cross, who conformed themselves here in this life to Christ crucified on the cross, shall go to Christ their Judge with great faith and trust in Him.

Why dost thou dread to take the cross, sith it is the very way to the kingdom of heaven, and none but that?   In the cross is health, in the cross is life, in the cross is defence from our enemies, in the cross is the infusion of heavenly sweetness, in the cross is the strength of mind, the joy of spirit, the highness of virtue, and the full perfection of all holiness: and there is no health of soul nor hope of everlasting life but through virtue of the cross.   Take the cross, therefore, and follow Jesus, and thou shalt go into the life everlasting.   He hath gone before thee bearing His cross, and died for thee upon the cross, that

[1] Matt. xvi. 24.   [2] Matt. xxv. 41.

thou shouldst in like wise bear with Him the cross of penance and tribulation, and that thou shouldst be ready for His love to suffer death, if need require, as He hath done for thee. If thou die with Him, thou shalt live with Him: and if thou be fellow with Him in pain, thou shalt be with Him in glory.

Behold, then, how in the cross standeth all, and how in dying to the world lieth all our health. And there is no other way to true and inward peace but the way of the cross, and of daily mortifying of the body to the spirit. Go whither thou wilt, and seek what thou list, and thou shalt never find above thee, or beneath thee, within thee or without thee, a higher, more excellent, or surer way to Christ than the way of the holy cross. Dispose everything after thy will, and thou shalt ever find that thou must of necessity suffer somewhat, either with thy will or against thy will, and thou shalt always find the cross: for either thou shalt feel pain in thy body, or in thy soul thou shalt have trouble of spirit.

Thou shalt be sometimes as thou were forsaken of God. Sometimes thou shalt be vexed with thy neighbour, and, what is more painful, thou shalt sometimes be grievous to thyself. Neither shalt thou find means to be delivered, but that it behoveth thee to suffer till it shall please Almighty God of His goodness otherwise to dispose for thee: for He willeth that thou shalt learn to suffer tribulation without consolation, that thou mayest wholly submit thyself to Him, and by tribulation be made more meek. No

man feeleth the Passion of Christ so effectuously as
he that feeleth like pain as Christ did. This cross is
always ready, and everywhere it abideth thee, and
thou mayest not flee nor fully escape it, wheresoever
thou goest; for in what place soever thou art, thou
shalt bear thyself about with thee, and so always
shalt thou find thyself. Turn thee where thou wilt,
above thee, beneath thee, within thee, and without
thee, and thou shalt find this cross on every side, so
that it shall be necessary for thee that thou always
keep thee in patience ; and this it behoveth thee to
do if thou wilt have inward peace, and deserve the
perpetual crown in heaven.

If thou wilt gladly bear the cross, it shall bear thee,
and bring thee to the end that thou desirest, where
thou shalt never after have anything to suffer. If
thou bear the cross against thy will, thou makest a
great burden for thyself, and it will be the more
grievous to thee: and yet it behoveth thee to bear it.
If it happen thee to put away one cross, that is to say,
one tribulation, yet surely another will come, and
haply more grievous than the first was.

Trowest thou to escape that which never yet any
mortal man might escape? What Saint in this
world hath been without this cross, and without
some trouble? Truly our Lord Jesus was not one
hour without some sorrow and pain as long as He
lived here, for it behoved Him to suffer death, and
to rise again, and so enter into His glory.[1] And how

---

[1] Luke xxiv. 26, 46.

is it then that thou seekest any other way to heaven than this plain way of the cross?

All the life of Christ was cross and martyrdom; and thou seekest pleasure and joy. Thou errest greatly, if thou seek any other thing than to suffer: for all this mortal life is full of miseries, and is all beset about and marked with crosses. And the more highly that a man profiteth in spirit, the more painful crosses shall he find; for by the soothfastness of Christ's love, wherein he daily increaseth, daily appeareth unto him more and more the pain of his exile.

Nevertheless, a man thus vexed with pain is not left wholly without all comfort, for he seeth well that great fruit and high reward shall grow unto him by the bearing of his cross. And when a man freely submitteth himself to such tribulation, then all the burden of tribulation is suddenly turned into a great trust of heavenly consolation. The more the flesh is punished with tribulation, the more is the soul strengthened daily by inward consolation. And sometimes the soul shall feel such comfort in adversities, that for the love and desire that it hath to be conformed to Christ crucified, it would not be without sorrow and trouble: for it considereth well that the more it may suffer for His love here, the more acceptable shall it be to Him in the life to come. But it is not of the power of man, but through the grace of God, that a frail man should take and love that which his bodily kind abhorreth and flieth.

For it is not in the power of man gladly to bear

the cross, to love the cross, to chastise the body, and to make it obedient to the will of the spirit: to flee honours, gladly to sustain reproofs, to despise himself, and to covet to be despised; patiently to suffer adversities with all the displeasures thereof, and not to desire any manner of profit in this world. If thou trust in thyself thou shalt never bring this about; but if thou trust in God, He shall send thee strength from heaven, and the world and the flesh shall be made subject to thee. Yea, if thou be strongly armed with faith, and be marked with the cross of Christ, as His household servant, thou shalt not need to fear thy ghostly enemy, for he shall also be made subject to thee, so that he shall have no power against thee.

Purpose thyself, therefore, as a true faithful servant of God, manfully to bear the cross of thy Lord Jesus, Who for thy love was crucified on the cross. Prepare thyself to suffer all manner of adversities and discommodities in this wretched life, for so shall it be with thee wheresoever thou hide thee. And there is no remedy to escape, but that thou must keep thyself always in patience. If thou desire to be a dear and well-beloved friend of Christ, drink effectuously with Him a draught of the chalice of His tribulation. As for consolations, commit them to His will, that He order them as He knoweth most expedient for thee: but as for thyself, dispose thee to suffer, and when tribulations come, take them as special consolations, saying with the Apostle thus: '*The sufferings of this present time are not worthy to be*

comparea with the glory which shall be revealed in us';[1]
yea, though thou thyself mightest suffer as much as
all men do.'

When thou comest to that degree of patience, that
tribulation is sweet to thee, and for the love of God
is savoury and pleasant in thy sight, then mayest thou
trust that it is well with thee, and that thou art in
good estate; for thou hast found paradise on earth.
But as long as it is grievous to thee to suffer, and thou
seekest to flee, so long it shall not be well with thee,
and thou shalt not be in the perfect way of patience.

But if thou couldst bring thyself to that estate at
which thou shouldst be, that is to suffer gladly for
God and to die fully to the world, then should it
shortly be better with thee, and thou wouldst find
great peace. Yet although thou were rapt with Saint
Paul into the third heaven, thou wouldst not therefore be free from all adversity: for our Saviour,
speaking of Saint Paul, said thus of him: '*I will shew
him how great things he must suffer for my name's sake.*'[2]
To suffer therefore to thee remaineth, if thou wilt
love thy Lord Jesus, and serve Him perpetually.
Would to God that thou wert worthy to suffer somewhat for His love! O how great joy would it be to
thee to suffer for Him! What gladness to all the
Saints of heaven! How great edifying to thy neighbour! All men commend patience, and yet few men
will to suffer. Righteously oughtest thou, that sufferest much for the world, to suffer some little thing
for God.   [1] Rom. viii. 18.   [2] Acts ix 16.

Thomas à Kempis

Know this for certain, that it behoveth thee to lead a dying life, and the more that thou canst die to thyself here, the more thou beginnest to live to God. No man is apt to receive the heavenly reward, but he has first learned to bear adversities for the love of Christ. Nothing is more acceptable to God, or more profitable to man in this world, than to be glad to suffer for Christ. Insomuch that if it were put in thy election, thou shouldst rather choose adversity than prosperity · for then, by the patient suffering thereof thou wouldst be more like to Christ, and the more conformed to all His Saints. Our merit and our perfection of life standeth not in consolations and sweetness, but rather in suffering of great adversities and grievous tribulations.

For if there had been any nearer or better way for the health of man's soul than to suffer, our Lord Jesus would have shewed it by word and by example. But as there was not, therefore He openly exhorted the disciples that followed Him, and all others that desired to follow Him, to forsake their own will and to take the cross of penance, and follow Him, saying: '*If any man will come after me, let him deny himself, and take up his cross, and follow me.*'[1] Therefore, all things searched and read, be this the final conclusion, that by many tribulations it behoveth us to enter into the kingdom of heaven.

To the which bring us our Lord Jesu. Amen.

[1] Matt xvi 24.

The third book
Of internal consolation

The Third Book
Of internal consolation

The First Chapter: Of the inward speaking of Christ to a faithful soul.

'I WILL hear,' saith a devout soul, '*what God the Lord will speak.*'[1] Blessed is that man who heareth Jesus speaking in his soul, and that taketh of His mouth some word of comfort. Blessed be the ears that hear the secret breathings of Jesus, and heed not the deceitful whisperings of this world. And blessed indeed be the ears that heed not the outward speech, but rather take heed what God speaketh and teacheth inwardly in the soul. Blessed also be the eyes that be shut from the sight of outward vanities, and that take heed of the inward movings of God. Blessed be they that get themselves virtues, and prepare themselves by good bodily and ghostly works to receive daily more and more the secret inspirations and inward teachings of God. Also, blessed be they that set themselves wholly to serve God, and for His service set apart all lettings of the world. O thou my soul! take heed to that which has been said, and shut the

---

[1] Ps. lxxxv. 8.

doors of thy sensuality, which are thy five wits, that thou mayest hear inwardly what our Lord Jesus speaketh in thy soul.

Thus saith thy Beloved: I am thy health, I am thy peace, I am thy life; keep thee with Me, and thou shalt find peace in Me. Forsake the love of transitory things, and seek things that be everlasting. What be all temporal things but deceivable? And what may any creature help thee, if thy Lord Jesus forsake thee? Therefore, all creatures and all worldly things forsaken and left, do that in thee is to make thee pleasant in His sight, that after this life thou mayest come to the life everlasting in the kingdom of heaven. Amen.

The Second Chapter: How Almighty God speaketh inwardly to man's soul, without sound of words. ¶ '*Speak, Lord; for thy servant heareth.*'[1] '*I am thy servant; give me understanding, that I may know thy testimonies.*'[2] Bow my heart to follow the words of Thy holy teachings, that they may distil into my soul as dew into the grass. The children of Israel said to Moses: '*Speak thou with us, and we will hear: but let not God speak with us, lest we die.*'[3] Not so, Lord, not so, I beseech Thee, but rather I ask meekly with Samuel the Prophet that Thou vouchsafe to speak to me Thyself, and I shall gladly hear Thee. Let not Moses, or any other of the Prophets, speak to me, but rather Thou, Lord, Who art the inward inspirer and giver of light to all Prophets; for Thou

[1] 1 Sam. iii. 9.　　[2] Ps. cxix 125　　[3] Ex xx 19

alone without them mayest fully inform and instruct me. They without Thee may little profit me.

They speak Thy words, but they give not the spirit to understand the words. They speak fair, but if Thou be still, they kindle not the heart. They shew fair letters, but Thou declarest the sentence. They bring forth great high mysteries, but Thou openest thereof the true understanding; they declare Thy commandments, but Thou helpest to perform them. They show the way, but Thou givest comfort to walk therein. They do all outwardly, but Thou illuminest and informest the heart within. They water only outwardly, but it is Thou that givest the inward growing. They cry all in words, but Thou givest to the hearers understanding of the words that be hard.

Let not Moses, therefore, speak to me, but Thou, my Lord Jesu, Who art the everlasting Truth, lest haply I die and be made as a man without fruit, warmed outwardly, but not inflamed inwardly; and so to have the harder judgment, for that I have heard Thy word, and not done it; known it, and not loved it; believed it, and not fulfilled it. Speak, therefore, to me Thyself, for I Thy servant am ready to hear Thee. '*Thou hast the words of eternal life*';[1] speak then to me to the full comfort of my soul, and give me amendment of all my life past; to Thy joy, honour, and glory everlastingly. *Amen.*

[1] John vi 68

The Third Chapter: That the words of God are to be heard with great meekness, and that there be but few that ponder them as they ought to do. ¶ 'My son,' saith our Lord, 'hear My words and follow them, for they be most sweet, far passing the wisdom and cunning of all philosophers and wise men of the world. My words be spiritual and ghostly, and cannot be fully comprehended by man's wit. Neither are they to be turned or applied to the vain pleasure of the hearer, but are to be heard in silence with great meekness, and with great inward affection of the heart; as also in great rest and quietness of body and soul.' O blessed is he, Lord, whom Thou informest and teachest, so that Thou mayest be meek and merciful unto him in the evil day, that is to say, in the day of the most dreadful judgment, that he be not then left desolate and comfortless in the land of damnation!

Then saith our Lord again. 'I have taught Prophets from the beginning, and yet cease I not to speak to every creature; but many be deaf and will not hear, and many hear the world more gladly than Me, and more lightly follow the appetite of the flesh than the pleasure of God.' The world promiseth temporal things of small value, and yet is he served with great affection: but God promiseth high things, and things eternal, and the hearts of the people be slow and dull. O who serveth and obeyeth God in all things with so great a desire as he doth the world, and as worldly princes be served and obeyed? I trow, none. Why is this? For a little prebend great journeys be taken; but for the life everlasting the people will scarcely lift their feet once from the ground. A thing that is of small price many times is busily sought, and for a penny there is sometimes great strife; for the promise of a little worldly profit men eschew not to swink and sweat both day and night.

But, alas for sorrow! for the goods everlasting, and for the reward that may not be esteemed by man's heart, for the high honour and glory that never shall have an end, men be slow to take any manner of pain and labour. Be thou therefore ashamed, thou slow servant of God, that they be found more ready to works of death than thou art to works of life, and that they joy more in vanity than thou in truth · and yet they be oft deceived in that in which they have most trust, but My promise deceiveth no man, and leaveth no man that trusteth in Me without some comfort. That I have promised I will perform, and that I have said I will fulfil to every person, so that they abide faithfully in My love and dread unto the end; for I am the rewarder of all good men, and a strong prover of all devout souls.

Write My words therefore in thy heart diligently, and oft think upon them; for they shall be in time of temptation much necessary unto thee. That thou understandest not when thou readest it, thou shalt understand in the time of My visitation. I am wont to visit My servants two manner of ways, that is to say, with temptation and with consolation. And two

lessons daily I read unto them, one whereby I rebuke
their vices, another whereby I stir them to increase
in virtues.   He that knoweth My words and despiseth them, hath that that shall judge him in the
last day.

A Prayer to obtain the grace of devotion.   ¶ O Lord
Jesu! Thou art all my riches, and all that I have, I
have it of Thee.   But what am I, Lord, that I dare
thus speak to Thee?   I am Thy poorest servant, and
a worm most abject, more poor and more despicable
than I can or dare say.   Behold, Lord, that I am
nought, that I have nought, and of myself I am nought
worth; Thou alone art good, righteous, and holy;
Thou orderest all things, Thou givest all things, Thou
fulfillest all things with Thy goodness, leaving only
the wretched sinner barren and void of heavenly comfort.   Remember Thy mercies, and fill my heart with
Thy manifold graces, for Thou wilt not that Thy
works in me be made in vain.   How may I bear the
miseries of this life, unless Thy grace and mercy do
comfort me therein?   Turn not Thy face from me;
defer not Thy visitings of me; ne withdraw not Thy
comforts from me, lest haply my soul be made as dry
earth without the water of grace, and as it were a
thing unprofitable to Thee.   Teach me, Lord, to fulfil Thy will, and to live meekly and worthily before
Thee ; for Thou art all my wisdom and cunning.
Thou art He that knowest me as I am, and that knewest me before the world was made, and before that I
was born or brought into this life.

Of the Imitation of Christ

The Fourth Chapter: How we ought to be conversant before God in truth and meekness.

¶ My son, saith our Lord Jesus, walk before Me in truth, and seek Me always in simpleness and plainness of heart. He that walketh in truth shall be defended from all perils and dangers, and truth shall deliver him from all deceivers, and from all evil sayings of wicked people. If truth deliver thee thou art very free, and thou shalt little care for the vain sayings of the people.

Lord! it is true all Thou sayest; be it done to me after Thy saying. I beseech Thee that Thy truth may teach me and keep me, and finally lead me to a blessed ending; that it may deliver me from all evil affections, and from all inordinate love, that I may walk with Thee in freedom of spirit and liberty of heart.

Then Truth saith again · I shall teach thee what is acceptable and liking to Me. Think on thy sins past with great displeasure and sorrow of heart, and never think thyself worthy to be called holy or virtuous for any good deeds that thou hast done, but think how great a sinner thou art, belapped and bound with great and manifold sins and passions; that of thyself thou drawest to nought, soon fallest, soon art overcome, soon art troubled, and soon art broken with labour and pain. Thou hast nothing whereof thou mayest righteously glorify thyself, but many things thou hast wherefor thou oughtest to despise thyself; for thou art more unstable and more weak to ghostly works than thou knowest or mayest think.

Let nothing therefore seem great to thee, nothing precious, nothing worthy any reputation, nor worthy to be praised in thy sight, but that is everlasting. Let the everlasting truth be most liking and most pleasant to thee above all other things, and that thine own sin and vileness be most misliking and most displeasing to thee. Dread nothing so much, reprove nothing so much, let nothing be to thee so hateful, and flee nothing so much as thy sins and wickedness; for they should more displease thee than should the loss of all worldly things. Some there be that walk not purely before Me, for they through pride and curiosity desire to search and know high things of My Godhead, forgetting themselves and the health of their own souls. Such persons fall ofttimes into great temptations and grievous sins by their pride and curiosity, for the which I am turned against them and leave them to themselves without help and counsel of Me.

Dread, therefore, the judgments of God, and the wrath of Him that is Almighty, and discuss not, nor search His secrets; but search well thine own iniquities, how oft and how grievously thou hast offended Him, and how many good deeds thou hast negligently omitted and left undone, which thou mightest well have done. Some persons bear their devotion in books, some in images, some in outward tokens and figures; some have Me in their mouth, but little in their hearts. But some there be that have their reason clearly illumined with the light of true understanding, whereby their affection is so purged and purified from

Of the Imitation of Christ

love of earthly things, that they may always covet and desire heavenly things; insomuch as it is grievous to them to hear of earthly likings, and it is to them also a right great pain to serve the necessities of the body, and they think all the time as lost wherein they go about it. Such persons feel and know well what the spirit of truth speaketh in their souls, for it teacheth them to despise earthly things, and to love heavenly things; to forsake the world that is transitory, and to desire, both day and night, to come thither where is joy everlasting. *To the which bring us, our Lord Jesu! Amen.*

The Fifth Chapter: Of the marvellous effect of the love of God. ❡ Blessed be Thou, heavenly Father, the Father of my Lord Jesus Christ, for Thou hast vouchsafed to remember me Thy poorest servant; and sometimes dost comfort me with Thy gracious presence, that am unworthy all comfort. I bless Thee and glorify Thee always with Thy only-begotten Son, and the Holy Ghost, without ending. Amen.

O my Lord God, most faithful lover, when Thou comest into my heart, all mine inward parts do joy. Thou art my glory, and the joy of my heart, my hope and whole refuge in all my troubles. But forasmuch as I am yet feeble in love and unperfect in virtue; therefore I have need of more comfort and help of Thee. Vouchsafe, therefore, ofttimes to visit and instruct me with Thy holy teachings. Deliver me from all evil passions, and heal my sick heart from all inordinate affections, that I may be inwardly healed and purged from all inordinate affections and vices, and be made apt and able to love Thee, strong to suffer for Thee, and stable to persevere in Thee.

Love is a great thing and a good, and alone maketh heavy burdens light, and beareth in like balance things pleasant and unpleasant ; it beareth a heavy burden and feeleth it not, and maketh bitter things to be savoury and sweet. The noble love of Jesus perfectly printed in the soul maketh a man to do great things, and stirreth him always to desire perfection, growing more and more in grace and goodness. Love will always have his mind upward to God, and will not be occupied with love of the world. Love will also be free from all worldly affections, that the inward sight of the soul be not darked or let, nor that his affection to heavenly things be put from his free liberty by inordinate winning or losing of worldly things. Nothing, therefore, is more sweet than love, nothing higher, nothing stronger, nothing larger, nothing more joyful, nothing fuller, nor anything better in heaven or in earth ; for love descendeth from God, and may not rest finally in anything lower than God.

Such a lover flieth high, he runneth swiftly, he is merry in God, he is free in soul, he giveth all for all, and hath all in all ; for he resteth in one high Goodness above all things, of Whom all goodness floweth and proceedeth. He beholdeth not only the gift, but the Giver above all gifts. Love knoweth no measure, but is fervent without measure. He feeleth no burden, he regardeth no labour, he desireth more than he may attain, he complaineth of no impossibility ; for he thinketh all things that may be done for his Beloved, possible and lawful unto him. Love, therefore, doth many great things, and bringeth them to effect, wherein he that is no lover fainteth and faileth.

Love waketh much and sleepeth little, and sleeping sleepeth not ; he fainteth and is not weary ; is restrained of liberty, and is in great freedom. He seeth causes of fear and feareth not, but as a quick brand or sparkle of fire flameth always upward by fervour of love unto God, and through the especial help of grace is delivered from all perils and dangers. He that is thus a ghostly lover knoweth well what his voice meaneth, which sayeth thus : Thou, Lord God, art my whole love and my desire, Thou art all mine, and I all Thine.

Spread Thou my heart into Thy love, that I may taste and feel how sweet it is to serve Thee, and how joyful it is to laud Thee, and to be as I were all molten into Thy love. O I am bounden in love, and go far above myself ; for the wonderful great fervour that I feel of Thy unspeakable goodness! I shall sing to Thee the song of love, and I shall follow Thee, my Beloved, by highness of thought, wheresoever Thou go ; and my soul shall never be weary to praise Thee with the joyful song of ghostly love that I shall sing to Thee. I shall love Thee more than myself, and not myself but for Thee, and all other in Thee and for Thee, as the law of love commandeth, which is given by Thee. Love is swift, pure, meek, joyous and glad, strong, patient, faithful, wise, forbearing, manly, and never seeking himself or his own will; for whensoever a man seeketh himself, he falleth from love. Also, love is circumspect, meek, righteous; not tender, not light, nor heeding vain things; sober, chaste, stable, quiet, and well stabled in his outward wits. Love is subject and obedient to his prelate, vile and despicable in his own sight, devout and thankful to God, trusting and always hoping in Him, and that when he hath but little devotion or little savour in him; for without some sorrow or pain no man may live in love.

He that is not always ready to suffer, and to stand fully at the will of his Beloved, is not worthy to be called a lover, for it behoveth a lover to suffer gladly all hard and bitter things for his Beloved, and not to decline from his love for any contrarious thing that may befall unto him.

The Sixth Chapter: Of the proof of a true lover of God.

¶ My son, saith our Saviour Christ, thou art not yet a strong and a wise lover.

Why, Lord?

For a little adversity thou leavest anon that thou hast begun in My service, and with great desire thou seekest outward consolations. But a strong and faithful lover of God standeth stable in all adversities, and giveth little heed to the deceitful persuasions of the enemy, and as I please him in prosperity, so I displease him not in adversity.

A wise lover considereth not so much the gift of

his lover as he doth the love of the giver. He regardeth more the love than the gift, and accounteth all gifts little in comparison of his Beloved, who giveth them to him. A noble lover resteth not in the gift, but in Me above all gifts. Furthermore, it is not all lost, though thou sometimes feel less devotion to Me and to My Saints than thou wouldst do. And on the other side, the sweet ghostly desire that thou feelest sometimes to thy Lord Jesus is the feelable gift of grace given to thy comfort in this life, and a taste of the heavenly glory in the life to come; but it is not good that thou lean overmuch to such comforts, for they lightly come and go after the will of the giver. But to strive always without ceasing against all evil motions of sin, and to despise all the suggestions of the enemy, is a token of perfect love, and of great merit and singular grace.

Let no vanities or any strange phantasies trouble thee, of what matter soever they be. Keep thine intent and thy purpose always whole and strong to Me, and think not that it is an illusion, that thou art suddenly ravished into excess of mind, and that thou art soon after turned again to thy first lightness of heart; for thou sufferest such lightness rather against thy will than with thy will, and, therefore, if thou be displeased therewith, it shall be to thee great merit and no perdition.

Know that the old ancient enemy, the fiend, will essay to let thy good will, and to extinguish the good desire that thou hast to Me, and he will also hinder thee from all good works and devout exercises if he may; that is to say, from the honour and worship that thou art bound to give to Me, and to My Saints, from mind of My Passion, from the remembrance of thine own sins, from the diligent keeping of thy heart in good meditations, and from a steadfast purpose to profit in virtue. He will also put into thy mind many idle thoughts, to make thee irk and soon weary of prayer and holy reading. A meek confession displeaseth him much, and, if he can, he will so let a man that he shall not be houseled.[1] Believe him not, and care not for him, though he assail thee ever so much. Make all his malice return to himself again, and say to him thus: Go from me, thou wicked spirit, and be thou ashamed, for thou art foul and ugly, that wouldst bring such things into my mind. Go from me, thou false deceiver of mankind, thou shalt have no part in me; for my Saviour Jesus standeth by me as a mighty warrior and a strong champion, and thou shalt fly away to thy confusion. I had liefer suffer the most cruel death than to consent to thy malicious stirrings. Be still, therefore, thou cursed fiend, and cease thy malice, for I shall never assent to thee, though thou vex me ever so much. '*The Lord is my light and my salvation; whom shall I fear? The Lord is the strength of my life; of whom shall I be afraid? . . . Though an host should encamp against me, my heart shall not fear.*'[2] Why? God is my Helper and my Redeemer!

Always then, saith our Lord again to such a soul,

---

[1] *i.e.* receive the Holy Communion.   [2] Ps. xxvii 1, 3.

strive as a true knight against all the stirrings of the
enemy. And if sometimes through thy frailty thou
be overcome, rise soon again, and take more strength
than thou hadst first, and trust verily to have more
grace and more comfort of God than thou hadst before. But beware always of vain-glory and pride, for
thereby many persons have fallen into great errors,
and into great blindness of soul, so far that it hath
been right nigh incurable. Let, therefore, the fall
and ruin of such proud folks as have foolishly presumed of themselves, and have in the end perished
by their presumption, be to thee a great example, and
a matter of perpetual meekness.

The Seventh Chapter: How grace is to be
kept close through the virtue of meekness. ¶ My son, it
is much more expedient, and a surer way for thee,
that thou hide the grace of devotion and speak not
much of it, or regard it much, but rather to despise
thyself the more for it, and to think thyself unworthy
any such gracious gift of God. And it is not good to
cleave much to such affections as may be soon turned
into the contrary. When thou hast the grace of devotion, consider how wretched and needy thou wert
wont to be, when thou hadst no such grace. The
profit and increase of life spiritual is not only when
thou hast devotion, but rather when thou canst meekly and patiently bear the withdrawing and absenting
thereof; so as not then to leave off thy prayers, and
leave undone the other good deeds that thou art accustomed to do. But that to thy power, and so far

as in thee is, thou dost thy best therein, and forgettest
not thy duty, and art not negligent, for any dulness
or unquietness of mind that thou feelest.

Nevertheless, there be many persons that when
any adversity falleth to them, they be anon unpatient,
and made thereby very slow and dull to do any good
deed, thus hindering themselves greatly. For it is
not in the power of man, the way that he shall take;
but it is only in the grace of God to dispose this after
His will; to send comfort when He will, as much as
He will, to whom He will, and not otherwise than it
shall please Him.

Some unwary persons, through an indiscreet desire
that they have had to have the grace of devotion, have
destroyed themselves; for they would do more than
their power was to do, and not knowing the measure
of their gift or the littleness of their own strength,
they rather would follow the pride of their heart,
than the judgment of reason.

And because they presumed to do greater things
than was pleasing to God, therefore they lost anon
the grace that they had before. They were left needy
and without comfort, who thought to have builded
their nests in heaven, and so were taught not to presume of themselves, but meekly to trust in God and
in His goodness.

Such persons also as be beginners, and lack yet experience in ghostly travail, may lightly err and be deceived, unless they will be ruled by counsel of other.
And if they will needly follow their own counsel, and

will in nowise be removed from their own will, it will
be very perilous to them in the end. They that be
wise and cunning in their own sight, will seldom be
meekly ruled or ordered by other. It is better to have
little cunning with meekness, than great cunning with
vain liking therein ; and it is better to have little cunning with grace, than much cunning whereof thou
shouldst be proud. Also, he doth not discreetly, that
in time of devotion setteth himself also to spiritual
mirth, and as it were to a heavenly gladness, forgetting his former desolation and the meek dread of
God. Neither doth he well or virtuously, who in time
of trouble, and in any manner of adversity, beareth
himself desperately, and doth not feel or think so
faithfully of Me as he ought to do.

He that in time of peace and ghostly comfort will
think himself overmuch sure, commonly in time of
battle and of temptation shall be found overmuch de-
ject and fearful. But if thou couldst always abide
meek and little in thine own sight, and couldst order
well the motions of thine own soul, thou wouldst not
so soon fall into presumption or despair, or so lightly
offend Almighty God. Wherefore, this is good and
wholesome counsel, that when thou hast the spirit of
fervour, thou think how thou shalt do when that fervour is past. And when it happeneth so with thee, that
thou then think the light may soon come again, which
to My honour and thy proving I have withdrawn for
a time.

It is more profitable to thee that thou shouldst be so

proved, than that thou shouldst always have prosperous things after thy will. Merits are not to be thought great in any person, because he hath many visions, or many ghostly comforts, or that he hath clear understanding of Scripture, or that he is set in high degree. But if he be stably grounded in meekness and fulfilled with charity; if he seek wholly the worship of God and in nothing regardeth himself; if fully in his heart he can despise himself, and also coveteth to be despised of other, then may he have good trust, that he hath somewhat profited in grace, and that he shall in the end have great reward of God for his good travail. Amen.

The Eighth Chapter: How we should think through meekness ourselves to be vile and abject in the sight of God. ¶ Shall I, Lord Jesu, dare speak to Thee, that am but dust and ashes? Verily, if I think myself any better than ashes and dust, Thou standest against me; and mine own sins also bear witness against me, that I may not withsay it. But if I despise myself and set myself at nought, and think myself but ashes and dust as I am; then Thy grace shall be nigh unto me and the light of true understanding shall enter into my heart, so that all presumption and pride in me shall be drowned in the vale of meekness, through perfect knowing of my wretchedness. Through meekness Thou shalt show unto me what I am, what I have been, and from whence I came; for I am nought, and knew it not. If I be left to myself, then am I nought, and all is feebleness and imperfec-

tion. But if Thou vouchsafe a little to behold me,
anon I am made strong and am filled with a new joy,
and marvel it is that I, wretch, am so soon lifted up
from my unstableness into the beholding of heavenly
things, and that I am so lovingly lifted up by Thee,
that of myself fall down always to earthly things.

But Thy love, Lord, causeth all this, which preventeth me, and helpeth me in all my necessities, and
keepeth me warily from all perils and dangers, that I
daily am like to fall into. I have lost Thee and also
myself by inordinate love that I have had to myself,
and in seeking of Thee again I have found both Thee
and me ; therefore I will more deeply from henceforth set myself at nought, and more diligently seek
Thee than in times past I have done ; for Thou, Lord
Jesu, Thou dost to me above all my merits, and above
all that I can ask or desire.

But blessed be Thou in all Thy works, for though
I be unworthy any good things, yet Thy goodness
never ceaseth to do well to me, and also to many
others, that be unkind to Thee, and are turned right
far from Thee. Turn us, Lord, to Thee again, that
we may henceforward be loving and thankful, meek
and devout to Thee, for Thou art our health, Thou
art our virtue, and all our strength in body and soul,
and none but Thou.

To Thee therefore be joy and glory everlastingly in the
bliss of heaven.   Amen.

The Ninth Chapter: How all things are to be referred to God as the end of every work. ¶ My son, saith our Saviour Christ, I must be the end of all thy works, if thou desire to be happy and blessed; and if thou refer all goodness to Me, from Whom all goodness cometh, then shall be purged and made clean in thee thine inward affections, which else would be evil inclined to thyself, to other creatures. If thou seek thyself in anything as the end of thy work, anon thou failest in thy doing, and waxest dry and barren from all moisture of grace. Wherefore, thou must refer all things to Me, for I give all. Behold, therefore, all things as they be, flowing and springing out of My sovereign goodness, and reduce all things to Me as to their original beginning; for of Me both small and great, poor and rich, as of a quick-springing well, draw water of life.

He that serveth Me freely and with good will shall receive grace for grace. But he that will glorify himself in himself, or wilfully joy in anything beside Me, shall not be stablished in perfect joy, or be dilated in soul; but he shall be letted and anguished many ways from the true freedom of spirit. Thou shalt therefore ascribe no goodness to thyself, nor shalt thou think that any person hath any goodness of himself; but yield thou always the goodness to Me, without Whom man hath nothing. I have given all, and all will I have again, and with great straitness will I look to have thankings therefor.

This is the truth whereby is driven away all manner of vain-glory and pride of heart. If heavenly grace and perfect charity enter into thy heart, then shall there be no envy nor unquietness of mind, neither shall any private love have rule in thee. For the charity of God shall overcome all things, and shall dilate and inflame all the powers of thy soul. Wherefore, if thou understandest aright, thou shalt never joy but in Me, and in Me only thou shalt have full trust, for no man is good but God alone, Who is above all things to be honoured, and in all things to be blessed.

The Tenth Chapter: That it is sweet and delectable to serve God, and to forsake the world. ¶ Now shall I speak again to Thee, my Lord Jesu, and not cease. And I shall say in the ears of my Lord, my God and King that is in heaven, 'Oh how great is *thy goodness, which thou hast laid up for them that fear thee!*'[1] But what is it then to them that love Thee, and that with all their heart do serve Thee? Verily, it is the unspeakable sweetness of contemplation, that Thou givest to them that love Thee. In this, Lord, Thou hast most shewed the sweetness of Thy charity to me, that when I was not, Thou madest me, and when I erred far from Thee, Thou broughtest me again to serve Thee, and Thou commandest me also that I shall love Thee.

O Fountain of love everlasting! what shall I say of Thee? How may I forget Thee, that hast vouchsafed so lovingly to remember me? When I was

[1] Ps. xxxi. 19

like to have perished, Thou shewedst Thy mercy to me above all that I could think and desire, and hast sent me of Thy grace and love above my merits. But what shall I give Thee again for all this goodness? It is not given to all men to forsake the world, and to take a solitary life, and only to serve Thee. Yet it is no great thing to serve Thee, Whom every creature is bound to serve. It ought not therefore to seem any great thing to me to serve Thee, but rather it should seem marvel and wonder to me, that Thou wilt vouchsafe to receive so poor and so unworthy a creature as I am into Thy service, and that Thou wilt join me to Thy well-beloved servants.

Lo! Lord, all things that I have, and all that I do Thee service with, is Thine; and yet Thy goodness is such that Thou rather servest me than I Thee. For, lo heaven and earth, planets and stars with their contents, which Thou hast created to serve man, be ready at Thy bidding, and do daily that Thou hast commanded. And Thou hast also ordained Angels to the ministry of man. But above all this Thou hast vouchsafed to serve man Thyself, and hast promised to give Thyself unto him.

What shall I then give to Thee again for this thousandfold goodness? Would to God that I might serve Thee all the days of my life, or at least that I might for one day be able to do Thee faithful service; for Thou art worthy all honour, service, and praising for ever. Thou art my Lord and my God, and I Thy poorest servant, most bound before all other to love

Of the Imitation of Christ

Thee and praise Thee, and I never ought to wax weary of the praising of Thee. This it is that I ask, and I desire, that is to say, that I may always laud and praise Thee. Vouchsafe, therefore, most merciful Lord, to supply that wanteth in me, for it is great honour to serve Thee, and all earthly things to despise for the love of Thee.

They shall have great grace that freely submit themselves to Thy holy service. And they shall find also the most sweet consolation of the Holy Ghost, and shall have great freedom of spirit, that here forsake all worldly business, and choose a hard and strait life in this world for Thy Name.

O free and joyful service of God, by which a man is made free, holy, and also blessed in the sight of God! O holy state of religion, which maketh a man like to Angels, pleasant to God, dreadful to wicked spirits, and to all faithful people right highly commendable! O service much to be embraced, and always to be desired, by which the high goodness is won, and the everlasting joy and gladness is gotten without end!

The Eleventh Chapter : That the desires of the heart ought to be well examined and moderated.

¶ My son, saith our Lord, it behoveth thee to learn many things that thou hast not yet well learned.

What be they, Lord?

That thou order thy desires and affections wholly after My pleasure, and that thou be not a lover of thyself, but a desirous follower of My will in all

115

things. I know well that desires oft move to this thing or to that ; but consider well whether thou be moved principally for Mine honour, or for thine own. If I be the cause, thou shalt be well contented whatsoever I do with thee; but if anything remain in thy heart of thine own will, that is it that letteth and hindereth thee.

Beware, therefore, that thou lean not much to thine own desire without My counsel, lest haply it repent thee, and displease thee in the end, that which first pleased thee. Every affection and desire of man's heart that seemeth good and holy, is not forthwith to be followed, nor is every contrarious affection or desire hastily to be refused. It is sometimes right expedient that a man refrain his affections and desires, though they be good, lest haply by his importunity he fall into unquietness of mind, or that he be a let to other, or be letted by other, and so fail in his doing.

Sometimes it behoveth us to use, as it were, a violence to ourself, and strongly to resist and break down our sensual appetite, and not regard what the flesh will or will not; but always to take heed that it be made subject to the will of the spirit, and that it be so long chastised and compelled to serve, till it be ready to all things that the soul commandeth, and till it can learn to be content with a little, and can delight in simple things, and not murmur or grudge for any contrarious things that may befall unto it.

Of the Imitation of Christ

The Twelfth Chapter: How we should keep
patience, and continually strive against all concupiscence.
¶ O my Lord God, as I hear say, patience is much necessary unto me, because of many contrarious things
which in this life daily chance. I see well that howsoever I do order myself for peace, yet my life cannot be without some battle and sorrow.

My son, it is true what thou sayest; wherefore I
will not that thou seek to have such peace as wanteth
temptations, or as feeleth not some contradiction;
but that thou trow and believe that thou hast found
peace when thou hast many troubles, and art proved
with many contrarious things in this world. And if
thou say thou mayest not suffer such things, how
shalt thou then suffer the fire of purgatory? Of two
evils, the less evil is to be taken. Suffer, therefore,
patiently the little pains of this world, that thou mayest hereafter escape the greater in the world to come.
Trowest thou that worldly men suffer little or nothing? Yes, truly, thou shalt find none without some
trouble, though thou seek the most delicate persons
that be.

But percase thou sayest to Me again : They have
many delectations, and follow their own pleasure so
much, that they ponder but little all their adversities.

Well, I will it be as thou sayest, that they have all
that they can desire ; but how long, trowest thou,
that it shall endure? Soothly, it shall suddenly vanish
away as smoke in the air, so that there shall not be left
any remembrance of their joys past. And yet, when

they lived they were not without great bitterness and grief; for ofttimes of the same thing wherein they had their greatest pleasure, received they afterwards great trouble and pain. Righteously came this unto them, that forasmuch as they sought delectations and pleasures inordinately, they should not fulfil their desire therein but with great bitterness and sorrow.

O how short, how false, and inordinate be all the pleasures of this world! Soothly, for drunkenship and blindness of heart worldly people perceive it not ; but as dumb beasts, for a little pleasure of this corruptible life, they run headlong into everlasting death. Therefore, My son, '*go not after thy lusts, but turn away from thy own will.*'[1] '*Delight thyself also in the Lord,*' and fix thy love strongly in Him, '*and he shall give thee the desires of thine heart.*'[2]

And if thou wilt have consolation abundantly, and wilt receive the soothfast comfort that cometh of God, dispose thyself fully to despise this world, and put from thee wholly all inordinate delectations, and thou shalt have plenteously the comfort of God. And the more that thou withdrawest thee from the consolation of all creatures, the more sweet and blessed consolations shalt thou receive of thy Creator. But soothly thou canst not at the first come to such consolations, but with heaviness and labour going before. Thy old custom will somewhat withstand thee, but with a better custom it may be overcome. The flesh will murmur against thee, but with fervour

1 Ecclus xviii 30   2 Ps. xxxvii. 4.

of spirit it shall be restrained. The old ancient enemy, the fiend, will let thee if he can, but with devout prayer he shall be driven away, and with good bodily and ghostly labours his way shall be stopped, so that he shall not dare come nigh unto thee.

The Thirteenth Chapter: Of the obedience of a meek subject, after the example of our Lord Jesus Christ.

¶ My son, saith our Saviour Christ, he that laboureth to withdraw himself from obedience, withdraweth himself from grace; and he that seeketh to have private things, loseth the things that be in common. If a man cannot gladly submit himself to his superior, it is a token that his flesh is not yet fully obedient to the spirit, but that it oft rebelleth and murmureth. Therefore, if thou desire to overcome thyself, and to make thy flesh obey meekly to the will of the spirit, learn first to obey gladly thy superior. The outward enemy is the sooner overcome, if the inner man, that is, the soul, be not feebled or wasted. There is no worse or any more grievous enemy to the soul, than thyself, if thy flesh be not well-agreeing to the will of the spirit. It behoveth thee, therefore, that thou have a true despising and contempt of thyself, if thou wilt prevail against thy flesh and blood. But forasmuch as thou yet lovest thyself inordinately, therefore thou fearest to resign thy will wholly to another man's will.

But what great thing is it to thee that art but dust and nought, if thou subdue thyself to man for My sake, when I, that am Almighty and Most High God,

Maker of all things, subdued Myself meekly to man
for thy sake? I made Myself most meek and most
low of all men, that thou shouldst learn to overcome
thy pride through My meekness. Learn, therefore,
thou ashes, to be tractable; learn, thou earth and
dust, to be meek, and to bow thyself under every
man's foot for My sake; learn to break thine own
will, and to be subject to all men in thine heart.

Rise in great wrath against thyself, and suffer not
pride to reign in thee, but show thyself so little and
obedient, and so naughty in thine own sight, that all
men may righteously, as thou thinkest, go over thee,
and tread upon thee, as upon earth or clay. O vain
man! of what hast thou to complain? O thou foul
sinner! what mayest thou righteously say against
them that reprove thee, sith thou hast so oft offended
God, and hast also so oft deserved the pains of hell?
But, nevertheless, My eye of mercy hath spared thee,
for thy soul is precious in My sight; that thou mightest thereby know the great love that I have to thee,
and be therefore the more thankful to Me again, and
give thyself to perfect and true subjection and meekness, and be ready in heart patiently to suffer for My
sake thine own contempts and despisings, whensoever they happen to fall unto thee. *Amen*.

The Fourteenth Chapter: Of the secret and
hidden judgments of God to be considered, that we be
not proud of our good deeds. ¶ Lord, Thou soundest
Thy judgments terribly upon me, and fillest my body
and bones with great fear and dread; my soul also

trembleth very sore, for I am greatly astonied, for that I see that '*the heavens are not clean in thy sight.*'[1] Sith Thou foundest default in angels, and sparedst them not, what shall become of me, that am but vile? Stars fell from heaven, and I, dust and ashes, what should I presume? Some also that seemed to have great works of virtue, have fallen full low ; and such as were fed with meat of angels, I have seen after delight in swine's meat, that is to say, in fleshly pleasures.

Wherefore, it may be well said and verified that there is no holiness or goodness in us, if Thou with-draw Thy hand of mercy from us. No wisdom may avail us, if Thou, Lord, govern it not ; nor any strength help, if Thou cease to preserve us. No sure chastity can be, if Thou, Lord, defend it not ; nor may any sure keeping profit us, if Thy holy watch-fulness be not present ; for if we be forsaken of Thee, anon we are drowned and perish. But if Thou visit us a little with Thy grace, we anon live, and be lifted up again. We are unstable unless Thou confirm us ; we are cold and dull but if by Thee we be stirred to fervour of spirit.

O how meekly and abjectly ought I therefore to judge of myself, and how much ought I in my heart to despise myself, though I be holden ever so good and holy in sight of the world ! How profoundly ought I to submit me to Thy deep and profound judgments, sith I find in myself nothing else but nought and

[1] Job xv. 15.

nought! O Substance that may not be pondered! O Sea that may not be sailed! in Thee and by Thee I find that my substance is nothing, and over all nought. Where is now the shadow of this worldly glory, and where is the trust that I had in it? Truly it is vanished away through the deepness of Thy secret and hidden judgments upon me.

What is flesh in Thy sight? How may clay glorify himself against his Maker? How may he be deceived with vain praises whose heart in Truth is subject to God? All the world may not lift him up into pride, whom Truth, that God is, hath perfectly made subject unto Him; nor may he be deceived with any flattering that putteth his whole trust in God. For he seeth well that they that speak be vain and nought, and that *'their memorial is perished with them,'* but *'the Lord shall endure for ever.'*[1]

The Fifteenth Chapter: How man shall order himself in his desires. ¶ My son, saith our Saviour Christ, thus shalt thou say in everything that thou desirest: 'Lord, if it be Thy will, be it done as I ask, and if it be to Thy praising, be it fulfilled in Thy Name. And if Thou see it good and profitable to me, give me grace to use it to Thy honour. But if Thou know it hurtful to me, and not profitable to the health of my soul, then take from me such desire.' Every desire cometh not of the Holy Ghost, though it seem righteous and good, for it is sometimes full hard to judge whether a good spirit or an evil moveth thee to

[1] Ps. ix. 6, 7.

Of the Imitation of Christ

this thing or to that ; or whether thou be moved of thine own spirit. Many be deceived in the end, who first seemed to have been moved of the Holy Ghost.

Therefore with dread of God and with meekness of heart, we are to desire and ask whatsoever cometh to our mind to be desired and asked ; and with a whole forsaking of ourself to commit all things to God, and to say thus · 'Lord, Thou knowest what thing is to me most profitable, do this or that after Thy will. Give me what Thou wilt, as much as Thou wilt, and when Thou wilt. Do with me as Thou knowest best to be done, and as it shall please Thee, and be most to Thy honour. Put me where Thou wilt, and freely do with me in all things after Thy will. I am in Thine hands, lead me and turn me where Thou wilt. Lo ! I am Thy servant, ready to all things that Thou command-est, for I desire not to live to myself but to Thee. Would that it might be worthily and profitably, and to thy honour! *Amen.*

A Prayer that the will of God be always fulfilled.

¶ Most benign Lord Jesu, grant me Thy grace, that it may be always with me, and work with me, and per-severe with me unto the end. And that I may ever desire and will that is most pleasant and acceptable to Thee, Thy will be my will, and let my will always follow Thy will, and best accord therewith. Be there always in me one will and one desire with Thee. And that I may have no power to will or not will, but as Thou wilt or wilt not, grant me that I may die to all things that be in the world, and for Thee

123

to love to be despised, and to be as a man unknown
in this world. Grant me also, above all things that
can be desired, that I may rest me in Thee, and
fully in Thee pacify my heart; for Thou, Lord, art
the very true peace of heart, and the perfect rest
of body and soul, and without Thee all things be
grievous and unquiet. Wherefore, in that peace that
is, in Thee, the one high, one blessed, and one endless
Goodness, shall I always rest me.[1] So may it be.
Amen.

**The Sixteenth Chapter : That the very true
solace and comfort is in God.** ¶ Whatsoever I may
desire or think to my comfort, I abide it not here, but
I trust to have it hereafter ; for if I alone might have
all the solace and comfort, of this world, and might use
the delights thereof after mine own desire without sin,
it is certain that they might not long endure. Wherefore my soul may not fully be comforted, nor perfectly
refreshed, but in God only, Who is the comfort of the
poor in spirit, and the embracer of the meek and lowly
in heart. Abide, my soul, abide the promise of God,
and thou shalt have abundance of all goodness in
heaven. If thou inordinately covet these goods present, thou shalt lose the goodness eternal. Have
therefore present goods in use, and the eternal in
desire. Thou mayest in no manner be satiate with
temporal goods, for thou art not created so to use
them as to rest thee in them. If thou alone hadst
all the goods that ever were created and made, thou

[1] Ps iv. 8

mightest not therefore be happy and blessed; but thy blessedness and full felicity standeth only in God, that hath made all things of nought. And that is not such felicity as is commended of the foolish lovers of the world, but such as good Christian men and women hope to have in the bliss of heaven, and such as some ghostly persons, clean and pure in heart, whose '*conversation is in heaven*,'[1] sometimes do taste here in this present life. All worldly solace and all man's comfort is vain and short, but that comfort is blessed and soothfast that is received from Truth inwardly in the heart. A devout follower of God beareth always about with him his comforter, that is Jesus, and sayeth thus unto Him : 'My Lord Jesu, I beseech Thee that Thou be with me in every place and every time, and that it be to me a special solace gladly for Thy love to want all man's solace ; and if Thy solace want also, that Thy will and Thy righteous proving and assaying of me may be to me a singular comfort and a high solace.' '*Thou wilt not always chide; neither wilt thou keep thy anger for ever.*'[2] So may it be. *Amen.*

The Seventeenth Chapter : That all our study and business of mind ought to be put in God.

¶ My son, saith our Lord to His servant, suffer Me to do with thee what I will, for I know what is best and most expedient for thee. Thou workest in many things after thy kindly reason, and after as thy affection and thy worldly policy stirreth thee, and so thou mayest lightly err and be deceived.

[1] Phil. iii. 20.   [2] Ps. ciii. 9

Thomas à Kempis

O Lord! it is true all that Thou sayest. Thy providence is much better for me than all I can do or say of myself. Wherefore it may well be said, that he standeth very casually that setteth not his whole trust in Thee. Therefore, Lord, while my wit abideth steadfast and stable, do with me in all things as it pleaseth Thee, for it may not be but well all that Thou dost. If Thou wilt that I be in light, be Thou blessed; and if Thou wilt that I be in darkness, be Thou also blessed. If Thou vouchsafe to comfort me, be Thou highly blessed; and if Thou wilt that I shall live in trouble and without all comfort, be Thou in like wise much blessed.

My son, so it behoveth to be with thee, if thou wilt walk with Me; as ready must thou be to suffer as to joy, and as gladly be needy and poor as wealthy and rich.

Lord, I will gladly suffer for Thee whatsoever Thou wilt shall fall upon me. Indifferently will I take of Thy hand good and bad, bitter and sweet, gladness and sorrow, and for all things that shall befall unto me, heartily will I thank Thee. Keep me, Lord, from sin, and I shall dread neither death nor hell. Put not my name out of the book of life, and it shall not grieve me what trouble soever befall me.

The Eighteenth Chapter: That all temporal miseries are gladly to be borne through the example of Christ. ¶ My son, saith our Lord, I descended from heaven, and for thy health have I taken thy miseries, not compelled thereto of necessity, but of My charity;

that thou mightest learn to have patience with Me, and not to disdain to bear the miseries and wretchedness of this life, as I have done for thee. For from the first hour of My birth unto My death upon the cross, I was never without some sorrow or pain. I had great lack of temporal things; I heard great complaints made on Me; I suffered benignly many shames and rebukes; for My benefits I received unkindness; for My miracles, blasphemies; and for My true doctrine, many reproofs.

O Lord! forasmuch as Thou wert found patient in Thy life, fulfilling in that most specially the will of Thy Father, it is seeming that I, most wretched sinner, bear me patiently after Thy will in all things, and that, as long as Thou wilt, I bear for mine own health the burden of this corruptible life. For though this life be tedious and as a heavy burden to the soul, yet nevertheless it is now through Thy grace made very meritorious; and by example of Thee and of Thy holy Saints, it is now made to weak persons more sufferable and clear. And also much more comfortable than it was in the Old Law, when the gates of heaven were shut, and the way thitherward was dark, and so few did covet to seek it. And yet they that were then righteous, and were ordained to be saved, before Thy blessed Passion and Death could never come thither.

O what thanks am I bound therefore to yield to Thee, that so lovingly hast vouchsafed to show to me, and to all faithful people that will follow Thee, the very true and straight way to Thy kingdom. Thy holy life is our way, and by holy patience we walk to Thee, Who art our head and governor. And if Thou, Lord, hadst not gone before and showed us the way, who would have endeavoured him to have followed? How many would have tarried behind, if they had not seen Thy blessed example going before? We are yet slow and dull, now we have seen and heard Thy signs and doctrines; what would we then have been, if we had seen no such Light going before us? *Truly, we should have fixed our mind and love wholly in worldly things. From the which keep us, Lord, of Thy great goodness! Amen.*

The Nineteenth Chapter: Of patient suffering of injuries and wrongs, and who is truly patient. ¶ My son, what is it that thou speakest? Why complainest thou thus? Cease, cease, complain no more, consider My Passion, and the passions of My Saints, and thou shalt well see that it is right little that thou sufferest for Me. Thou hast not yet suffered to the shedding of thy blood, and truly thou hast little suffered in comparison of them that have suffered so many things for Me in time past, and that have been so strongly tempted, so grievously troubled, and so many ways proved. It behoveth thee, therefore, to remember the great grievous things that others have suffered for Me, that thou mayest the more lightly bear thy little griefs; and if they seem not little to thee, look thy impatience cause it not: but, nevertheless, whether they be little or great, study always to bear them patiently, without grudging or complaining, if thou may.

The better that thou canst dispose thee to suffer them, the wiselier thou dost, and the more merit shalt thou have; thy burden shall also be the lighter by reason of thy good custom and thy good will. Thou shalt never say: 'I cannot suffer this thing of such a person, nor is it for me to suffer it; he hath done me great wrong, and layeth unto my charge that I never thought; but of another man I will suffer as I shall think.' Such sayings be not good, for they consider not the virtue of patience, nor of Whom it will be crowned, but they consider rather the persons and the offences done unto them.

Therefore he is not truly patient that will not suffer but as much as he will, and of whom he will; for a true patient man forceth not of whom he suffereth, whether of his prelate, or of his fellow that is equal unto him, or of any other that is under him; whether he be a good man and a holy, or an evil man and an unworthy. But whensoever any adversity or wrong falleth unto him, whatsoever it be, and of whomsoever, and how oft soever, he taketh all thankfully as of the hand of God, and accounteth it as a rich gift and a great benefit: for he knoweth well, that there is nothing that a man may suffer for God, that may pass without great merit.

Be thou therefore ready to battle if thou wilt have victory. Without battle thou mayest not come to the crown of patience, and if thou wilt not suffer thou refusest to be crowned. Wherefore, if thou wilt needly be crowned, resist strongly and suffer patiently; for without labour no man may come to rest, nor without battle may any man come to victory.

O Lord Jesu! make it possible to me by grace, that is impossible to me by nature. Thou knowest well that I may little suffer, and that I am cast down anon with a little adversity. Wherefore I beseech Thee, that trouble and adversity may hereafter for Thy Name be beloved and desired of me; for truly to suffer and to be vexed for Thee is very good and profitable to the health of my soul.

The Twentieth Chapter: Of the acknow-ledging of our own infirmities, and of the miseries of this life. ¶ '*I will acknowledge my sin unto Thee*,'[1] and I will confess to Thee, Lord, all the unstableness of my heart.

Ofttimes it is but a little thing that casteth me down, and maketh me dull and slow to all good works. I purpose to stand strongly; but when a little temptation cometh it is to me great anguish and grief. Of a right little thing sometimes riseth a grievous temptation, and when I think myself to be somewhat surer, and I have the higher hand as it seemeth, suddenly I feel myself near-hand overcome by a light temptation.

Behold therefore, good Lord, behold my weakness and my frailness, best known to Thee before all other. Have mercy on me, O Lord, and '*deliver me out of the*

---

[1] Ps. xxxii 5.

mire[1] of sin, that my feet be never fixed in it. But this it is that oft grudgeth me sore, and in manner confoundeth me before Thee, that I am so unstable and weak, so frail to resist my passions. And though they draw me not always to consent, yet nevertheless their cruel assaults be very grievous unto me, so that it is in a manner tedious to me to live in such battle: but yet such battle is not all unprofitable to me, for thereby I know the better mine own infirmities, in that I see well that such wicked fantasies do rise in me much sooner than they go away. But would to God that Thou, most strong God of Israel, the lover of all faithful souls, wouldst vouchsafe to behold the labour and sorrow of me Thy poorest servant, and that Thou wouldst assist me in all things that I have to do! Strengthen me, Lord, with heavenly strength, so that the old enemy the fiend, or my wretched flesh, which is not yet fully subject to the spirit, have not power or lordship over me; for against them I must fight continually, while I shall live in this miserable life. But alas, what life is this, where no trouble or misery wanteth, where also every place is full of snares and of mortal enemies! For one trouble or temptation going away another cometh; and the first conflict yet during, many others suddenly rise, more than can be thought.

How may this life therefore be loved that hath such bitterness, and that is subject to so many miseries? And how may it be called a life, that bringeth forth

[1] Ps. lxix. 14.

so many deaths, and so many ghostly infections?
And yet it is beloved and much delighted of in many
persons. The world is oft reproved, that it is deceitful and vain, and yet it is not lightly forsaken, especially when the concupiscences of the flesh be suffered
to have rule. Some things stir a man to love the
world, and some things to despise it. *'The lust of the
flesh, and the lust of the eyes, and the pride of life'*[1] stir
man to love the world. But the pains and miseries
that follow them cause again hatred and tediousness
of it.

But alas for sorrow, a little delectation overcometh
the mind of them that be much set to love the world,
and driveth out of their hearts all heavenly desires;
insomuch that many account it as a joy of paradise
to live under such sensible pleasures, because they
neither have seen nor tasted the sweetness in God, and
the inward gladness that cometh of virtues. But
they that perfectly despise the world, and that study
to live under holy discipline, be not ignorant of the
heavenly sweetness that is promised unto ghostly
livers; they also see how grievously the world erreth,
and how grievously it is deceived in divers manners.

**The Twenty-first Chapter: How a man
should rest in God above all things.** ¶ Above all
things and in all things rest thou, my soul, in thy
Lord God, for He is the eternal rest of all Angels
and Saints.

Give me, Lord Jesu, this special grace, to rest me

[1] 1 John ii. 16.

in Thee above all creatures ; above all health and
fairness, above all glory and honour, above all dignity
and power, above all cunning and policy, above all
riches and crafts, above all gladness of body and
soul, above all fame and praising, above all sweetness and consolation, above all hope and promise,
above all merit and desire ; above all gifts and rewards
that Thou mayest give or send beside Thyself, and
above all joy and mirth that man's heart or mind may
take or feel. Also above all Angels and Archangels,
and above the company of heavenly spirits, above all
things visible and invisible, and above all thing that
is not Thyself.

For Thou, O Lord God, art the best, most high,
most mighty, most sufficient, and most full of goodness, most sweet, most comfortable, most fair, most
loving, most noble, and most glorious above all
things ; in Whom all goodness together perfectly
and fully is, hath been, and shall be. And therefore,
whatsoever Thou givest me beside Thyself, it is little
and insufficient to me ; for my heart may not rest
nor fully be pacified but in Thee, so that it ascendeth
above all gifts, and also above all things that be
created.

O my Lord Jesu Christ, most loving spouse, most
pure lover and governor of every creature, who shall
give me wings of perfect liberty that I may fly high
and rest me in Thee ? O when shall I fully tend to
Thee, and see and feel how sweet Thou art ! When
shall I wholly gather myself together in Thee so per-

fectly, that I shall not for Thy love feel myself, but
Thee alone above myself and above all bodily things,
and that Thou shalt visit me in such wise as Thou
dost visit Thy faithful lovers! Now I oft mourn and
complain the miseries of this life, and with sorrow
and woe bear them with right great heaviness; for
many evil things happen daily in this life, which ofttimes trouble me, and make me very heavy, and
greatly darken mine understanding; very often they
hinder me greatly, and put my mind from Thee, and
so encumber me many ways, that I cannot have free
mind and clean desire to Thee, nor have the sweet
embracings that to Thy blessed Saints be always present. Wherefore I beseech thee, Lord Christ Jesu,
that the sighings and the inward desires of my heart,
with my manifold desolations, may somewhat move
Thee and incline Thee to hear me.

O Jesu, the light and brightness of everlasting
glory, the joy and comfort of all Christian people that
are walking and labouring as pilgrims in the wilderness of this world, my heart crieth to Thee by still
desires without voice, and my silence speaketh unto
Thee, and saith thus: 'How long tarrieth my Lord
God to come to me? Verily, I trust that He will
shortly come to me, His poorest servant, and comfort me, and make me joyous and glad in Him; that
He will deliver me from all anguish and sorrow.
Come, Lord, come, for without Thee I have no glad
day nor hour; for Thou art all my joy, and without
Thee my soul is barren and void. I am a wretch,

and in manner in prison, and bound with fetters, till Thou, through the light of Thy gracious presence, vouchsafe to visit me and refresh me, and to bring me again to liberty of spirit, and Thou vouchsafe to shew Thy favourable and loving countenance unto me.

'Let others seek what they will, but truly there is nothing that I will seek, or that shall please me, but Thou, my Lord God, my hope and everlasting health. I will not cease of prayer till Thy grace return to me again, and Thou speak inwardly to my soul, and say thus:

'"Lo, I am here! I am come to thee, for thou hast called Me. Thy tears, and the desire of thy heart, thy meekness and thy contrition, have bowed Me down and brought Me to thee."'

And I shall say again: 'Lord, I have called Thee, and I have desired to have Thee, ready to forsake all things for Thee, sith Thou first stirred me to seek Thee. Wherefore, be Thou always blessed that hast shewed such goodness to me after the multitude of Thy mercy. What hath Thy servant, Lord, more to do or say, but that he meeken himself before Thy Majesty, and ever have in mind his own iniquity? There is none like to Thee, Lord, in heaven or in earth. Thy works be good, Thy judgments be righteous, and by Thy Providence all things be governed. Wherefore to Thee, Who art the Wisdom of the Father, be everlasting joy and glory! And I humbly beseech Thee, that my body and soul, my heart and tongue, and all Thy creatures, may ever laud Thee and bless Thee.' *Amen.*

The Twenty-second Chapter: Of remembering the great and manifold benefits of God. ¶ Open mine heart, Lord, into the beholding of Thy laws, and in Thy commandments teach me to walk. Give me grace to know and to understand Thy will, and with great reverence and diligent consideration to remember Thy manifold benefits; that from henceforth I may yield to Thee due thanks for them again. But I know and confess it for truth, that I am not able to yield to Thee condign thankings for the least benefit that thou hast given me, for I am less than the least benefit that Thou hast given. And when I behold Thy nobleness and worthiness, my spirit dreadeth and trembleth very sore for the greatness thereof.

O Lord! all that we have in body and in soul, inwardly and outwardly, naturally or supernaturally, they are Thy benefits, and show Thee openly to be a blessed and good benefactor, of Whom we have received such gifts. And though one hath received more and another less, yet they all are Thy gifts, and without Thee the least cannot be had. He that hath more received, may not rightfully glorify himself therein, as though he had gotten it by his own merit, nor exalt himself above other, nor disdain other, nor despise his inferiors; for he is greatest and most acceptable to Thee, that least ascribeth to himself, and that is for such gifts the more meek and devout in yielding thanks to Thee for them. And he that through meekness can hold himself most vile, and most unworthy of all other, is the more apt to receive of Thy hand larger gifts.

He that hath received the fewer gifts ought not therefore to be heavy, or to disdain at it, nor to be envious against them that have received the greater; but rather he ought to lift his mind upward to Thee, and highly to laud and praise Thy Name, that Thou so liberally, so lovingly, and so freely, without accepting of persons, departest Thy gifts among Thy people. All things come of Thee, and therefore Thou art in all things to be blessed. Thou knowest what is expedient to be given to every person, and why one hath less and another more; it is not for us to reason or discuss, but to Thee only, by Whom the merits of every man shall be discussed.

Wherefore, Lord, I account it for a great benefit not to have many gifts whereby outwardly, and after man's judgment, laud and praising should follow. And over that, as meseemeth, although a man consider and behold his own poverty, and the vileness of his own person, he ought not therefor to take grief, heaviness, and dejection, but rather to conceive thereby great gladness of soul; for Thou hast chosen, and daily dost choose, poor meek persons, and such as be despised in the world, to be Thy familiar and household servants. Witness Thy Apostles, whom Thou madest princes of all the world. Nevertheless they were conversant among the people without complaining or missaying; so meek and simple without all malice or deceit, that they joyed to suffer reproofs for Thy Name; so far forth, that such things as the world abhorreth and flieth, they coveted with great desire.

Thus it appeareth that nothing ought so much to comfort and glad Thy lover, and him that hath received Thy benefits, as that Thy will and pleasure be fulfilled in him after Thy eternal disposition of him from the beginning. Wherewith he ought to be so well contented and pleased, that he would as gladly be holden least as others would be holden most. As peaceful would he be and as well pleased in the lowest place, as in the highest; as glad to be despised, and abject, and of no name or reputation in the world, as others to be nobler or greater. For Thy will, Lord, and the honour of Thy Name, ought to excel all things; and more ought it to please and comfort Thy lover, than all other benefits given, or that might be given unto him.

The Twenty-third Chapter: Of four things that bring peace into the soul. ¶ My son, now shall I teach thee the very true way of peace and of perfect liberty.

O Lord Jesu, do as Thou sayest, for that is right joyous for me to hear.

Study, My son, rather to fulfil another man's will than thine own.

Choose always to have little worldly riches, rather than much.

Seek always the lowest place, and desire to be under other rather than above.

Of the Imitation of Christ

Covet always, and pray that the will of God be wholly done in thee.

Lo! such a person entereth soothfastly into the very true way of peace and inward quietness.

O Lord, this short lesson that Thou hast taught me, containeth in itself much high perfection. It is short in words, but it is full of sentence and fruitful in virtue; for if it were well and faithfully kept of me, unrestfulness would not so lightly spring in me as it hath done. For as oft as I feel myself unrestful and not contented, I find that I have gone from this lesson and from this good doctrine. But Thou, Lord Jesu, Who hast all things under Thy governance, and always lovest the health of man's soul, increase more grace in me, that I may from henceforth fulfil these teachings, and that I may do always what shall be to Thy honour and to the health of my soul. *Amen.*

A Prayer against evil thoughts. ¶ My Lord Jesu! I beseech Thee, be not far from me, but come shortly and help me, for vain thoughts have risen in mine heart, and worldly dreads have troubled me very sore. How shall I break them down? How shall I pass unhurt without Thy help?

'I shall go before thee,' Thou sayest, Lord, 'and I shall drive away the pride of thy heart, then shall I set open to thee the gates of ghostly knowledge, and shall shew to thee the privities of My secrets.'[1]

O Lord, do as Thou sayest, and then shall flee from me all wicked fantasies. Truly this is my hope and

---

[1] See Isa. xlv. 2, 3

my only comfort, to flee to Thee in every trouble, steadfastly to trust in Thee, inwardly to call to Thee, and patiently to abide Thy coming and Thy heavenly consolations, which I trust will shortly come to me. *Amen.*

A Prayer for the clarifying of man's mind. ¶ Clarify me, Lord Jesu, with the clearness of the everlasting light, and drive out of my heart all manner of darkness and all vain imaginations. Fight strongly for me, and drive away the evil beasts, *that is to say, all my evil and wicked concupiscences*, that peace of conscience may enter and have full rule in me, and that abundance of laud and praising of Thy Name may sound continually in the chamber of my soul, *that is to say, in a pure and clean conscience.* Command the winds and tempests of pride to cease; bid the sea of worldly covetise to be in rest; and charge the north wind, *that is to say, the fiend's temptation*, that it blow not; and then shall be great tranquillity and peace in me.

'*O send out thy light and thy truth*'[1] of ghostly knowledge, that it may shine upon the earth barren and dry. Send down Thy grace from above, and therewith anoint my dry heart; give me the water of inward devotion to moist therewith the dryness of my soul, that it may bring forth some good fruit, that shall be liking and pleasant to Thee. Raise up my mind that is sore oppressed with the heavy burden of sin, and lift up my desire to the love of heavenly things,

[1] Ps. xliii. 3.

that by a taste of the heavenly felicity it may loathe to think on any earthly thing.

Take me, Lord, and deliver me from the vile consolation of creatures, which must of necessity shortly perish and fail. For there is nothing created that may fully satisfy mine appetite. Join me, therefore, to Thee, with a sure bond of heavenly love, for Thou alone sufficest to Thy lover. And without Thee all things be vain and of no substance.

The Twenty-fourth Chapter: That it is not good to search curiously another man's life. ¶My son, saith our Lord, look thou be not curious in searching of any other man's life, neither do thou busy thyself with those things which do not belong unto thee. What is this or that to thee? Follow thou Me. What is it to thee whether this man be good or bad; whether he say or do this or that? Thou needest not to answer for another man's deeds, but for thine own thou must needly answer. Why then dost thou meddle where it needeth not? I know every man, and every thing under the sun I see and behold. How it is with every person, what he thinketh, what he willeth, and to what end his work draweth, is open to Me. Therefore all things are to be referred to Me. Keep thyself always in good peace, and suffer him that will always search another man's life to be as busy as he will. And in the end it shall fall upon him as he hath done and said, for he cannot deceive Me whatsoever he be.

If thou admonish any person for his soul-health,

look thou do it not to get thee thereby any name or fame in the world; nor to have the familiarity or private love of any person, for such things cause much unquietness of mind, and will make thee also to lose the reward that thou shouldst have of God, and will bring great darkness into thy soul. I would gladly speak to thee My words, and open to thee the secret mysteries of fraternal correction, if thou wouldst prepare thy soul against My coming, and thou wouldst open the mouth of thy heart faithfully to Me. Be thou provident, wake diligently in prayer, humble thyself in everything, and thou shalt find great comfort in God.

The Twenty-fifth Chapter: In what thing the peace of heart and greatest profit of man standeth.

¶ My son, saith our Lord Jesus, I said to My disciples thus: '*Peace I leave with you, my peace I give unto you: not as the world giveth, give I unto you,*'[1] but much more than it may give. All men desire peace, but all men will not do that belongeth to peace. My peace is with the meek and mild in heart. Thy peace shall be in much patience. If thou wilt hear Me and follow My words, thou shalt have great plenty of peace.

O Lord, what shall I do to come to that peace?

Thou shalt in all thy works take good heed what thou dost and sayest, and thou shalt set thy whole intent to please Me, and nothing shalt thou covet or seek without Me. But of other men's deeds thou

[1] John xiv. 27.

shalt not judge presumptuously, neither shalt thou meddle with things that pertain not to thee; if thou do thus, it may be that thou shalt little or seldom be troubled. But never to feel any manner of trouble, nor to suffer any heaviness in body or in soul, is not the state of this life, but of the life to come.

Think not therefore that thou hast found the true peace when thou feelest no grief; nor that all is well with thee when thou hast no adversity; nor that all is perfect for that everything cometh after thy mind. Nor yet that thou art great in God's sight, or specially beloved of Him, because thou hast great fervour in devotion, and great sweetness in contemplation, for a true lover of virtue is not known by all these things, nor doth the true perfection of man stand in them.

Wherein then, Lord?

In a man offering his heart wholly to God; not seeking himself either in great things or in small, in time or in eternity. So that he abide always one, and yield always like thanks to God for things pleasant and unpleasant; weighing them all in the one like balance of His love. Also, if he be so strong in God that, when inward consolation is withdrawn, he can yet stir his heart to suffer more if God so will; and yet justifieth not himself, nor praiseth himself as holy and righteous. He walketh then in the very true way of Peace, and he may then have a sure and perfect hope that he shall see Me face to face in the everlasting joy and fruition of the kingdom of heaven. And if he can come to a perfect despising of himself, then he shall have a full abundance of rest and peace in the joy everlasting, after the measure of his gift. *Amen.*

The Twenty-sixth Chapter: Of the excellence and worthiness of a free mind. ¶ Lord, it is the work of a perfect man not to sequester his mind from the beholding of heavenly things; and amongst many cares, to go as if he were without care, not in the manner of an idle or of a desolate person, but by the special prerogative of a free mind always busy in God's service, and not cleaving by inordinate affection to any creature.

I beseech Thee, therefore, my Lord Jesu, most meek and merciful, that Thou keep me from the business and cares of the world; and that I be not overmuch unquieted with the necessities of the bodily kind, nor taken with the voluptuous pleasures of the world and the flesh; likewise that Thou preserve me from all hindrance of the soul, that so I be not broken with overmuch heaviness, sorrow, and worldly dread. And by these petitions I ask to be delivered not only from such vanities as the world desireth, but also from such miseries as grieve the soul of me, Thy servant, with the common malediction of mankind, that is, with the corruption of the body, whereby I am so grieved and letted, that I may not have liberty of spirit to behold Thee when I would.

O Lord God, that art sweetness unspeakable, turn into bitterness to me all fleshly delights, which would draw me from the love of eternal things to the love of a short and a vile delectable pleasure. Let not flesh and blood overcome me, nor the world with his short glory deceive me, nor the fiend with his thousandfold crafts supplant me; but give me ghostly strength in resisting, patience in suffering, and constancy in persevering. Give me also, for all worldly consolations, the most sweet consolations of the Holy Ghost; and for all fleshly love, send into my soul the love of Thy Holy Name.

Lo! meat, drink, clothing, and all other necessaries for the body be painful and troublesome to a fervent spirit, which, if it might, would always rest in God and in ghostly things. Grant me grace, therefore, to use such bodily necessaries temperately, and that I be not deceived with overmuch desire to them. To forsake all things is not lawful, for the bodily kind must be preserved; but to seek superfluous things more for pleasure than for necessity, Thy holy law prohibiteth; for so the flesh would rebel against the spirit. Wherefore, Lord, I beseech Thee, that Thy hand of grace so govern and teach me, that I exceed not by any manner of superfluity. *Amen.*

The Twenty-seventh Chapter : That private love most letteth a man from God.

¶ My son, saith our Lord, it behoveth thee to give all for all, and to keep nothing to thee of thine own love; for the love of thyself more hurteth thee than any other thing in this world. After thy love and after thine affection everything cleaveth to thee more or less. If thy love be pure, simple, and well ordered, thou shalt be with-

out inordinate affection to any creature. Covet nothing therefore that it is not lawful for thee to have,
and have nothing that may let thee from ghostly
travail, or that may take from thee inward liberty of
soul. It is marvel that thou committest not thyself
fully to Me with all thy heart, together with all things
that thou mayest have or desire.

Why art thou thus consumed with vain sorrow?
Why art thou wearied with superfluous cares? Stand
at My will, and thou shalt find nothing that shall hurt
or hinder thee. But if thou seek this thing or that,
and wouldst be in this place or in that, for thine own
profit and for thine own pleasure, thou shalt never
be at rest, nor ever free from some trouble of mind ;
for in every place shall be found something that will
mislike thee.

Transitory things when they be had and greatly
multiplied in the world, do not always help man's soul
to peace ; but rather when they be despised and fully
cut out of the love and desire of the heart. This is
not to be understood only of gold and silver, and
other worldly riches, but also of the desire of honours
and praisings of the world, which shortly vanish and
pass away, as does the smoke with the wind.

The place helpeth little if the spirit of fervour be
away. The peace also that a man getteth outwardly
shall not long stand whole, if it be void from the true
inward Peace of heart. That is to say, though thou
change thy place, yet it shall little amend thee, unless thou stand steadfast in Me. For by new occa-

sions that shall daily rise, thou shalt find that thou
hast fled ; and percase much more perilous and much
more grievous things than the first were.

A Prayer for the purging of man's soul, and for heavenly wisdom and the grace of God to be obtained and had.
¶ Confirm me, Lord, by the grace of the Holy Ghost.
Give me grace to be strong in soul, and avoid out
thereof all unprofitable business of the world and of
the flesh, that it may not be led by unstable desires of
earthly things ; that I may behold all things as they
be, transitory and of short abiding ; and myself as
also to go with them : for nothing under the sun may
long abide, but all is vanity and affliction of spirit. O
how wise is he that feeleth and understandeth this!

Give me, Lord, heavenly wisdom, that I may learn
to seek Thee and to find Thee, and above all things
to love Thee; and to understand and know all other
things as they be, after the order of Thy wisdom and
none otherwise. Give me grace also wisely to withdraw me from them that flatter me, and patiently to
suffer them that grieve me ; for it is great wisdom
not to be moved with every blast of words, nor to give
ear to him that flattereth, as doth the mermaid. The
way that is thus begun shall bring him that walketh
in it to a good and blessed ending.

The Twenty-eighth Chapter : Against the evil
sayings of detractors. ¶ My son, saith our Saviour
Christ, thou shalt not take it to grief, because some
persons think evil of thee, or say of thee that thou
dost not gladly hear ; for thou shalt yet think worse

of thyself, and that no man is so evil as thou art. If thou be well ordered inwardly thou shalt not much care for such flying words. It is no little wisdom for a man to keep himself in silence and in good peace, when evil words be spoken, and to turn his heart to God, and not to be troubled with man's judgment.

Let not thy peace be in the hearts of men; for whatsoever they say of thee, good or bad, thou art not therefore another man : but as thou art, thou art. Where are the true peace and glory? Are they not in Me? Yes, truly. Therefore he that neither desireth to please man, nor dreadeth to displease him, shall have great plenty of peace ; for of inordinate love and vain dread cometh all unquietness of heart and unrestfulness of mind.

The Twenty-ninth Chapter : How Almighty God is to be inwardly called unto in time of tribulation.
¶ Lord, Thy Name be blessed for ever,[1] that wouldst that this temptation and tribulation should fall upon me! I may not escape it; but of necessity I am driven to flee to Thee, that Thou vouchsafe to help me, and to turn all into ghostly profit. O Lord, I am now in trouble, and it is not well with me, for I am greatly vexed with this present passion. And now, most beloved Father, what shall I say? I am now taken with anguishes and troubles on every side. Save me in this hour. Yet I trust that I am come into this hour that Thou mightest be lauded and praised when I am made perfectly meek before Thee, and clearly delivered by

[1] See Ps cxiii 2.

Of the Imitation of Christ

Thee. Be it therefore pleasing to Thee to deliver me;[1] for what may I, most sinful wretch, do, or whither may I go without Thee? Give me patience now in all my troubles. Help me, my Lord God, and I shall not fear or dread what troubles soever fall upon me.

And now what shall I say, but that Thy will be done in me? I have deserved to be troubled and grieved, and therefore it behoveth that I suffer as long as it shall please Thee. Would to God that I might suffer gladly till the furious tempests were overpast, and quietness of heart were come again! Thy mighty hand, Lord, is strong enough to take this trouble from me, and to assuage the cruel assaults thereof, so that I do not utterly fail; for thus hast Thou ofttimes done to me before this time. The more hard it is to me, the more light it is to Thee. And when I am delivered by Thee, then shall I say: 'This is the changing of the right hand of Him that is Highest; *that is, of the Blessed Trinity, to Whom be joy, honour, and glory everlastingly.*' *Amen.*

The Thirtieth Chapter: Of the help of God to be asked, and of a full trust to recover through devout prayer our former grace. ¶ My son, I am the Lord, that sendeth comfort in time of tribulation. Come therefore to Me, when it is not well with thee. This it is that letteth thee most, that thou turnest thee over slowly to Me; for before thou pray heartily to Me, thou seekest many other comforts, and refreshest thy

[1] See Ps. xl. 14.

149

spirits in outward things. And therefore all that thou dost little availeth thee, till thou canst behold and see that I am He that sendeth comfort to all that faithfully do call to Me, and that there is not without Me any profitable counsel or perfect remedy. But now take a good spirit to thee, and after thy troubles be thou comforted in Me, and in the light of My Mercy have thou full trust; for I am near to thee to help thee, and to restore thee again, not only to like grace, as thou hadst first, but also to much more, and in great abundance.

Is there anything hard or impossible to Me? Or am I like to him that sayeth a thing, and doth it not? Where is thy faith? Stand strongly and perseverantly in Me. Be steadfast, abiding My promise, and thou shalt have comfort in such time as shall be most expedient for thee. Abide, abide, and tarry for Me, and I shall come soon and help thee. It is temptation that vexeth thee, and a vain dread that feareth thee much. But what availeth such fear of dread for things that perchance will never come, but that the ghostly enemy would that thou shouldst have sorrow upon sorrow. Bear therefore patiently thy troubles that be present, and dread not overmuch those that are to come, for '*Sufficient unto the day is the evil thereof.*'[1] It is a vain thing and unprofitable to be heavy or glad for things that perchance will never happen.

But it is the unstableness of man that he is deceived, and that he so lightly follows the suggestion of the

[1] Matt. vi. 34

enemy, who careth not whether he deceive thee by
true suggestions or by false ; whether it be by love of
things present, or by dread of things to come. Therefore be thou not troubled, neither dread ; but trust
strongly in Me, and in My mercy have perfect hope ;
for when thou weenest that thou art right far from
Me, ofttimes I am right near unto thee, and when thou
weenest that all is lost, then ofttimes followeth the
greater reward. All is not therefore lost, though
something happen against thy will ; for thou shalt not
judge therein after thy outward feeling. Neither shalt
thou take any grief so sore to heart, but that thou shalt
have good trust to escape it.

Think not thyself wholly forsaken of Me, though
I send thee for a time some heaviness and trouble, for
this is the surer way to the kingdom of heaven. And
doubtless it is more expedient to thee and to other of
My servants, that ye sometimes be proved with adversity, than that ye always have all things after your
wits.[1] I know the hidden thoughts of man, and that it
is much expedient to the health of the soul that she be
left sometimes to herself without ghostly favour or
comfort, lest haply she be raised up into pride, and
think herself better than she is. That I have given, I
may take away, and may restore it again when it listeth
Me.

When I give a thing to any person it is Mine own
that I have given, and when I take it away again, I take
none of his, for every good gift and every perfect

[1] desires

151

reward cometh of Me. If I send to thee trouble or heaviness, in what wise soever it be, take it gladly and disdain it not; neither let thy heart fail thee therein, for I may anon lift thee up again, and turn thy heaviness into great joy and ghostly gladness. And verily, I am righteous and much to be lauded and praised when I do so with thee.

If thou understand aright, and behold thyself truly as thou art, thou shalt never be so heavy for any adversity, but thou shalt rather joy therein, and think it the greatest gift, that I spare not to scourge thee with such trouble and adversity. '*As the Father hath loved me, so have I loved you,*'[1] I said to My disciples; and yet I sent them not forth into the world to have temporal joys, but to have great battles; not to have honours, but despites; not to be idle, but to labour; not to rest, but to bring forth much good fruit in patience and good works. My son, remember well these words that I have spoken to thee, for they are true and cannot be denied.

The Thirty-first Chapter: How we should forget all creatures, that we may find our Creator.
¶ Lord, I have great need of Thy grace, or[2] that I may come thither where no creature shall let or hinder me from perfect beholding of Thee; for as long as any transitory thing holdeth me, or hath rule in me, I may not fly freely to Thee. He coveted to fly without let that said thus: '*Oh that I had wings like a dove! for then would I fly*' into the bosom of my Saviour, and into the

[1] John xv. 9. [2] in order

152

holes of His Blessed Wounds, '*and be at rest.*'[1]   I see
well that no man is more restful or more liking in this
world, than is that man who always hath his mind and
whole intent upward to God, and nothing desireth of
the world.   It behoveth him therefore that would perfectly forsake himself and behold Thee, to surmount
all creatures and himself also ; and through excess of
mind to see and behold that Thou, Maker of all things,
hast nothing among all creatures like unto Thee. But[2]
a man be clearly delivered from the love of creatures,
he may not fully tend to his Creator.   And this is the
greatest cause why there be so few contemplatives,
because so few there be that will willingly sequester
themselves from the love of creatures.

To contemplation is great grace required, for it
lifteth up the soul and ravisheth it up in spirit above
itself.   And except a man be lifted up in spirit above
himself, and be delivered in his love from all creatures,
and be perfectly united to God ; whatsoever he can,
or whatsoever he hath either in virtue or cunning, it is
but little worth afore God.   Therefore he shall have
but little virtue, and long shall he lie still in earthly
things, that accounteth anything great or worthy to
be praised, but God alone ; for all other things besides
God are nought, and for nought are to be accounted.
There is a great difference between the wisdom of a
devout man lightened by grace, and the cunning of a
subtle and studious clerk.   That learning is much
more noble and much more worthy that cometh by

<hr>

[1] Ps. lv 6.   [2] Unless

the influence and gracious gift of God, than that which is gotten by the labour and study of man.

Many desire to have the gift of contemplation, but they will not use such things as be required to contemplation. One great let of contemplation is that we stand so long in outward signs and in sensible things, and take no heed of perfect mortifying our body to the spirit. I wot not how it is, by what spirit we be led, nor what we pretend, we that be called spiritual persons, that we take greater labour and study for transitory things than we do to know the inward state of our own soul.

Alas for sorrow! anon as we have made a little recollection to God we run forth to outward things, and do not search our own conscience with due examination, as we should do. We heed not where our affection resteth, and we sorrow not that our deeds be so evil and so unclean as they be. The people corrupted themselves with fleshly uncleanness; and therefore followed the great flood. Verily, when our inward affection is corrupted, it is necessary that our deeds following thereupon be also corrupted; for from a clean heart springeth the fruit of a good life.

It is ofttimes asked what deeds such a man hath done; but of what zeal, of what intent he did them, is little regarded. It is oft inquired whether a man be rich, strong, fair, able, a good writer, a good singer, or a good labourer; but how poor he is in spirit, how patient and meek, how devout, and how inwardly turned to God, is little regarded. Nature holdeth the outward deed, but grace turneth her to the inward intent of the deed. The first is oft deceived, but the second putteth her trust wholly in God, and is not deceived.

The Thirty-second Chapter: How we should forsake ourselves, and thrust all covetise out of our hearts. ¶ My son, saith our Lord, thou shalt not have perfect liberty of mind, unless thou wholly forsake thyself. All proprietaries, and all lovers of themselves, all covetous persons, curious, vain-glorious, all runners about, and such as seek things soft and delectable in this world, and not those of Jesus Christ, oft saying and greedily seeking that which will not long endure, be as men fettered and bound with chains, and have no perfect liberty or freedom of spirit; for all things shall perish that be not wrought of God. Hold well in thy mind this short word. *Forsake all things and thou shalt find all things; forsake covetise and thou shalt find great rest.* Print well in thy mind that I have said, for when thou hast fulfilled it, thou shalt well know that it is true.

Lord, this lesson is not one day's work, nor a play for children; for in it is contained the full perfection of all religion.

My son, thou oughtest not to be turned from God, nor to be anything discouraged from His service, when thou hearest the strait life of perfect men; but rather thou oughtest to be provoked thereby to higher perfection, and at least to desire in heart that thou mightest come thereto. But would to God thou were first come to this point, that thou were not a lover of thyself, but that thou wouldst keep My commandments, and the commandments of him that I have appointed to be thy father spiritual; for then thou shouldst please Me greatly, and all thy life should pass forth in joy and peace. Thou hast yet many things to forsake, which, unless thou canst wholly forsake, thou shalt not get that thou desirest. And therefore '*I counsel thee to buy of me gold tried in the fire,*'[1] that is to say, heavenly wisdom, that despiseth all earthly things. Cast from thee all worldly wisdom, all man's comfort, and all thine own affections; choose also to have vile and abject things, rather than those that are precious and high in the sight of the world.

The true heavenly wisdom seemeth to many to be vile and little, and well-nigh forgotten. Many can say with their mouth that it is good not to desire to be magnified in the world, but their life followeth not their saying. But yet it is the precious margaret[2] and the high virtue that is hid from much people for their presumption.

Get it whoso may.

The Thirty-third Chapter: Of the unstableness of man's heart, and that our final intent in all things should be to God. ¶ My son, look thou believe not thine own affection, for it changeth oft from one to another. As long as thou livest thou shalt be subject to changeableness, whether thou wilt or not: now glad, now sorrowful; now pleased, now dis-

[1] Rev iii 18.   [2] pearl.

pleased ; now devout, now undevout ; now lusty, now slothful; now heavy, now lightsome. But a wise man, that is well taught in ghostly travail, standeth stable in all such things, and forceth little what he feeleth, or on what side the wind of unstableness bloweth ; for the whole intent and study of his mind is, how he may profit most in virtue, and come finally to the most fruitful and most blessed end. By such a whole intent fully directed to God, a man may abide steadfast and stable in himself among many adversities.

The more pure and the more clean is his intent, the more stable shall he be in every storm. But alas for sorrow ! the eye of man's soul is anon darkened, for it beholdeth lightly delectable things that come of the world and of the flesh. Insomuch that there is seldom found any person that is free and clear from the venomous desire of hearing tales or other fantasies ; and that by their own seeking. In such manner came the Jews into Bethany to Martha and to Mary Magdalen, not for the love of our Lord Jesus, but to see Lazarus, whom He had raised from death to life. Wherefore the eye of the soul is to be kept full bright, that it be always pure and clean, and that it be above all passing things wholly directed to Me.

The which grant unto us, O Lord. Amen.

The Thirty-fourth Chapter : How our Lord God savoureth to His lover sweetly above all things and in all things. ¶ Our Lord God is to me all in all ! And sith He is so, what would I have more, or

what can I desire more ?   O this is a savoury word
and a sweet, to say that our Lord is to me all in all !
But it is to him that loveth the Word and not the
world. To him that understandeth this word, is said
enough ; but yet to repeat it oft is liking to him that
loveth.   I may therefore more plainly speak of this
matter, and say : ' Lord, when Thou art present to
me all thing is pleasant and liking, but when Thou
art absent all things are grievous and greatly misliking. When Thou comest Thou makest mine heart
restful, and bringest into it a new joy. Thou makest
Thy lover to feel and understand the Truth, and to
have a true judgment in all things, and in all things
to laud and praise Thee.   O Lord, without Thee
nothing may be for long liking or pleasant ; for if anything should be liking or savoury, it must be through
help of Thy grace, and be tempered with the spicery
of Thy wisdom.

To him to whom Thou savourest well, what shall
not savour well ?   And to him that Thou savourest
not well unto, what may be joyful or liking?   But
worldly-wise men, and they that savour the delights
of the flesh, fail of this wisdom ; for in worldly wisdom
is found great vanity, and in fleshly pleasures is everlasting death.   Therefore, they that follow Thee,
Lord, by despising of the world, and by perfect mortifying of the lusts of the flesh, are known to be very
wise ; for they be led from vanity to Truth, and from
fleshly liking to spiritual cleanness. To such persons
God savoureth wondrous sweet, and whatsoever they

find in creatures, they refer it all to the laud and praising of the Creator; for they see well, that there is great difference betwixt the Creator and creatures, eternity and time, and betwixt the light made and the light unmade.

O everlasting Light! far passing all things that are made, send down the beams of Thy lightnings from above, and purify, glad, and clarify in me all the inward parts of my heart. Quicken my spirit with all the powers thereof, that it may cleave fast and be joined to Thee in joyful gladness of ghostly ravishings. O when shall that blessed hour come that Thou shalt visit me and glad me with Thy blessed presence, so that Thou be to me all in all? As long as that gift is not given to me, that Thou be to me all in all, there shall be no full joy in me. But alas for sorrow! mine old man, *that is, my fleshly liking*, yet liveth in me, and is not yet fully crucified, nor perfectly dead in me; for yet striveth the flesh strongly against the spirit, and moveth great inward battle against me, and suffereth not the kingdom of my soul to live in peace.

But Thou, good Lord, that hast the lordship over all the power of the sea, and *'rulest the raging'* [1] thereof, arise and help me, break down the power of mine enemies, who always move this battle in me. Shew the greatness of Thy goodness, and let the power of Thy right hand be glorified in me; for there is to

[1] Ps lxxxix. 9

me none other hope or refuge, but in Thee only, my Lord, my God !

To Whom be joy, honour, and glory everlastingly. Amen.

The Thirty-fifth Chapter: That there is no full surety from temptation in this life. ¶ Our Lord sayeth to His servant thus: Thou shalt never be sure from temptation and tribulation in this life. And therefore armour spiritual shall always, as long as thou livest, be necessary for thee. Thou art among thine enemies, and shalt be troubled and vexed by them on every side ; and unless thou use in every place the shield of patience, thou shalt not long keep thyself unmoved. And over that, if thou set not thy heart strongly in Me, with a ready will to suffer all things patiently for Me, thou mayest not long bear this ardour, nor come to the reward of blessed Saints. It behoveth thee therefore manly to pass over many things, and to use a strong hand against all the thwartings of the enemy. To the overcomer is promised Angel's Food,[1] and to him that is overcome is left much misery.

If thou seek rest in this life, how then shalt thou come to the rest everlasting ? Set not thyself to have rest here, but to have patience, and seek soothfast rest not in earth but in heaven ; not in man, or any creature, but in God only, where it is. For the love of God thou oughtest to suffer gladly all things, that is to say, all labours, sorrows, temptations, vexations,

[1] See Rev 11 17

anguishes, neediness, sickness, injuries, evil sayings, reprovings, oppressions, confusions, corrections, and despisings. These help a man greatly to virtue, these prove the true knight of Christ, and make ready for him the heavenly crown. And I shall yield him everlasting reward for this short labour, and infinite glory for this transitory confusion.

Trowest thou that thou shalt have always spiritual comforts after thy will? Nay, nay; My Saints had them not, but many great griefs, and divers temptations, and great desolations, but they bore all with great patience, and more trusted in Me than in themselves: for they knew well *'that the sufferings of this present time are not worthy to be compared with the glory which shall be revealed in us.'*[1] Wilt thou look to have anon that which others could not get but with great weepings and labours? *'Wait on the Lord; be of good courage, and he shall strengthen thy heart; wait, I say, on the Lord'*;[2] mistrust Him not; and go not back from His service for pain or for dread : but lay forth thy body and soul constantly to His honour in all good bodily and ghostly labours. And He shall reward thee again most plenteously for thy good travail, and He shall be with thee and help thee in every trouble that shall befall unto thee.

So may it be. Amen.

The Thirty-sixth Chapter: Against the vain judgments of men. ¶ My son, fix thy heart steadfastly in God, and dread not the judgments of man, when

---

[1] Rom viii. 18.   [2] Ps. xxvii. 14.

thine own conscience witnesseth thee to be innocent
and clear. It is right good and blessed sometimes to
suffer such sayings, and it shall not be grievous to a
meek heart, which trusteth more in God than in himself. Many folk can say many things, and yet little
faith is to be given to their sayings. But to please all
men it is not possible. For though St. Paul laboured
all that he might to have pleased all people in God,
and did to all men all that he could for their salvation, yet nevertheless he could not let but that he was
sometime judged of other.

He did for the edifying and health of other as much
as in him was, but that he should not sometime be
judged of other, or be despised of other, he could not
let; wherefore he committed all to God that knoweth
all thing, and armed himself with patience and meekness against all things that might be untruly spoken
against him. Nevertheless sometimes he answered
again, lest by his silence hurt or hindrance might have
grown to others.

What art thou then that dreadest so sore a mortal
man? This day he is, and to-morrow he appeareth
not. Dread God, and thou shalt not need to dread
man. What may man do with thee in words or injuries? He hurteth himself more than thee; and in
the end he shall not flee the judgment of God, whatsoever he be. Have always God before the eye of thy
soul, and strive not again by multiplying of words.
And if thou seem for a time to suffer confusion that
thou hast not deserved, disdain thou not therefor,

nor through impatience minish thy reward. But rather lift up thy heart to God in heaven, for He is able to deliver thee from all confusion and wrongs, and to reward every man after his desert, and much more than he can deserve.

The Thirty-seventh Chapter: Of a pure and a whole forsaking of ourself and our own will, that we may get freedom of spirit and follow the will of God.

My son, saith our Lord, forsake thyself, and thou shalt find Me. Stand without following of thine own will, and without all propriety,[1] and thou shalt much profit in grace; and if thou wholly resign thyself into My hands, and take nothing to thee again, thou shalt have the more grace of Me.

O Lord, how oft shall I resign me unto Thee, and in what things shall I forsake myself?

Always and in every hour, in great things and in small. I except nothing, for in all things I will to find thee naked, and very poor, and void of thine own will. Else how mayest thou be Mine, and I thine, unless thou be clearly bereft of thine own will, within and without? The sooner thou canst bring it about, so much the sooner shall it be better with thee; and the more perfectly and the more clearly thou canst do it, the more fully shalt thou please Me, and the more shalt thou win.

Some persons resign themselves unto Me, but it is with some exception, for they trust not fully to Me,

---

[1] *i e.* property   This was addressed to those who, having taken the vow of poverty, had left all things.

and therefore they study to provide for themselves. And some at the beginning offer themselves to Me, but after, when any temptation cometh, they soon turn again to their own will and to that which they promised to forsake; therefore they profit little in virtue. Truly such persons shall never come to perfect cleanness and freedom of heart, nor to the grace of familiarity with Me, but through a perfect forsaking of themselves, and through a daily offering of themselves and all that they have wholly to Me; for without this no man may have perfect fruition and uniting with Me.

I have said to thee many times before, and yet I say to thee again : *Forsake thyself, and resign thyself wholly to Me, and thou shalt have great inward peace in Me.* Give all for all, and nothing keep to thyself of thine own will, but stand purely and stably in Me, and thou shalt have Me, and thou shalt be so free in heart and in soul, that neither darkness of conscience nor thraldom of sin shall ever have power in thee. Endeavour thyself therefore to get this freedom of spirit that I speak of, pray for it, study for it, and always desire in thy heart that thou mayest clearly be spoiled and bereft of all property and of thine own will, so that being naked of all worldly things thou mayest follow Me that hung naked for thee upon the cross : also that in thy love thou mayest die to thyself and to all worldly things, and blessedly live to Me. If thou do thus, then all vanities, all fantasies, all superfluous cares of the world and of the flesh shall fail, and fade, and go away. Then also immoderate dread and inordinate love shall die in thee, and thou shalt blessedly live in Me and I in thee. *Amen.*

The Thirty-eighth Chapter: How a man shall rule himself in outward things, and how he ought to call to God for help in all perils and dangers. ¶ Our Lord Jesu sayeth to His servant thus: Thou oughtest to take heed diligently that in every place, in every deed, and in every outward occupation that thou dost, thou be inwardly free in thy soul, and have the rule over thyself, and that all things be under thee, and not thou under them; that thou be lord and governor over thy deeds, not a servant or a bond-man; but rather exempted[1] as a true Hebrew, and going into the number and into the freedom of the children of God, who stand upon things present and look towards things everlasting, who behold things transitory with their left eye, and things everlasting with their right eye; whom worldly goods cannot draw down to the love of them, but who rather draw worldly goods to serve in such wise as they be ordained of God, and as they be instituted to do by the high Maker of all things, Who leaveth nothing inordinate in His creatures.

Also, if in every adventure and doubt that shall happen unto thee, thou stand not to the judgment of thy outward appearance, but anon enterest into thine own soul by devout prayer, as Moses did into the Tabernacle[2] to ask counsel of God, thou shalt hear

---

[1] *i e.* free.   [2] See Ex. xxxiii 8-11.

anon the answer of our Lord, which shall instruct
thee sufficiently in many things both present and to
come. It is read that Moses had always recourse to
the tabernacle of God for the solving of doubts and
questions, and that he there asked the help of God
through devout prayer, for the perils and dangers,
as well of himself as of the people. So shouldst thou
enter into the secret tabernacle of thine own heart,
and there ask inwardly with good devotion the help
of God in all such doubts and perils. We read that
Joshua and the children of Israel were deceived by
the Gibeonites, because they gave light credence to
their sayings, and did not first ask counsel of God,
as they should have done ; and so by the fair words
of the Gibeonites, and through false pity, Joshua and
the children of Israel were illuded and greatly deceived.[1]

The Thirty-ninth Chapter: That a man should not be importune in his business. ¶ My son,

saith our Lord, commit always thy cause to Me, and
I shall well dispose it for thee, when the time shall
come. Abide Mine ordinance and direction, and
thou shalt find thereby great profit and help.

O Lord, gladly will I commit all things to Thee,
for it is little that I can do for myself. Would to God
that I did not cleave to desires of worldly things, but
that I might always offer myself wholly to Thy will
and pleasure.

So it is good for thee to do, My son, for oftentimes

[1] See Jos. ix.

a man that trusteth much in himself and in his own will, setteth his mind to bring about this thing or that, as he desireth ; but when he has attained to what he desired, he beginneth then to feel towards it all otherwise than he did before: for the affections and desires of men are not always one, but oft drive a man from one thing to another. It is therefore no small thing for a man fully to forsake himself, though it be in right little things.

For truly, the very perfection of man is a perfect denying and a full forsaking of himself. And such a man is very free and beloved of God. But the old enemy the fiend, who resisteth goodness all that he may, ceaseth not long from temptation, but day and night he maketh grievous assaults to see if he may catch any unwary person in his snare of deceit. '*Watch and pray, that ye enter not into temptation.*'[1]

⚙ɦe ⚙ortieth Chapter: ⚙hat a man hath no goodness of himself, and that he may not rightfully glorify himself in anything. ¶ Lord, '*what is man, that thou art mindful of him?*'[2] Or what hath he done for Thee that Thou shouldst visit him with grace? Of what may I complain, though Thou sometimes forsake me? Or what may I righteously say, though Thou grant me not that I ask? Truly, I may well think and say thus: 'I am nought; of myself I have no goodness; but in all things I am of myself all insufficient and tend to nought. And unless I be holpen of Thee, and be inwardly informed and taught by

[1] Matt xxvi. 41   [2] Ps. viii. 4.

Thee, I shall be altogether slothful and to all things unprofitable.'

O Lord, Thou art always One, ever shalt be One; always good, always righteous and holy; doing all things well, righteously, and blessedly ; disposing all things after Thy Wisdom. But I, wretch, that am always more ready and prone to evil than to good, I am not always abiding in one, for seven times be changed upon me ! Nevertheless, it will be better with me when it shall please Thee to put forth Thy helping hand ; for Thou alone art He that without man's aid mayest help me, and so confirm and stable me in Thee, that mine heart shall not lightly be changed from Thee, but be wholly fixed in Thee, and finally rest in Thee.

Verily if I could cast away from me all man's comfort, either to get devotion, or because of necessity I am compelled thereto (for that I find no comfort in man), then might I well trust in Thy grace to have of Thee new visitations and new heavenly consolation.

But I confess it for truth, that I am unworthy to have any such consolations, and I thank Thee as oft as any good thing cometh to me, for all that is good cometh of Thee. I am but vanity and nought before Thee, an inconstant man and a feeble. Whereof then may I righteously glorify myself, or why should I look to be magnified? Truly vain glory is a perilous sickness, a grievous pestilence, and a right great vanity ; for it draweth a man from the true joy that he should have in God, and robbeth him clearly of all heavenly grace. For when a man pleaseth himself, he displeaseth Thee, and when he delighteth in man's praisings, he is deprived of true virtue.

True steadfast joy and gladness is to joy in Thee and not in himself; in Thy name and not in his own virtue or in any creature. Therefore Thy Name be praised, and not mine; Thy works be magnified, and not mine; let Thy goodness be always blessed, but to me let nothing be given of the laud and praising of man. Thou art my glory and the joy of my heart. In Thee I will glory and will joy always; but in myself I will glory in nothing but in my infirmities.

Let the Jews seek glory among themselves, but I will seek none but that is of Thee alone. For all man's glory, all temporal honour, and all worldly highness to Thy eternal glory compared, is but foolishness and a great vanity. O Truth! O Mercy! O Blessed Trinity! to Thee be laud, honour, and glory everlastingly. *Amen.*

The Forty-first Chapter: how all temporal honour is to be despised. ¶ My son, take it not to grief, though thou see other men honoured and exalted, and thyself despised and set at nought. If thou raise up thine heart to Me in heaven, the despites of man on earth shall little grieve thee.

O Lord, we are here in great darkness and are soon deceived with vanities. Verily if I beheld myself well, I should openly see that there was never

any wrong done to me by any creature, nor have I
anything whereof I may righteously complain. But
inasmuch as I have oft sinned and grievously offended
against Thee, therefore all creatures be armed against
me. To me therefore is due confusion and despite;
to Thee laud, honour, and glory. And unless I can
bring myself to this point, that I would gladly be
despised and forsaken of all creatures, and utterly to
seem as nought in the world, I may not be inwardly
pacified and stablished in Thee, nor be spiritually
illumined, nor yet fully united to Thee.

The Forty-second Chapter: That our trust
is not to be put in worldly people. ¶ My son, if thou
set thy peace in any person for thine own pleasure or
worldly friendship, thou shalt always be unstable,
and never shalt thou be contented; but if thou
always have recourse to the Truth everlasting, that
is God Himself, then the death or going away of thy
dearest friend, whatsoever he be, shall little grieve
thee. The love of thy friend ought always to be referred to Me; and for Me he is to be beloved, how
good and how profitable soever he seem unto thee in
this life. Without Me friendship is nought worth,
and may not long endure; nor is that love true and
clean that is not knit by Me. Thou oughtest therefore to be so mortified in all such affections of worldly
men, that, inasmuch as in thee is, thou wouldst covet
to be without all man's comfort.

So much a man draweth nearer to God, as he can
withdraw himself from the world and from all world-

ly comforts; and so much higher he ascendeth to God, as he can descend lower in himself, and can wax vile and abject in his own sight.

He that ascribeth any goodness to himself, withstandeth the grace of God, and letteth[1] it to live in him; for the grace of the Holy Ghost seeketh always a meek and humble heart. If thou couldst perfectly annihilate thyself, and wholly put out of thy heart all human and create love, then should I dwell in thee with great abundance of My grace. But when thou lookest to creatures, then is righteously drawn from thee the sight of the Creator. Learn therefore to overcome thyself for the love of Him that made thee like to Himself, and thou shalt anon come to great ghostly knowledge. How little soever the thing be that a man loveth, if he love it inordinately, it hindereth and letteth him greatly from the true and perfect love that he should have to God.

The Forty-third Chapter: That we should eschew vain secular cunning. ¶ My son, saith our Lord, let not fair and subtle words move thee, *'for the kingdom of God is not in word, but in power.'*[2] Take heed to My words, for they inflame the heart, and lighten the understanding; they bring also compunction of heart for sins past, and ofttimes cause great heavenly comfort suddenly to come into the soul. Never read in any science to the intent thou wouldst be called wise, but study rather to mortify in thee all stirrings of sins, and that shall be more

[1] preventeth. [2] 1 Cor. iv 20.

profitable to thee than the knowledge of many hard and subtle questions.

When thou hast read and understood many doubts, yet nevertheless it behoveth thee to come to One Who is the beginning of all things, God Himself; or else thy knowledge shall little avail thee. I am He that teacheth a man cunning, and do give more understanding to meek persons, than can be taught by man's teaching. He to whom I speak shall soon be made wise; and much shall he profit in spirit, when pain and woe shall be to them that only seek for curious learning, taking little heed to the way of serving God. The time will come when Christ, Lord of Angels, and Master of all masters, shall appear to hear the lesson of every creature, that is, to examine the conscience of every person. And then shall Jerusalem, *that is, man's soul*, be searched with lanterns [1] and lights of God's high knowledge and rightful judgments. Then also shall be made open the deeds and thoughts of every man; all excuses and vain arguments shall cease and be utterly set apart.

I am He also that suddenly illumine and lift up a meek soul, so that it shall be made able in short time to take and to receive the true reason of the Wisdom of God more perfectly, than another that studieth ten years in Schools and lacketh meekness. I teach without sound of words, without diversity of opinions, without desire of honour, and without strife of arguments. I am He that teach all to despise earthly

[1] Sophonias 1. 12.

things, to loathe things that be present, to seek and
to savour eternal things, to flee honours, to bear
patiently all evil words and speakings, to put their
trust wholly in Me, nothing to covet without Me,
and above all things burningly to love Me.

Some folks, through an inward love that they have
had to Me, have learned many great things, and have
spoken high mysteries of My Godhead. They profited more in forsaking all things than in studying
high and subtle learning. But to some men I speak
common things, to others special things ; to some I
appear sweetly in signs and figures, to others I give
great understanding of Scripture, and open to them
high secret mysteries.

There is in books one voice and one letter that is
read, but it informeth not all alike; for I am within
secretly hidden in the letter, the Teacher of Truth,
the searcher of man's heart, the knower of thoughts,
the promoter of good works, and the rewarder of all
men, after as My Wisdom and Goodness judgeth
them to have deserved, and none otherwise.

The Forty-fourth Chapter: That we should
not regard much outward things, and ponder but little
the judgment of man. ¶ My son, it is profitable to
thee to be ignorant in many things, and to think thyself as dead to the world, and one to whom all the
world is crucified. Thou must also let many things
pass with a deaf ear, as if thou neither heard them nor
saw them, and rather to think on such things as shall
cause thee an inward peace of soul. It is also more

profitable to thee that thou turn the eye of thy soul
from things that displease thee, and to let every man
hold the opinion that to him seemeth best, rather
than to strive again with froward words. And truly,
if thou were well stabled in God, and beheld His
judgments aright, thou wouldst be content to be
judged of other, and to be overcome by other, as our
Lord Jesus was for thee in time of His Passion.

O Lord! what shall become of us that heed worldly
things so much, and beweep so greatly a little temporal
loss? We labour and run for worldly profit with all
our might, but our spiritual profit and the health of
our own souls we little regard. Such a thing as little
or nothing profiteth us is much set by ; but that which
is most necessary to us is nigh forgotten. Why? Because men run gladly into outward things, and unless
they shortly turn back again, they gladly rest in them.
The which shall be to them in the end great peril and
danger.

**The Forty-fifth Chapter: That men be not
always worthy of belief, for that they so lightly offend
in words.** ¶ Lord, '*give us help from trouble: for
vain is the help of man.*'[1] How often have I not found
friendship, where I thought I should have found it?
And how often have I found it, where I least presumed to have found it? Wherefore it is a vain thing
to trust in man, for the true and soothfast trust and
health of righteous men is in Thee alone. Blessed
therefore be Thou, Lord, in all things that happen

[1] Ps lx. 11.

unto us ; for we are weak and unstable, soon deceived
and soon changed from one thing to another.

Who may so warily and so assuredly keep himself
in everything, as not to fall sometimes into some deceit or into some perplexity ? Truly very few. But
he that trusteth in Thee, and that seeketh Thee with
a clean heart, slideth not so lightly from Thee. And
if it happen him to fall into any trouble or perplexity,
whatsoever it be and how grievous soever it be, he
shall anon either be delivered by Thee, or be comforted by Thee ; for Thou never forsakest him that
trusteth in Thee. It is right hard to find so true and
faithful a friend that will persevere with his friend in
all his troubles; but Thou, Lord, art most faithful in
all things, and like to Thee none can be found.

O how well that holy soul[1] savoured in ghostly
things that said thus: '*My mind is stablished in God,
and is fully grounded in Christ.*' Truly if it were so
with me, the dread of man would not so lightly enter
into me, nor would other men's words so soon move
me. Who may foresee all things ? Or who may prevent all evils that are to come ? And if things foreseen
ofttimes do great hurt, what then shall those things
do that be not foreseen ? But why have not I, wretch,
better seen to myself ? And why have I so lightly believed other men's sayings ? Truly for that we are
but men, and but frail men, though we be esteemed
and thought of many to be as Angels in our conversation. Whom may I believe but only Thee ? Thou

[1] St Agatha.

art the Truth that deceivest no man; nor mayest Thou be deceived. And on the other side, every man is a liar, weak, unstable, and sliding most especially in words; so that what seemeth openly to be true may scarcely be believed.

How prudently therefore hast Thou warned us to beware of the lightness of man,[1] and also that our familiar servants may be our enemies.[2] Hence, though one should say, *Lo, here is thy friend*; or, *Lo, there is thy friend;* he is not to be believed, as mine own hurt hath taught me. Would to God it might be as a warning to me, and not to my more folly!

Some one says to me · 'Beware, beware, keep close to thyself what I shall shew thee.' And when I keep it close and believe it to be secret, he cannot be secret in that he himself desired, but anon betrayeth both himself and me, and goeth his way. From such tales and from such unstable men Lord defend me, that I fall not into their hands, or ever commit any such thing ! A true and a stable word, Lord, give unto my mouth, and a deceitful tongue drive far away from me; for that I would not have done to myself, I ought to be wary that I do it not to other.

O how good and how peaceful it is to keep silence of other men's words and deeds, and not to give full credence till the truth be tried ; not to report lightly to other all that we hear or see, nor to open our heart fully but to very few ; always to seek Thee, Who art the beholder of man's heart, and not to be moved with

[1] Matt. x. 17.   [2] *Ib* x 36.

every flake of words, but to desire in heart that all things in us inwardly and outwardly may be fulfilled after Thy Will. How sure a thing is it also for the keeping of heavenly grace to flee the conversation of worldly people all that we may, and not to desire things that seem outwardly to be pleasant and liking; but with all the study of our heart to seek such things as bring fervour of spirit and amendment of life. A virtue known and over-timely praised hath been truly a great hurt to many persons; and contrariwise, a grace kept in silence, and not lightly reported to others, hath been in this frail life, that is full of temptation and private envy, right profitable to some.

The Forty-sixth Chapter: That we shall put all our confidence in God when evil words be spoken to us. ¶ My son, saith our Lord, stand strongly, and trust faithfully in Me. What be words but words? They fly in the air, but they hurt not a stone on the ground. And if thou know thyself not guilty, think that thou wilt gladly suffer such words for God. It is but a little thing for thee to suffer sometimes a hasty word, sith thou art not yet able to suffer hard strokes. But why is it that so little a thing goeth so nigh thy heart, but that thou art yet carnal, and heedest to please men more than thou shouldst? And because thou dreadest to be despised, thou wilt not gladly be reproved for thine offences, and therefore searchest busily and with great study how thou mayest be excused.

M   177

Thomas à Kempis

But behold thyself well, and thou shalt see that the world yet liveth in thee, and also a vain love to please man. When thou refusest to be rebuked and punished for thy defaults, it appeareth evidently that thou art not soothfastly meek, and that thou art not yet dead to the world, nor the world to thee yet truly crucified. But hear My words, and thou shalt not need to care for the words of ten thousand men. Lo, if all things were said against thee that could be most maliciously and untruly feigned against thee, what would they hurt, if thou suffered them to overpass and go away? Truly, no more than a straw under thy foot. Besides, could they take from thee one hair of thy head? No, forsooth.

He that hath not a man's heart within him, nor setteth God before the eye of his soul, is soon moved with a sharp word; but he that trusteth in Me, and will not stand to his own judgment, shall be free from all man's dread. For I am the Judge that knoweth all secrets; I know how everything is done, and I know also both him that doth the wrong, and him to whom it is done. Of Me this thing is wrought, and by My sufferance it is come about, so that the thoughts of men's hearts may be known. When the time cometh I shall judge both the innocent and him that is guilty: but through this My righteous examination I will first prove them both.

The witness of man ofttimes deceiveth, but My judgment is always true, and shall not be subverted. Howbeit it is sometimes hid, and known but to few,

178

yet it is ever true, and erreth not; neither may it err, though in the sight of some persons it seemeth not right. Therefore in every doubt it behoveth thee to run to Me, and not to lean much on thine own judgment. Be content with everything that I shall send thee; for a righteous man is never troubled with anything that I shall suffer to fall unto him. Insomuch that though a thing were untruly spoken against him, he would not care much for it. Neither would he much joy though he were sometimes reasonably excused; for he thinketh always that I am He Who searcheth man's heart, and that I judge not according to outward appearance. Indeed ofttimes it shall be found in My sight worthy to be blamed, that in man's sight seemeth much worthy to be praised.

O Lord God, most righteous judge, strong and patient, Who knowest the frailty and malice of man, be Thou my strength and whole comfort in all my necessities; for mine own conscience sufficeth me not, sith Thou knowest in me that I know not. Therefore in every reproof I ought always to meeken myself, and after Thy pleasure patiently to suffer all things in charity. Forgive me, Lord, as oft as I have not so done, and give me grace of great sufferance in time to come. Thy mercy is more profitable to me, and a more sure way to the getting of pardon and forgiveness of my sins, than a trust in mine own works, through defence of my dark conscience. *'For I know nothing by myself; yet am I not hereby justified,'*[1]

[1] 1 Cor. iv. 4.

for, Thy mercy removed and taken away, no man may be justified nor appear righteous in Thy sight.

The Forty-seventh Chapter: How all grievous things in this life are gladly to be suffered, for winning of the life that is to come. ❡ My son, saith our Lord, be not broken by impatience with the labour that thou hast taken for My sake; nor suffer thou tribulation to cast thee into despair, or into unreasonable anguish in anywise. But be thou comforted and strengthened in every chance by My promises and behests; for I am able and of power to reward thee and other My servants abundantly more than ye can think or desire. Thou shalt not labour long here, nor always be grieved with heaviness. Tarry awhile My promises, and thou shalt shortly see an end of all thy troubles. An hour shall come when all thy labours and troubles shall cease. And truly that hour will shortly come, for all is short that passeth with time.

Do therefore as thou dost, labour busily and faithfully in My vineyard, and I shall shortly be thy reward. Write, read, sing, mourn, be still, pray, and suffer adversity gladly, for the kingdom of heaven is more worth than all these things, and much greater things than they are. Peace shall come one day which is to Me known, and that shall not be the day of this life but a day everlasting, with infinite clearness, steadfast peace, and sure rest without ending. Then thou shalt not say: '*Who shall deliver me from the body of this death?*[1] Neither shalt thou need to cry: '*Woe is me,*'[2] that my coming to the kingdom of heaven is thus prolonged! For death shall then be destroyed, and health of body and soul shall be without end; insomuch that no manner of unrestfulness shall be, but blessed joy, and sweetest and fairest company.

Oh! if thou sawest the everlasting crowns of My Saints in heaven, in how great joy and glory they are, that sometime seemed to be vile persons, and as men despisable in the world, thou wouldst anon meeken thyself low to the ground, and wouldst rather covet to be subject to all men, than to have sovereignty over any one person. Thou wouldst not desire to have mirth and solace in this world, but rather tribulation and pain, and thou wouldst account it as a great winning to be despised and taken as nought among the people.

O if these things savoured well to thee, and deeply pierced into thy heart, thou wouldst not once dare complain for any trouble that should befall unto thee. Are not all painful things and most grievous labours gladly to be suffered for the joys everlasting? Yes, verily, for it is no little thing to win or lose the kingdom of heaven. Lift up thy face therefore into heaven, and behold how I and all My Saints that be with Me had in this world great battle, and now they joy with Me, and be comforted in Me, and be sure of abiding with Me in the kingdom of My Father without ending. *Amen.*

[1] Rom vii. 24. [2] Ps. cxx 5

Thomas à Kempis

The Forty-eighth Chapter: Of the Day of Eternity, and of the miseries of this life. ¶ O blessed mansion of the Heavenly City! O most clear day of Eternity, which the night may not darken, but the high Truth, that is God, illumineth and cleareth. Day always merry, always sure, and never changing its state into the contrary. Would to God that this day might once appear and shine upon us, and that these temporal things were at an end. This blessed day shineth to Saints in heaven with everlasting brightness and clarity, but to us pilgrims on earth it shineth not but afar off, as through a glass.

The heavenly citizens know well how joyous this day is: but we outlaws, the children of Eve, do weep and wail the bitterness and tediousness of the day of this present life, short and evil, full of sorrows and anguishes ; where a man is oftentimes defiled with sin, encumbered with passions, unquieted with dreads, bounden with cares, busied with vanities, blinded with errors, overcharged with labours, vexed with temptations, overcome with delights of the world, and sometimes grievously tormented with penury and need.

O Lord, when shall the end come of all these miseries? When shall I be delivered from the bondage of sin? When, Lord, shall I only have mind on Thee, and be fully made glad and merry in Thee? When shall I be free without letting, and in perfect liberty without grief of body and soul? When shall I have solid peace without trouble, peace within and without, on every side steadfast and sure? O Lord

Jesu, when shall I stand and behold Thee, and have
full sight and contemplation of Thy glory? When
wilt Thou be to me all in all? And when shall I be
with Thee in Thy kingdom, which Thou hast ordained to Thy elect people from the beginning? I am
left here poor and as an outlaw in the land of mine
enemies, where daily be battles and great misfortunes.

Comfort my exile, assuage my sorrow, for all my
desire crieth to Thee; for it is to me a grievous
burden, whatsoever the world offereth me here to my
solace. I desire to have inward fruition of Thee, but
I cannot attain thereto. I covet to cleave fast to
heavenly things, but temporal things and passions
unmortified pull me away downward. In mind I
would be above all temporal things, but whether I
will or not, I am compelled through mine own default
to be subject to my flesh. Thus I, most wretched
man, fight in myself, and am made grievous to myself, whiles my spirit desireth to be upward and my
flesh downward.

O what suffer I inwardly, when in my mind I behold heavenly things, and anon a great multitude
of carnal thoughts enter into my soul? Therefore,
'*O God, be not far from me,*'[1] '*hide not thy face far from
me; put not thy servant away in anger.*'[2] Send to me
the lightning of Thy grace, and break down in me
all carnal thoughts. Send forth the darts of Thy
love, and break therewith all fantasies of the enemy.
Gather the wits and powers of my soul together in

[1] Ps lxxi. 12.   [2] Ps xxvii 9.

Thomas à Kempis

Thee. Make me forget all worldly things, and grant
me to cast away and wholly to despise all fantasies of
sin. Help me, Thou everlasting Truth, that hereafter no worldly vanity have power in me. Come
also, Thou heavenly Sweetness, and let all bitterness
of sin fly far from me. Pardon me, and mercifully
forgive me, when I think in my prayer of anything
but of Thee ; for I confess for truth that in time
past I have used myself very unstable therein ; for
many times I am not there where I stand or sit, but
rather I am there where my thoughts lead me.
There I am where my thought is, and where my
thought is accustomed to be, there is that which I
love. And that ofttimes cometh into my mind, that
by custom pleaseth me best, and that most desireth
me to think upon.

Wherefore Thou that art everlasting Truth sayest:
'*Where your treasure is, there will your heart be also.*'[1]
Wherefore, if I love heaven, I speak gladly of heavenly things, and of such things as be of God. If I love
the world, I joy anon at worldly felicity, and sorrow
anon at his adversity. If I love the flesh, I imagine
ofttimes that which pleaseth the flesh. If I love my
soul, I delight much to speak and to hear of things
that be to my soul-health. And so whatsoever I love,
of them I gladly hear and speak, and bear the images
of them oft in my mind. Blessed is that man that for
Thee, O Lord, forgetteth all creatures and learneth
truly to overcome himself, and with fervour of spirit

[1] Matt. vi. 21.

184

crucifieth his flesh ; so that in a clean and pure conscience he may offer his prayers to Thee, and (all
earthly things excluded from him and fully set apart)
he may be worthy to have the company of Blessed
Angels. *Amen.*

The Forty-ninth Chapter: Of the desire of everlasting life, and of the great reward that is promised to them that strongly fight against sin. ¶ My son,
when thou feelest that a desire of everlasting bliss is
given unto thee, and thou covetest to go out of the
tabernacle of thy mortal body that thou mayest without shadow behold My clearness, open thine heart,
and with all the desires of thy soul take thou this holy
inspiration ; yielding most large thanks to the high
goodness of God, that so worthily doth to thee, so
benignly visiteth thee, so brenningly stirreth thee,
and so mightily beareth thee up, that through thine
own burden thou fall not down to earthly things.
Think not that this desire cometh of thyself or of
thine own working, but rather that it cometh of the
gift of grace and of a lovely beholding of God upon
thee ; that thou shouldst profit thereby in meekness
and virtue, and shouldst prepare thee also to be ready
against another time for battles that are to come ; that
thou shouldst more surely cleave to Me with all the
desire and affection of thy heart, and study with all thy
power how thou mayest most purely and most devoutly serve Me.

Son, take heed of this common proverb : '*The fire
doth oft burn, but the flame doth not ascend without smoke.*'

So likewise the desire of some men draweth to heavenly things, and yet they are not all free from the smoke of carnal affections. And therefore they do it not always purely for the honour and love of God that they ask so desirously of Him. Such ofttimes is thy desire, that thou hast shewn to be so importune. For the desire is not clean and perfect, which is mixed with thine own commodity.

Ask not therefore what is delectable and profitable to thee, but what is acceptable to Me, and is to Mine honour ; for if thou do well and judge aright, thou shalt prefer My ordinance and My will before all thy desires, and before all things that may be desired beside Me. I know well thy desire : thou wouldst now be in liberty of the glory of the sons of God the everlasting home, and the heavenly country full of joy and glory, now delight thee much ; but that time cometh not yet, for there is yet another time to come, that is to say, a time of labour and of proof. Thou desirest to be fulfilled with the highest good in heaven ; but thou mayest not yet come thereto. I am the full reward of man ; abide Me till I come, and thou shalt have Me to thy reward.

Thou art yet to be proved here upon earth, and more thoroughly to be assayed in many things. Some comfort shall be given to thee, but the fulness thereof shall not yet be granted. Be thou therefore comforted in Me, and be thou strong as well in doing as in suffering things contrary to thy will. It behoveth thee to be clothed with the new man, and to be changed

into another man. Ofttimes thou must do that thou
wouldst not do, and that thou wouldst do, thou must
forsake and leave undone. That shall please other
shall go well forward, and that shall please thee shall
have no speed. That other men say shall be well
heard, and that thou shalt say shall be set at nought.
Others shall ask and have their asking, thou shalt ask
and be denied.

Others shall be great and have the laud and praise
of the people, but of thee no word shall be spoken.
To other this office or that shall be committed, but
thou shalt be judged unprofitable in everything. For
these and other like things nature will murmur and
grudge, and thou shalt have a great battle in thyself,
if thou bear them secret in thy heart without complaining and missaying. Nevertheless in such things,
and other like, My faithful servants are wont to be
proved how they can deny themselves, and how they
can in all things break their own wills. There is nothing wherein thou shalt need so much to overcome
thyself, as to learn to be contented not to be set any
price by in the world, and to suffer such things as be
most contrary to thy will, especially when such things
be commanded to be done as in thy sight seem unprofitable.[1]

But, my son, consider well the profit and fruit of all
these labours, the speedy end and the great reward;
and thou shalt feel no grief or pain in all thy labours,
but the sweetest comfort of the Holy Ghost through

[1] The verse 'Et quia non audes,' etc. is omitted by Whytford

187

thy good will. And for that little will that thou forsakest here, thou shalt always have thy will in heaven, where thou shalt have all that thou canst or mayest desire. There shalt thou have full possession of all goodness, without dread to lose it. There thy will shall be ever one with My Will, and it shall covet no strange nor private things. There no man shall resist thee, no man shall complain of thee, no man shall let thee, and nothing shall withstand thee ; but all things that thou canst desire shall be there present, and shall fulfil all the powers of thy soul. There shall I yield glory for reproofs ; and a pall of laud for thy heaviness of soul; and for the lowest place here a seat in heaven for ever. There shall appear the fruit of obedience ; the labour of penance shall joy ; and humble subjection shall be crowned gloriously.

Bow thee therefore meekly now under every man's hand, and force little who saith this, or who commandeth this to be done. But with all thy study take heed that whether thy prelate or thy fellow, or any other lower than thou, ask anything of thee, or will anything to be done by thee, that thou take it always to the best, and with a glad will study to fulfil it. Let this man seek this thing, and another that; let this man joy in this thing and another in that, and let them be lauded and praised a thousand times; but joy thou neither in this thing nor in that, but only in thine own despising, and in My Will to be fulfilled, and that I may always, whether it be by life or death, be lauded and honoured in thee and by thee. *Amen.*

Of the Imitation of Christ

The Fiftieth Chapter: How a man that is desolate ought to offer himself wholly to God.

¶Lord, holy Father, be Thou blessed now and for ever, for as Thou wilt so it is done, and that Thou dost is always well. Let me, Thy poorest servant and most unworthy, joy in Thee and not in myself, nor in anything else beside Thee; for Thou, Lord, art my gladness, Thou art my hope, my crown, my joy, and all my honour. What hath Thy servant but that he hath of Thee, and that without his desert? All things be Thine. '*I am afflicted and ready to die from my youth up*';[1] and my soul hath been in great heaviness with weeping and tears, and sometimes it hath been troubled in itself through manifold passions that come of the world and of the flesh.

Wherefore, Lord, I desire that I may have of Thee the joy of inward peace, and I ask for the rest of Thy chosen children, that be fed and nourished of Thee in the light of heavenly comforts; but without Thy help I cannot come thereto. If Thou, O Lord, give peace, or if Thou give inward joy, my soul shall be anon full of heavenly melody, and be devout and fervent in Thy lauds and praisings; but if Thou withdraw Thyself from me, as Thou hast sometime done, then may not Thy servant run the way of Thy commandments, as he did first; but he is then compelled to bow his knees and knock his breast, for it is not with him as it was before, when the lantern of Thy ghostly presence shone upon his head,[2] and he was

[1] Ps lxxxviii. 15. [2] Job xxix. 3

defended under the shadow of Thy mercy from all perils and dangers.

O righteous Father ever to be praised, the time is come that Thou wilt Thy servant be proved; and righteously is it done that I now suffer somewhat for Thee! Now is the hour come that Thou hast known from the beginning, that Thy servant for a time should outwardly be set at nought, but live to Thee inwardly; that he should be for a little despised in the sight of the world, and be broken with passions and sickness, that he might after rise with Thee into a new light, and be clarified, and made glorious in the kingdom of heaven.

O Holy Father, Thou hast ordained it so to be, and it is done as Thou hast commanded: this is Thy grace to Thy friend, to suffer and to be troubled in this world for Thy love, how oft soever it be, of what person soever it be, and in what manner soever Thou suffer it to fall unto him. Without Thy counsel and providence, and without cause, nothing is done upon earth. '*It is good for me,*' Lord, '*that I have been afflicted; that I might learn thy statutes,*'[1] and put from me all manner of presumption and highness of mind. And it is very profitable to me that confusion hath covered my face, that I may learn thereby to seek for help and succour to Thee rather than to man. I have thereby learned to dread Thy secret and terrible judgments, Who scourgest the righteous man with the sinner, but not without equity and justice.

[1] Ps cxix. 71.

Of the Imitation of Christ

I yield thanks to Thee, that Thou hast not spared my sins, but hast punished me with scourges of love, and hast sent me sorrows and anguishes within and without; so that there is no creature under heaven that may comfort me, but Thou, Lord God, the heavenly Leech[1] of man's soul, '*For thou scourgest, and thou savest: thou leadest down to hell, and bringest up again*';[2] that he may thereby learn to know the littleness of his own power, and the more fully to trust in Thee. Thy discipline is fallen upon me, and Thy rod of correction hath taught me.

Under that rod I wholly submit me, beloved Father; strike my back and bones as it shall please Thee, and make me to bow my crooked will unto Thy Will; make me a meek and humble disciple, as Thou hast sometimes done with me, that I may walk wholly after Thy Will. To Thee I commit myself and all mine to be corrected, for better it is to be corrected by Thee here than in time to come. Thou knowest all things, and nothing is hidden from Thee that is in man's conscience. Thou knowest things to come before they fall, and it is not needful that any man teach Thee, or warn Thee of anything that is done upon the earth. Thou knowest what is speedful for me, and how much tribulation helpeth to purge the rust of sin in me: do with me after Thy pleasure, and disdain not my sinful life, to none so well known as it is to Thee.

Grant me grace, Lord, that to know that is neces-

[1] Physician   [2] Tobias xiii. 2

191

sary to be known, that to love that is to be loved, that to praise that highly pleaseth Thee, that to regard that appeareth precious in Thy sight, and that to refuse that is vile before Thee. Suffer me not to judge after my outward wits, nor to give sentence after the hearing of uncunning men; but in true judgment to discern things visible and invisible, and above all things always to search and follow Thy will and pleasure.

The outward wits of men be oft deceived in their judgments; and in like wise the lovers of the world be deceived through loving only of visible things. What is a man the better, for that he is taken to be greater than others? Truly nothing. For a deceitful man deceiveth another, a vain man deceiveth another, and a blind and feeble creature deceiveth another when he exalteth him, and rather confoundeth him than praiseth him. For· '*How much soever a man be in the sight of God, so much he is and no more, how holy and how virtuous soever he be taken to be in the sight of the people,*' saith the meek St. Francis.

The Fifty-first Chapter: That it is good that a man give himself to meek bodily labours, when he feeleth not himself disposed to high works of devotion.
¶ My son, thou mayest not always stand in the high fervent desire of virtue, nor in the highest degree of contemplation; but thou must of necessity, through the corruption of the first sin, sometime descend to lower things, and to bear the burden of this corruptible body, even against thy will and with great tedi-

ousness. For as long as thou bearest this body of death, thou must need feel some tediousness and grief of heart. Ofttimes thou shalt beweep and mourn the burden of the flesh, and the contradiction of thy body to the soul; for thou mayest not, for the corruption thereof, persevere in spiritual studies and in heavenly contemplation as thou wouldst do.

Then it is good to thee to fly to meek bodily labours and to exercise thyself in good outward works; in a steadfast hope to abide My coming and My new heavenly visitation; to bear thy exile and the dryness of thy heart patiently, till thou be visited by Me again, and be delivered from all tediousness and unquietness of mind. When I come I shall make thee forget all thy former labours, and have inward rest and quietness of soul. I shall also lay before thee the flourishing meadow of Holy Scripture, and thou shalt, with great gladness of heart, and with new and blessed feeling, feel the very true understanding thereof, and then thou shalt run the way of My commandments.[1] Then shalt thou say in great spiritual gladness: '*The sufferings of this present time are not worthy to be compared with the glory which shall be revealed in us*'[2] in the bliss of heaven.

To the which bring us, Lord Jesu. Amen.

The Fifty-second Chapter: That a man shall not think himself worthy to have comfort, but rather to have sorrow and pain; and of the profit of contrition.

¶ Lord, I am not worthy to have Thy consolation,

---

[1] See Ps. cxix 32. [2] Rom. viii 18.

nor any spiritual visitation, and therefore Thou dost
righteously unto me, when Thou leavest me needy
and desolate; for though I might weep water of tears
like to the sea, yet were I not worthy to have Thy
consolation. For I am worthy to have nothing but
sorrow and pain, since I have so grievously and so oft
offended Thee, and in so many things greatly tres-
passed against Thee. Therefore I may well say and
confess for truth, that I am not worthy to have Thy
least consolation. But Thou, Lord, benign and merciful, that wilt not Thy works perish, to shew the
greatness of Thy goodness in the vessels of Thy
mercy, dost vouchsafe sometimes to comfort me,
Thy servant, above all my merits or desert, and also
more than I can think or devise.

Thy consolations be not like to men's fables, for
they are in themselves soothfast. But what have I
done, Lord, that Thou wilt vouchsafe to give me
any heavenly consolation? I know not that I have
done anything well as I should have done, but that I
have been prone and ready to sin and slow to amendment. This is true and I cannot deny it; for if I should
deny it Thou wouldst stand against me, and no man
might defend me. What have I then deserved but
hell and everlasting fire? I confess for truth that I am
worthy in this world of shame and despite, and that
it becometh not me to be conversant with devout
people. And though it be grievous to me to say thus,
yet (sith the truth is so) I will confess the truth as it
is, and openly will reprove myself of my defaults,

that I may the rather obtain of Thee mercy and forgiveness.

But what may I then say, Lord, that thus am guilty and full of confusion? Truly I have no mouth nor tongue to speak, but only this word: I have sinned, Lord, I have sinned ; have mercy on me, forgive me and forget my trespass. '*Let me alone, that I may take comfort a little, before I go whence I shall not return, even to the land of darkness and the shadow of death.*'[1] And what dost Thou, Lord, ask most of such a wretched sinner, but that he be contrite and meeken himself for his sin; for in true contrition and meekness of heart is found the very hope of forgiveness of sin, and the troubled conscience is thereby cleared, and the grace before lost is recovered again. Man also is thereby defended from the wrath to come, for Almighty God and the penitent soul meet lovingly together in holy kissings of heavenly love.

A meek contrition of heart is to Thee, Lord, a right acceptable sacrifice, more sweetly savouring in Thy sight than burning incense. It is also the precious ointment, that Thou wouldst should be shed upon Thy blessed feet, for '*a broken and a contrite heart, O God, thou wilt not despise.*'[2] This contrition is the place of refuge from the dread and wrath of the enemy, and thereby is washed and cleansed whatsoever is before misdone, or that is defiled through sin in any manner.

[1] Job x. 20, 21   [2] Ps. li. 17.

Thomas à Kempis

The Fifty-third Chapter: That grace will not be mixed with love of worldly things.

¶ My son, grace is a precious thing, and will not be mixed with any private love, nor with worldly comforts. It behoveth thee therefore to cast away all lettings[1] of grace, if thou wilt have the gracious gift thereof. Choose therefore a secret place, love to be alone, keep thee from hearing of vain tales ; and offer to God devout prayers, praying heartily that thou mayest have a contrite heart and a pure conscience. Think all the world as nought, and prefer My service before all other things, for thou mayest not have mind on Me and therewithal delight thee in transitory pleasures. It behoveth thee therefore to withdraw thee from thy dearest friends and from all thine acquaintance, and to sequester thy mind wholly from the inordinate desire of all worldly comfort, as much as thou mayest. Thus St. Peter prayed, that all Christian people might hold themselves as strangers and pilgrims upon earth,[2] for then they would set but little price by the comfort thereof.

O how sure a trust shall it be to a man at his departing out of this world, to feel in his soul that no worldly love, nor yet the affection of any passing or transitory thing, hath any rule in him. But a weak person, newly turned to God, may not so lightly have his heart severed from earthly liking, nor knoweth the carnal man the freedom of one that is inwardly turned to God. Therefore if a man will truly be

[1] hindrances.   [2] 1 Pet. ii. 11.

ghostly, he must renounce strangers as well as kinsfolk; and before all other he must be wary of himself,
for if he overcome himself perfectly, he shall the
sooner overcome all other enemies. The most noble
and the most perfect victory is for a man to have the
victory of himself. He therefore that holdeth himself so much subject, that the sensuality obeyeth to
reason, and reason in all things obeyeth to Me, he is
the true overcomer of himself and the lord of the
world.

But if thou covet to come to that point, thou must
begin manfully and set thy axe to the root of the tree,
and fully cut away and destroy in thee all the inordinate inclination that thou hast to thyself, or to any
private or material thing. For of that vice whereby
a man loveth himself inordinately, well-nigh dependeth all that ought groundly to be destroyed in man.
And if that be truly overcome, anon shall follow great
tranquillity and peace of conscience. But forasmuch
as there be but few that labour to die to themselves,
or overcome themselves perfectly, therefore they lie
still in their worldly comforts, and may in nowise rise
up in spirit above themselves; for it behoveth him
that will be free in heart and have contemplation of
Me, to mortify all the evil inclinations that he hath
to himself and to the world, and not to be bound to
any creature by inordinate or private love.

**The Fifty-fourth Chapter: Of the divers
movings between nature and grace.** ¶ My son, take
good heed of the motions of nature and grace; for

they be very subtle and much contrary the one to the other, and hardly may they be known asunder, but it be by a ghostly man, that through spiritual grace is inwardly lightened in soul. Every man desireth some goodness, and pretendeth somewhat of goodness in all his words and deeds; therefore under pretence of goodness many be deceived.

Nature is wily and draweth many to her, whom she oftentimes snareth and deceiveth, and ever beholdeth her own wealth as the end of her work. But grace walketh simply, she declineth from all evil, she pretendeth no guile, but all things she doth purely for God, in Whom finally she resteth.

Nature will not gladly die, nor be oppressed or overcome; neither will she gladly be under others, nor be kept in subjection. But grace studieth how she may be mortified to the world and to the flesh. She resisteth sensuality, seeketh to be subject, desireth to be overcome, and will not use her own liberty. She loveth to be holden under holy discipline, and coveteth not to have lordship over any one creature, but to live and stand always under the dread of God, and for His love to be always ready to bow herself meekly to every creature.

Nature laboureth for her own profit and advantage, and much beholdeth what winning cometh to her by other. But grace beholdeth not what is profitable to herself, but what is profitable to many.

Nature receiveth gladly honour and reverence ; but grace referreth all honour and reverence to God.

Nature dreadeth reprovings and despising. But grace joyeth for the name of Jesus to suffer them both, and taketh them when they come as special gifts of God.

Nature loveth idleness and bodily rest. But grace cannot be idle without doing some good deed, and therefore she seeketh gladly some profitable labours.

Nature desireth fair things and curious, and abhorreth vile things and gross. But grace delighteth in meek and simple things, she despiseth not hard things, nor refuseth to be clad in poor old clothing and simple garments.

Nature beholdeth gladly things temporal, she joyeth at worldly winnings, is heavy for worldly leesings,[1] and anon is moved with a sharp word. But grace beholdeth things everlasting and trusteth not in things temporal, neither is she troubled with the loss of them, or grieved with a froward word; for she hath laid her treasure in God, and in ghostly things which may not perish.

Nature is covetous and more gladly taketh than giveth, loveth much to have property and private things. But grace is pitiful and liberal to the poor, flieth private profit, is content with little, and judgeth it *'more blessed to give than to receive.'*[2]

Nature inclineth to the love of creatures, to the love of the flesh, to vanities, and to runnings about to see new things in the world. But grace draweth a man to the love of God and of virtue, renounceth

[1] losses   [2] Acts xx 35.

all creatures, flieth the world, hateth the desires of the flesh, restraineth the liberty of wandering about, and as much as she may escheweth to be seen among recourse of people.

Nature hath gladly some outward solace, wherein she may feelingly delight in her outward wits. But grace only seeketh to be comforted in God, and to delight her in His goodness above all things.

Nature doth all things for her own winning and special profit; she doth nothing free, but hopeth always to have a like profit or better, or at least the laud or favour of the people; for she coveteth much that her deeds be greatly pondered and praised. But grace seeketh no temporal thing, nor any other reward for her hire but only God; she wills no more of temporal goods than she shall need for the getting of the goods everlasting, and careth not for the vain praise of the world.

Nature joyeth greatly in many friends and kinsfolk, is glorified much of a noble place of birth, and of her noble blood and kindred; she joyeth with mighty men, flattereth rich men, and is merry with those that she thinketh like to her in nobleness of the world. But grace maketh a man to love his enemies; for she hath no pride in worldly friends, regardeth not the nobleness of kin or the house of her father, but if the more virtue be there. She favoureth more the poor than the rich, she hath more compassion of an innocent than of a mighty man; she joyeth ever in truth and not in falsehood; she always comforteth

good men to profit more and more, to grow in virtue
and goodness, and to seek daily higher gifts of grace,
that they may through good works be made like to
the Son of God.

Nature complaineth anon for wanting of a right
little thing that she would have, or for a little worldly
heaviness. But grace beareth gladly all neediness of
this world.

Nature inclineth all things to herself, argueth for
herself, striveth and fighteth for herself. But grace
rendereth all things to God, of Whom all things
originally do spring and flow; she ascribeth no goodness to herself, nor presumeth of herself; she striveth not, nor preferreth her opinion before other
men's, but in every sentence she submitteth herself
meekly to the eternal wisdom and judgment of God.

Nature coveteth to know secret things, and to hear
new things; she will that her works be outwardly
shewn, and that she have experience of many things
by her outward wits; she desireth also to be known,
and to do great things, wherefrom praising may
follow. But grace careth not for any new things, or
for curious things, whatsoever they be; for she knoweth well that all such vanities come of the corruption
of sin, and that no new thing may long endure upon
earth. She teacheth also to restrain the outward wits,
and to eschew all vain pleasure and outward show,
and meekly to keep those things secret which in the
world were greatly to be marvelled and praised. In
everything and in every science she seeketh some

spiritual profit for herself, but laud and honour to Almighty God. She will not that her good deeds nor her inward devotion be outwardly known, but most desireth that in all His works our Lord be blessed, Who of His high excellent charity freely giveth all things.

This grace is a light supernatural, and a spiritual gift of God, and it is the proper mark and token of the elect people, and the earnest-penny of the everlasting life ; for it ravisheth a man from love of earthly things to the love of heavenly things, and of a fleshly liver maketh a heavenly person. And the more that nature is oppressed and overcome, the more is grace given, and the soul through new gracious visitations is daily reformed more and more to the image of God.

The Fifty-fifth Chapter : Of the corruption of nature and the worthiness of grace. ¶ O Lord, Who hast made me to Thine image and likeness,[1] grant me this grace, that Thou hast shewed to me to be so great and so necessary to the health of my soul, that I may overcome this wretched nature, which always draweth me to sin, and to the losing of mine own soul. I feel in my flesh the law of sin fighting strongly against the law of my spirit, and leading me as a thrall to obey sensuality in many things : and I may not resist the passions thereof, unless Thy grace do assist me therein.

I have therefore great need of Thy grace, and of

[1] Gen. i 26

202

the great abundance of Thy grace, if I would overcome this wretched nature, which always from my
youth hath been ready to sin. For after nature was
vitiated and defiled by the sin of the first man Adam,
the pain thereof descended into all his posterity, so
that nature, which in the first-created was good and
righteous, is now taken for sin and corruption ; so
far forth, that the motions that are now left unto
nature always draw man into evil. And for this
reason, that the little strength and moving to goodness yet remaining in her is as a sparkle of fire that is
hid and overhilled with ashes. That is to say, the
natural reason of man, which is belapped with darkness of ignorance, hath nevertheless power yet to
judge betwixt good and evil, and to shew the diversity betwixt true and false. Howbeit that through
weakness it is not of itself able to fulfil all that it
approveth ; nor sith the first sin of Adam hath it
the full light of truth, or the sweetness of affections
to God, as it had first.

Of this it cometh, most merciful Lord, that in my
inward man, that is in the reason of my soul, I delight in Thy laws and in Thy teachings, knowing that
they are good and righteous and holy ; and also that
all sin is evil and to be eschewed. Yet in my outward
man, that is to say in my flesh, I serve the law of sin,
when I obey sensuality rather than reason. Of this it
followeth that I will good, but to perform it without
Thy grace I may not for weakness of myself. Sometimes I purpose also to do many good deeds, but for

that grace wanteth that should help me, I go back-
ward and fail in my doing. I know the way to perfection, and how I should do I see evidently, but for that
I am so oppressed with the heavy burden of this corrupt body of sin, I lie still and rise not to perfection.

O Lord! how necessary therefore is Thy grace to
me, to begin well, to continue well, and to end well;
for without Thee I may nothing do that good is. O
heavenly grace, come thou shortly and help me, sith
without thee our merits are nought worth, and the
gifts of nature nothing to be pondered; without
thee neither crafts nor riches are to be anything regarded, and neither beauty, nor strength, nor wit,
nor eloquence, may avail anything in the sight of
God. For the gifts of nature are common to good
men and to bad, but grace and love are the gifts of the
chosen, whereby they be marked and made worthy to
have the kingdom of heaven. This grace is of such
worthiness that neither the gift of prophecy, nor the
working of miracles, nor yet the gift of cunning and
knowledge may anything avail without her; nor yet
be faith, hope, or other virtues acceptable to Thee
without grace and charity.

O most blessed grace! that makest the poor in
spirit to be rich in virtue, and him that is rich in worldly goods makest meek and low in heart, come, descend
into my soul, and fulfil it with thy ghostly comforts,
that it fail not nor faint for weariness and dryness of
itself. I beseech Thee, Lord, that I may find grace
in Thy sight, for Thy grace shall suffice to me, though

Of the Imitation of Christ

I do want that nature desireth. Although I be tempted and vexed with troubles on every side, yet shall I not need to dread whiles Thy grace is with me; for she is my strength, she is my comfort, and she is my counsel and help; she is stronger than all mine enemies, and wiser than all the wisest of this world.

She is the mistress of truth, the teacher of discipline, the light of the heart, the comfort of trouble, the driver away of heaviness, the avoider of dread, the nourisher of devotion, the bringer of sweet tears and devout weepings. What am I then without grace, but a dry stock to be cast away? *Grant me therefore that Thy grace may prevent me, and follow me, and make me ever busy in good works unto my death.*[1]

So may it be. Amen.

The Fifty-sixth Chapter: That we ought to forsake ourselves, and to follow Christ by bearing His cross. ¶My son, as much as thou canst go out of thyself, so much mayest thou enter into Me. And as to desire nothing outwardly bringeth peace into a man's soul, so by an inward forsaking of himself a man joineth himself to God. I will therefore that thou learn to have a perfect forsaking and full resigning of thyself into My hands without withsaying and complaining. Follow Me: for '*I am the way, the truth, and the life.*'[2] Without a way no man may go, and without the truth no man may know, and without life no man may live. I am the Way in which thou oughtest to go, the Truth which thou oughtest to believe, and

---

[1] See Collect for Seventeenth Sunday after Trinity.   [2] John xiv. 6.

the Life for which thou oughtest to hope. I am the Way that cannot be defiled, the Truth which cannot be deceived, and the Life that never shall have an end. I am the Way most straight, the Truth most perfect, and the Life most soothfast. A blessed Life, and a Life unmade that made all things. If thou abide in My Way thou shalt know the Truth, and Truth shall deliver thee, and thou shalt come to everlasting Life.

If thou wilt come to that Life, keep My commandments.[1]

If thou wilt know the Truth, believe My teachings.

If thou wilt be perfect, sell all that thou hast.[2]

If thou wilt be My disciple, forsake thyself.[3]

If thou wilt have the Blessed Life, despise this present life.

If thou wilt be exalted in heaven, meek thee here on earth.

If thou wilt reign with Me, bear the cross with Me;[4] for truly only the servants of the cross shall find the Life of blessedness and of everlasting light.

O Lord Jesu! forasmuch as Thy Way is narrow and is also much despised in the world, give me grace to bear gladly the despisings of the world. There is no servant greater than his Lord, nor any disciple above his Master. Let Thy servant therefore be exercised in Thy ways, for therein is the health and the very perfection of life; whatsoever I read or hear beside that Way, it refresheth me not, nor delighteth me fully.

[1] Matt. xix. 17. [2] *Ib.* xix 21. [3] Luke ix. 23 [4] Luke xiv. 27.

Of the Imitation of Christ

My son, forasmuch as thou knowest these things, and hast read them all, thou shalt be blessed if thou fulfil them. *'He that hath my commandments, and keep-eth them, he it is that loveth me: and he that loveth me shall be loved of my Father, and I will love him, and will manifest myself to him,'*[1] and will make him sit with Me in the kingdom of My Father.

Lord Jesu, as Thou hast said and promised, so be it done to me. I have taken the cross of penance at Thy hand, and I will bear it unto my death, as Thou hast put it upon me. For the life of every good man is the cross, and it is also the leader to paradise. Now it is begun, it is not lawful for me to go back from it, nor is it behoveful for me to leave it.

Have done, therefore, my well-beloved brethren; go we forth together; Jesus will be with us. For Jesus we have taken this cross; for Jesus let us persevere. He will be our help, Who is our guide and leader. Lo, our King goeth before us, that will fight for us ! Follow we Him manfully, dread we no perils, but be we ready to die strongly in battle; that so we put no blot upon our glory, nor minish our reward by flying cowardly away from the cross.

The Fifty-seventh Chapter: That a man shall not be obermuch cast into heaviness, though he happen to fall into some defaults. ¶ My son, patience and meekness in adversity please Me more than much consolation and devotion in prosperity. Why art thou so heavy for a little word said or done against

[1] John xiv. 21.

thee? If it had been more, thou shouldst not have been moved therewith. But let it now overpass; it is not the first, and it shall not be the last, if thou live long. Thou art manful enough as long as no adversity falleth to thee; and thou canst well give counsel, and well canst thou comfort and strengthen other with thy words. But when adversity knocketh at thy door, thou failest anon both of counsel and strength. Behold well therefore thy great frailty, of which thou hast daily experience in little objects. Nevertheless it is for thy ghostly health that such and other like things are suffered to come unto thee.

Purpose in thy heart to do the best that lieth in thee, and then when such tribulations shall happen to fall unto thee, although it grieve thee, yet let it not wholly overthrow thee, nor let it long tarry with thee. At the least suffer it patiently, although thou may not suffer it gladly. Moreover, though thou be loth to hear such things, and feelest great indignation thereat in thy heart, yet thrust thyself down low in thine own sight, and suffer no inordinate word to pass out of thy mouth, whereby another might be hurt. Then all such indignation shall be soon appeased in thee, and that which before was taken to so great heaviness to thee shall anon be made sweet and pleasant in thy sight. For yet live I, saith our Lord, ready to help thee and to comfort thee, more than ever I did before, if thou wilt wholly trust in Me, and devoutly call to Me for help.

Be quiet in heart, prepare thyself yet to more suf-

ferance. For it is not all lost though thou feel thyself oft troubled and grievously tempted. Think that
thou art a man and not God; thou art flesh, and no
Angel. How mayest thou be in one state of virtue,
when that was wanting to Angels in heaven, and to
the first man in paradise, who stood not long? I am
He that raise up them that be sorrowful to health and
to comfort, and those that know their own unstableness I lift them up to be stabled in the sight of My
Godhead for ever.

Lord, '*how sweet are thy words unto my taste! yea,
sweeter than honey to my mouth!*'[1] What should I do
in all my troubles and heaviness, if Thou didst not
sometime comfort me with Thy wholesome and sweet
words? Therefore it shall not force what trouble or
adversity I suffer here for Thee, so that I may in the
end come to the port of everlasting health. Give me
a good end, and a blessed passage out of this world:
have a mind on me, my Lord, my God, and direct
me by a straight and ready way into Thy kingdom,
I beseech Thee. *Amen.*

The Fifty-eighth Chapter: That a man shall
not search the judgments of God. ¶ My son, beware
not to dispute of high matters, and of the secret judgments of God; why this man is so left and forsaken
of God, and why that man is taken to so great grace;
why also one man is so much troubled, and another
so greatly advanced. These things overpass all man's
knowledge, for to search God's judgment no man's

[1] Ps cxix 103.

reason, nor yet his disputation, may suffice. Therefore when the ghostly enemy stirreth thee to such
things, or if any curious men ask of thee such questions, answer with the Prophet David, and say thus:
'*Righteous art thou, O Lord, and upright are thy judgments.*'[1] And that other: '*The judgments of the Lord
are true and righteous altogether.*'[2] My judgments are
to be dreaded, and not to be discussed by man's wit,
for they are to man's wit incomprehensible.

Beware also that thou search not, nor reason of the
merits of the Saints, which of them was holier than
the other, or which of them is higher in heaven. Such
questions ofttimes nourish great strifes and unprofitable reasonings, and proceed of pride and vain-glory;
hence envy and dissensions spring forth when one
laboureth to prefer this Saint, and another that. And
truly a desire to know such things rather displeaseth
the Saints than pleaseth them. For I, saith our Lord,
am not the God of strife, but of peace; which peace
standeth rather in true meekness than in exalting of
themselves.

Some men are more stirred to love these or those
Saints, and that with much greater affection, but truly
that affection is ofttimes rather a manly than a godly
affection. Am I not He that have made all Saints?
Yes, truly. And over that I have given them grace,
and I have given them glory. I know all their merits,
and I prevented them with the sweetness of My blessings. I knew My beloved ones before the world was

[1] Ps. cxix 137.   [2] Ps xix. 9.

made; I have chosen them from the world, they have not chosen Me. I called them by My grace, I drew them by My mercy; I led them through temptations, I sent them inward comforts. I gave them persever-ance, I crowned their patience. I know the first man and the last, I love them all with an inestimable love.

Thus I am to be praised in all My Saints, and above all things I am to be blessed and honoured in all and every one of those whom I have so gloriously magni-fied and predestinated, without any merits of theirs going before. Therefore he that despiseth the least of My Saints, doth no honour to the greatest; for I have made both the less and the greater. And he that dispraiseth any of My Saints, he dispraiseth Me, and all other My Saints in the kingdom of heaven; for they are all one, fast united and knit together in one sure bond of perfect charity. They all feel one thing, they all will one thing, and they all love together unto one.

Yet they love Me much more than themselves or their own merits, for they are rapt above themselves, and are drawn from their own love, and are wholly turned into My love, in the which they rest by eternal fruition. There is nothing that may turn them from My love, nor thrust them down out of their glory, for they are full of eternal truth, and burn inwardly with fire of everlasting charity, that shall never be quenched. Let all therefore that be carnal and animal, and that cannot love but selfish joys, cease to search the state of My blessed Saints in heaven; for they take away or add to their merits as they favour, and not after the pleasure of the eternal truth of God.

In many folks there is great ignorance; but most specially in them that have so little light of ghostly understanding, that they cannot love any person with a clean love. Many also are moved by a natural affection, or by a worldly friendship, to love this man or that; and as they imagine in earthly things, so they imagine of heavenly things. But there is a distance incomparable betwixt things which imperfect men imagine by natural reason, and which men truly illumined with grace behold by heavenly contemplation.

Beware therefore, my son, to treat curiously of such things, for they pass thy knowledge, and endeavour that thou mayest be worthy to be numbered with the least Saint that shall come to heaven. And if percase a man might know who were holier, or who should be taken greater in the kingdom of heaven; what would that knowledge avail him, unless he should thereby the more meek himself, and the more rise thereby into the laud and praising of My Name? Truly nothing. Therefore he is much more acceptable to God that thinketh on the greatness of his sins and of the littleness of his virtues, and how far he is from the perfection of the least Saint that is in heaven, than he that argueth of their greatness or their littleness, forgetting himself. It is better also with devout prayers, and with weepings and tears, meekly to pray to Saints and to call to them for help, than vainly to search for their perfection.

Of the Imitation of Christ

They are very well contented with the joy that they have, if men would refrain themselves from such vain arguments. They glorify not themselves of their merits, nor do they ascribe any goodness to themselves; for they know well that I of My infinite goodness and charity have given all unto them. And they are so much filled with love of the Godhead and with overpassing joy, that no glory may want in them nor any felicity. And the higher that they be in heaven, the meeker be they in themselves, and the more nigh and the more loving to Me. Therefore it is written in the Apocalypse that Saints in heaven laid their crowns before God, and fell prostrate on their faces before the meek Lamb, that is Jesus, and they worshipped Him as their Lord God, Who is and shall be living evermore.[1] Amen.

Many search who is highest in the kingdom of heaven, that know not whether they shall be worthy to be numbered with the least that shall come thither. It is a great thing to be the least in heaven, where all are great; for all that shall come thither shall be called the sons of God, and so shall they be in deed. '*A little one shall become a thousand,*'[2] and '*the sinner being an hundred years old shall be accursed.*'[3] When the Apostles asked among themselves who should be greatest in the kingdom of heaven, they heard this answer of Christ: '*Except ye be converted, and become as little children, ye shall not enter into the kingdom of heaven.*

[1] See Rev. iv. 10.　　　　　　[2] Is lx 22
[3] Is lxv. 20.

213

Thomas à Kempis

Whosoever therefore shall humble himself as this little child, the same is greatest in the kingdom of heaven.'[1]

Woe then be to them that disdain to meek[2] themselves with little children, for the lowly gate of heaven will not suffer them to enter into it.

Woe also be unto the proud rich men that have their consolation here; for when the good poor man shall enter into the kingdom of God, they shall stand weeping and wailing without.

Joy ye then, ye that be meek and poor in spirit, for yours is the kingdom of heaven;[3] so that ye walk and hold your journey assuredly in the way of truth.

The Fifty-ninth Chapter: That all our hope and trust is to be put in God alone.

¶ Lord, what is the trust that I have in this life? or what is my greatest solace of all things under heaven? Is it not Thou, my Lord God, Whose mercy is without measure? Where hath it been well with me without Thee? Or when hath it not been well with me, Thou being present? I had liefer be poor with Thee, than rich without Thee. I had liefer be with Thee as a pilgrim in this world, than without Thee to be in heaven; for where Thou art there is heaven, and where Thou art not, there is both death and hell. Thou art to me all that I desire, and therefore it behoveth me to sigh to Thee, to cry to Thee, and heartily to pray to Thee. I have no one to trust in, that may help me in my necessities, but only Thee. Thou art my hope, Thou

---

[1] Matt. xviii. 3, 4.   [2] *i e.* humble.   [3] See Matt. v. 3.

art my trust, Thou art my comfort, and Thou art my faithful helper in every need.

Man seeketh that is his; but Thou seekest my health and profit, and turnest all things unto the best for me; for if Thou send temptations and other adversities Thou ordainest all to my profit, for Thou art wont by a thousand ways to prove Thy chosen people. In which proof Thou art no less to be lauded and praised than if Thou hadst fulfilled them with heavenly comforts.

In Thee, Lord, therefore I put my trust, and in Thee I bear patiently all my adversities; for I find nothing without Thee but unstableness and folly. For the multitude of worldly friends profiteth not, nor may strong helpers anything avail, nor wise counsellors give profitable counsel, nor the cunning of doctors give consolation, nor riches deliver in time of need, nor a secret place defend; if Thou, Lord, do not assist, help, comfort, counsel, inform, and defend.

All things that seem to be ordained to man's solace in this world, if Thou be absent, be nought worth, and may not bring to man any true felicity. For Thou art the end, Lord, of all good things, the highness of life, and the profound wisdom of all things that are in heaven and in earth. Wherefore to trust in Thee above all things is the greatest comfort to all Thy servants.

To Thee, therefore, I lift mine eyes, and in Thee only I put my trust, my Lord, my God, the Father of

Thomas à Kempis

Mercy. Bless Thou and hallow Thou my soul with Thy heavenly blessings, that it may be Thy dwelling-place, and the seat of Thy eternal glory ; so that nothing be found in me at any time that may offend the eye of Thy Majesty.

Behold me, Lord, after the greatness of Thy goodness and of Thy manifold mercies, and graciously hear the prayer of me, Thy poorest servant, outlawed and far exiled into the country of the shadow of death. Defend and keep me amidst the manifold dangers of this corruptible life ; and through Thy grace direct me by the way of peace into the country of everlasting clearness. *Amen.*

AFTER THE SAYDE THREE BOOKES

FOLOWETH

The Fourth Booke

WHICH WAS FIRST TRANSLATED OUT OF

FRENCHE INTO ENGLISHE

BY

The Right Noble and Excellent

Princes Margaret

late

Countesse of Richmonde and Darbye

MOTHER UNTO THE NOBLE PRINCE OF BLESSED MEMORIE
KINGE HENRY VII., FATHER UNTO OUR LATE SOVERAINE
LORD KINGE HENRY VIII

And for as muche as it was translated by the sayed noble
Princes out of Frenche, it coulde not folowe the Latin so
nigh, nor so directlie, as if it had bene translated out of Latin.
And therefore it is nowe translated out of Latin, and yet
neverthelesse it keepeth the substaunce and the effect of the
first translation out of Frenche.

The fourth book

Concerning the Sacrament

The Fourth Book
Concerning the Sacrament

'*OME unto me,*' saith our Lord, '*all ye that labour and are heavy laden, and I will give you rest.*'[1]

'*And the bread that I will give is my flesh, which I will give for the life of the world.*'[2]

'*Take, eat: this is my body, which is broken for you: this do in remembrance of me.*'[3]

'*He that eateth my flesh, and drinketh my blood, dwelleth in me, and I in him.*'[4]

'*The words that I speak unto you, they are spirit, and they are life.*'[5]

The First Chapter: With how great reverence Christ is to be received.

¶ O my Lord Jesu Christ, eternal Truth ! these words aforesaid be Thy words, albeit they were not said in one self time, nor written in one self place. And for that they be Thy words, I will thankfully and faithfully accept them. They be Thy words, and Thou hast spoken them, and they be now mine also ; for Thou hast said them for my health. I will gladly receive them of Thy mouth, to the end they may be the better sown and

---

[1] Matt. xi. 28.   [2] John vi. 51.   [3] 1 Cor. xi. 24.
[4] John vi. 56.   [5] John vi. 63.

planted in mine heart. Thy words of so great piety, full of sweetness and love, greatly excite me. But, Lord, my sins fear me greatly, and my conscience, not being pure enough to receive so great a mystery, draweth me sore aback. The sweetness of Thy words provoketh me, but the multitude of mine offences charge me very sore.

Thou commandest that I come unto Thee faithfully, if I would have part with Thee; and receive the nourishing of immortality, if I covet to obtain the glory and life eternal. Thou sayest, Lord: '*Come unto me, all ye that labour and are heavy laden, and I will give you rest.*'[1] O how sweet and how amiable a word is it in the ear of a sinner, that Thou, Lord God, shouldst bid me, that am so poor and needy, to the Communion of Thy most holy Body! But what am I, Lord, that I dare presume to come to Thee? Lo, heaven and earth may not comprehend Thee, and Thou sayest: '*Come ye all unto Me.*'

What meaneth this most meek worthiness, and this lovely and friendly bidding? How shall I dare come unto Thee, that knoweth that I have done nothing well? How shall I bring Thee into my house, that so oft have offended before Thy face? Angels and Archangels honour Thee, and righteous men dread Thee; and yet Thou sayest: '*Come ye all unto Me.*' But that Thou, Lord, hadst said it, who would believe it to be true? And but Thou hast commanded it, who dare attempt to go unto it?

[1] Matt. xi. 28.

Solomon the wisest of the
kings of Israel bestowed
seven years in building a ma-
-gnificent Temple to the praise
of Thy Name

Of the Imitation of Christ

Noah, that just man, laboured a hundred years to make a ship, to the end he might be saved with a few of his people. How may I prepare me then in an hour to receive Thee with due reverence, that art the Maker and Creator of all the world?

Moses, Thy servant, and great familiar, and special friend, made the ark of timber not corruptible, which he covered with right pure gold, and put in it the tables of the law. And I, a corrupt creature, how shall I dare so lightly to receive Thee, that art the Maker of the law, and Giver of grace and life unto all creatures?

Solomon, the most wise King of Israel, in the space of seven years, built a marvellous temple to the praising of Thy Name, and for eight days hallowed the Feast of the Dedication of the same; he offered a thousand peace-offerings, and put the ark of God in the place made ready for it, with great melody of clarions and trumpets. How dare I then, that am most poor among other creatures, receive Thee into mine house; I who scarcely have well spent one half-hour of time in my life?

O my good Lord, how much they studied to please Thee, and how little it is that I do! How little time I take when I dispose myself to be houseled.[1] Seldom am I gathered together in Thee, and more seldom am I purged from having my mind overmuch on worldly things. And certainly no unprofitable thoughts ought to come into the holy presence of the Godhead,

[1] to receive the Holy Communion.

nor ought any creatures to have place there; for I shall not receive an Angel but the Lord of Angels into my heart.

Nevertheless there is a great difference between the ark of God with its relics, and Thy most pure and precious Body with its virtues, which are more than can be spoken; and between the sacrifices of the Old Law that were but as figures of the New Law, and the true Host of Thy precious Body, which is the accomplishment of all the old sacrifices.

Why then am I not more inflamed to come to Thee? Why do I not prepare myself with greater diligence to receive this holy and blessed Sacrament, sith the holy ancient Fathers, the Patriarchs and Prophets, Kings and Princes, with all the people, have shewed so great affection towards Thy service in time passed?

The most devout and blessed King David went before the ark of God and honoured it with all his strength, always remembering the great benefits before given unto the Fathers; he made organs of divers manners, and also Psalms, which he ordained to be sung, and he himself sung them with great gladness; and ofttimes with his harp, he being fulfilled with the grace of the Holy Ghost, taught the people of Israel to laud and praise God with all their heart, and daily with their mouth to bless Him and preach His goodness. If there were shewed then so great devotion and remembrance of laud and praising to God before the ark of the Old Testament, how much reverence and devotion ought we then now to have in the presence of this holy Sacrament, and in the receiving of the most excellent Body of our Lord Jesus Christ?

Many run to divers places to visit relics of Saints, and marvel greatly when they hear of their blessed deeds; they see great buildings of temples, and behold how their holy bones be covered with silk and lapped in gold. And lo, Thou, my Lord God, Thou art present here with me upon the altar, the most holy Saint of Saints, Maker of all things, and Lord of Angels. Ofttimes there is great curiosity and vanity in the sight of such things, and little fruit and amendment is had thereby, specially where there is so light recourse, without any true contrition going before. But Thou, my Lord God, my Lord Jesus Christ, God and Man, art here wholly present in the Sacrament of the Altar, where the fruit of everlasting health is had plenteously, as oft as Thou art worthily and devoutly received. But if that shall be done fruitfully, there may be no lightness, curiosity, or sensuality; but steadfast faith, devout hope, and pure charity.

O God, invisible Maker of all the world, how marvellously doest Thou with us, how sweetly and how graciously disposest Thou all things to Thy chosen people, to whom Thou offerest Thyself to be taken in this glorious Sacrament. Certainly it surmounteth all understanding, and it draweth the hearts and kindleth the affections of all devout men. Thy true faithful people, that dispose all their life to amendment, receive ofttimes through this glorious Sacrament great grace of devotion, and great love of virtue.

O marvellous and secretly hidden grace of this Sacrament, which only the faithful people of Christ do know; for infidels and they that live in sin may have no manner of experience thereof! In this Sacrament spiritual grace is given, and the virtue that was lost in their soul is repaired, and the beauty that was deformed through sin returneth again. And the grace of this Sacrament sometimes is so much, that, of the fulness of devotion that cometh thereby, not only the mind, but also the feeble body, recover their former strength.

But verily it is greatly to be sorrowed, that we be slow and negligent, and that we are not stirred with greater affection to receive Christ; in Whom standeth all merit and hope of them that shall be saved. He is our health and our redemption; He is the comforter of all that live in this world, and the eternal rest of all Saints in heaven. This also is greatly to be sorrowed, that so many take so little heed of this high mystery, which gladdeth heaven and preserveth the world. Alas, the blindness and hardness of man's heart, that taketh not greater heed of so noble a gift, but by the daily using thereof is negligent and taketh little heed thereto.

If this most blessed Sacrament were ministered only in one place, and consecrated but by one priest in the world, with how great desire, thinkest thou, the people would run to that place and to that priest, that they might see there these heavenly mysteries? Now there be many priests, and Christ is offered in many places, that the grace and love of God to man may appear so much the greater, the more the holy Communion is spread abroad throughout the world.

Thankings be to Thee, therefore, my Lord Jesu, that Thou dost vouchsafe to refresh us poor outlaws with Thy Precious Blood, and to stir us with the words of Thine own mouth to receive this holy mystery, saying: *'Come unto me, all ye that labour and are heavy laden, and I will give you rest.'* [1]

The Second Chapter: That the great goodness and charity of God is given to man in this blessed Sacrament. ¶ O my Lord Jesu! trusting in Thy great goodness and mercy, I come to Thee, as a sick man to him that shall heal him, and as he that is hungry and thirsty to the fountain of life, as one that is needy to the King of Heaven, as a servant to his lord, a creature to his Creator, and as a desolate person to his meek and blessed comforter. But how is it that Thou comest to me? Who am I that Thou shouldst give Thyself unto me? How dare I, a sinner, appear before Thee? And how is it that Thou wilt vouchsafe to come to so sinful a creature? Thou knowest Thy servant, and seest well that of himself he hath no goodness wherefore Thou shouldst give this grace unto him. I confess therefore mine own unworthiness, and I acknowledge Thy goodness; I praise Thy

[1] Matt xi. 28

piety, and yield Thee thankings for Thy great charity. Verily Thou doest all this for Thine own goodness, and not for my merits; that Thy goodness may thereby the more appear, Thy charity the more largely be shewed, and Thy meekness the more highly be commended. Therefore, because this pleaseth Thee, and Thou hast commanded that it should thus be done, Thy goodness therein also pleaseth me; and would to God that mine iniquities resisted me not.

O my Lord Jesu! how great reverence and thankings, with perpetual praisings of Thy Name, ought to be given Thee for the receiving of Thy holy Body, Whose dignity no man is able to express. But what shall I think on in this Communion, and in going to my Lord God, Whom I cannot worship as I ought to do, and yet desire to receive devoutly? What may I think on better or more healthful to me, than wholly to meek myself before Thee, exalting Thy infinite goodness far above me? I laud Thee, my Lord God, and shall exalt Thee everlastingly. I despise myself and submit me to Thee, and sorrow greatly the deepness of mine iniquity.

Thou art the Saint of Saints, and I am the filth of all sinners: and yet Thou inclinest Thyself to me, that am not worthy to look toward Thee. Thou comest to me, Thou wilt be with me, Thou biddest me to Thy feast. Thou wilt give me this heavenly meat and this Angel's food to eat, which is plainly none other but Thyself, that art the lively bread which descendest from heaven and givest life to the world.

Of the Imitation of Christ

Behold, Lord, from whence all this love proceedeth, and how great goodness shineth upon us. How great thanks and praises are due to Thee therefor. O how healthful and profitable a counsel was it, when Thou ordainedst this glorious Sacrament! How sweet and joyous a feast was it when Thou gavest Thyself as meat to be eaten! O Lord, how marvellous is Thy work, how mighty is Thy virtue, and how far unspeakable is Thy truth! By Thy word all things were made, and all things were done as Thou hast commanded.

It is a marvellous thing, worthy to be believed, and far above the understanding of man, that Thou, Lord, that art God and very Man, art wholly contained under a little likeness of bread and wine, and art eaten without consuming, of him that taketh Thee; and that Thou, that art Lord of all things, and that needest nothing in this world, wouldst by this glorious Sacrament dwell in us. Keep Thou mine heart and my body immaculate, that in a glad and a pure conscience I may ofttimes celebrate Thy mysteries, and receive them to my everlasting health, which Thou hast ordained most specially to Thy honour and perpetual memory.

O my soul, be thou merry and glad for so noble a gift and so singular a comfort left to thee in this vale of misery, for as oft as thou rememberest this mystery and takest the Body of Christ, so oft thou workest the work of thy redemption, and art made partaker of all the merits of Christ. Truly the charity of Christ is never minished, and the greatness of His mercy is never consumed. Therefore thou oughtest always with a new renewing of mind to dispose thee to it, and with a well-advised and a deep consideration to think on this great mystery of health. It should seem to thee as new and as pleasant a joy and comfort when thou singest Mass or hearest it, as if Christ the same day first entered into the womb of the Virgin, and were made Man, or if He the same day suffered and died upon the cross for the health of mankind.

The Third Chapter: That it is very profitable oft to be houseled. ¶ Lord, I come to Thee, that it may be well with me through Thy gift, and that I may joy at the holy feast that Thou of Thy great goodness hast made ready for me. In Thee is all that I may or should desire, for Thou art my health and my redemption, my hope and my strength, my honour and my glory. Make me, Thy servant, this day merry and glad in Thee, for I have lifted my soul unto Thee. I desire now devoutly and reverently to receive Thee into mine house, that I may deserve with zeal to be blessed of Thee, and to be accounted among the children of Abraham. My soul coveteth to receive Thy body, my heart desireth to be united with Thee.

Betake Thyself to me, Lord, and it sufficeth; for without Thee there is no comfort. Without Thee I may not be; and without Thy visitation I may not live. And therefore it behoveth me ofttimes to go to Thee, and for my health to receive Thee, lest haply, if I be defrauded from that heavenly meat, I should fail in the way. So Thou sayedst Thyself, most merciful Jesu, as Thou wast preaching to the people, and healedst them of their sicknesses · '*I will not send them away fasting, lest they faint in the way*.'[1] Do with me therefore in like manner, Who hast left Thyself in this glorious Sacrament for the comfort of all faithful people. Thou alone art the true refection of the soul, and he that worthily eateth Thee shall be partaker and heir of eternal glory. It is necessary to me, that so oft do offend, so soon wax dull and slow, that by oftprayers and confessions I may renew myself, purify myself, and kindle myself to quickness and fervour of spirit, lest haply, by long abstaining, I might fall from that holy purpose.

For the wits of man and woman be from their youth proud and ready to evil ; and but if[2] this heavenly medicine do help, man may fall anon to worse and worse. This Holy Communion therefore draweth a man from evil, and comforteth him in goodness. If now I be ofttimes so negligent and slothful when I am commanded, what would I be, if I received not that blessed medicine, and sought not for that great help? And though I be not every day apt nor disposed to receive my Creator, nevertheless I shall take heed to receive Him at times convenient, so that I may be partaker of so great a grace. For it is one of the principal consolations of a faithful soul that, as long as he is as a pilgrim in this mortal body, he oft remember

1 Matt xv. 32.   2 unless.

his Lord God, and receive Him that is his only beloved above all things.

It is a marvellous goodness of the great pity which
Thou, Lord, hast towards us, that Thou, Creator and
giver of life to all spirits, vouchsafest to come to a
poor creature, and with Thy Godhead and Manhood
to refresh his hunger and need. O happy is that man,
and blessed is that soul that deserveth devoutly to
receive his Lord God, and in that receiving to be fulfilled with a spiritual joy ! O how great a Lord doth
he receive ; how well-beloved a guest doth he bring
into his house ; how joyous a fellow doth he receive;
how faithful a friend doth he accept; how noble a
spouse doth he embrace that receiveth Thee, for Thou
alone art to be beloved before all, and above all things!
Let heaven and earth, and all the ornaments of them,
be still in Thy presence, for whatsoever they have
worthy of laud or praise, they have that of the largess
of Thy gift, and yet they cannot be like to the honour
and glory of Thy Name, of Whose wisdom there is
no number or measure.

**The Fourth Chapter: That many commo=
dities be given to them that devoutly receive this holy
Sacrament.** ¶ O my Lord God ! prevent Thy servant
with the blessings of Thy sweetness, that he may deserve to go reverently and devoutly to this high
Sacrament. Stir up my heart unto a full beholding of
Thee, and deliver me from the great sloth and idleness in which I have been in time past. Visit me in
Thy goodness, and give me grace to taste in my soul

the sweetness that is secretly hid in this Blessed Sacrament, as in a most plenteous fountain. Illumine also mine eyes to see and behold so great a mystery, and strengthen me that I may always faithfully and undoubtedly believe it, for it is Thy operation and not the power of man, Thy holy institution and not man's invention. Therefore to take and to understand these things, no man is sufficient of himself, for they overpass the subtilty of all Angels and heavenly spirits. What then may I, most unworthy sinner, dust and ashes, search and talk of so high a secret?

Lord, in simpleness of heart, in a good, stable faith, and by Thy commandment, I come to Thee with meek hope and reverence, and verily believe that Thou art here present in this Sacrament, God and Man. Thou wilt therefore that I should receive Thee, and knit myself to Thee in perfect charity. Wherefore I ask Thee mercy, and desire that Thou give me Thy special grace, that I may from henceforth be fully molten into Thee, flow in Thy love, and never after intermit myself with any other comfort. This most high and most worthy Sacrament is the life of the soul and body, the medicine of all spiritual sickness, whereby all vices be cured, passions refrained, temptations overcome and diminished, greater grace is sent, virtue increased, and faith stablished, hope strengthened, charity kindled and spread abroad.

Thou hast given and ofttimes givest many great gifts by this Sacrament to Thy beloved servants that

devoutly receive, for Thou art thereby the strong up-
holder of my soul, the repairer of all the infirmities of
man, and the giver of all inward comfort in tribulation. From the deepness of their own dejection,
Thou raisest them again into a strong hope of Thy
preservation, renewest them, and lightest them inwardly with a new grace, so that they that felt themselves, before receiving of that Blessed Sacrament,
heavy and without affection, after, when they have
received it, have found themselves changed into a
great ghostly fervour. And all this Thou doest to
Thy elect people of Thy great goodness, that they may
see and know openly by experience that they have
nothing of themselves, but that all the grace and goodness that they have, they have received of Thee; for
of themselves they be cold, dull, and undevout, but by
Thee they be made fervent, quick in spirit, and devout
followers of Thy will. Who goeth meekly to the
fountain of sweetness, but he bringeth away with him
great plenty of sweetness? Or, who standeth by a
great fire, but he feeleth the great heat thereof? And
Thou, Lord, art the fountain of all sweetness, the fire
always brenning and never failing.

Therefore, though I may not draw the fulness of
that fountain, nor drink thereof to the full, I shall
nevertheless put my mouth to the hole of the heavenly
pipe, that I may take some little drop thereof to refresh my thirst, that so I be not all dried away. And
though I be not all heavenly and brenning in charity,
as the Seraphim and Cherubim be, nevertheless, I

shall endeavour me to set myself to devotion and to prepare mine heart, that I may get some little sparkle of the brenning of heavenly life, through the meek receiving of this living Sacrament. Whatsoever wanteth in me, I beseech Thee, my Lord Jesu, most holy and blessed, that Thou benignly and graciously supply in me, for Thou hast vouchsafed to call all to Thee, saying: '*Come unto me, all ye that labour and are heavy laden, and I will give you rest.*'[1]

I labour in the sweat of my body, and am troubled with the sorrow of mine heart; I am charged with sins, travailed with temptations, wrapped and oppressed with many evil passions; and there is none that may help or that may deliver me, nor that may make me safe, but Thou, Lord God, my only Saviour, to Whom I commit myself and all mine, that Thou keep me and lead me into life everlasting. Accept me, and take me into the laud and glory of Thy Name, that hast ordained to me Thy Body and Blood to be my meat and drink. '*Grant me, Lord, I beseech Thee, that by the oft receiving of Thy high mystery the fervour of devotion may daily increase in me.*'

The Fifth Chapter: Of the worthiness of the Sacrament of the altar, and of the state of the priesthood. ¶ If thou hadst the purity of Angels and the holiness of St. John Baptist, thou wouldst not for that be worthy to receive nor touch this holy Sacrament; for it is not granted for the merits of man, that a man should consecrate and touch the Sacrament of

[1] Matt xi 28

Christ, and take for his meat the Bread of Angels It is a great mystery; and great the dignity of priests, to whom it is granted that is not granted to Angels. For only priests that be duly ordained in the Church have power to sing Mass and to consecrate the Body of Christ. A priest is indeed the minister of God, using the word of consecration by the commandment and ordinance of God; but God is there the principal doer and invisible worker, to Whom is subject all that He willeth, and all obeyeth to that He commandeth.

Thou oughtest, therefore, more to believe Almighty God in this most excellent Sacrament, than thine own wit, or any other visible token or sign. And therefore with dread and reverence thou art to go to this blessed work. Take heed then diligently, and see from whence this ministry and service cometh that is given unto thee by the touching of the hands of the Bishop. Thou art now made a priest, and art consecrated to sing Mass. Take heed, therefore, that thou faithfully and devoutly offer thy Sacrifice to God in due time, and that thou keep thyself without reproof. Thou hast not made thy burden more light, but thou art now bound in a straiter bond of discipline, and of much higher perfection than thou wert before.

A priest ought to be adorned with all virtues, and to give others example of good life. His conversation should not be with the common people, nor in the common way of the world, but with Angels in heaven, or with perfect men in earth that be best disposed to serve God.

A priest clothed in holy vestments beareth the place of Christ, that he may humbly and meekly pray to our Lord for himself and for all the people. He hath before him and behind him the sign of the cross of Christ, that he may diligently remember His Passion. He beareth before him the cross that he may diligently behold the steps of Christ, and study fervently to follow them. Behind him also he is signed with the cross, that he may gladly and meekly suffer all adversities for the love of God. He beareth the cross before him that he may bewail his own sins; and he beareth it behind him, that he may through compassion beweep the sins of other, and know himself to be set as a mean between God and the whole people; and therefore not to cease of prayer and holy oblation, till he may deserve of Almighty God mercy and grace.

When a priest saith Mass, he honoureth God, he maketh Angels glad, he edifieth the Church, he helpeth the people that be alive, giveth rest to them that be dead, and maketh himself partaker of all good deeds.

The Sixth Chapter : Of the inward remembrance and exercise that a man ought to have afore the receiving of the Body of Christ. ¶ Lord, when I think of Thy worthiness, and of my great vileness, I tremble strongly, and am confounded in myself; for if I receive Thee not, I fly the eternal life, and if I unworthily receive Thee, I run into Thy wrath. What then shall I do, my good Lord, my helper, my protector, comforter, and right sure counsellor in all my necessities?

Teach me, good Lord, the right way, and purpose unto me some ready exercise convenable to the receiving of this holy mystery, for it is necessary unto me, and greatly profitable, to know how devoutly and reverently I ought to prepare mine heart to receive it, or to consecrate so great and so goodly a Sacrifice as it is.

The Seventh Chapter: Of the discussing of our own conscience, and of the purpose of amendment. ¶ It behoveth thee above all things with sovereign reverence and profound meekness of heart, with full faith and humble intent of the honour of God, to celebrate, take, and receive this holy Sacrament. Examine diligently thy conscience, and by true contrition and meek confession make it clean after thy power, so that thou know nothing that grieveth or biteth thy conscience, or that may let[1] thee to go freely unto it. Have displeasure of all thy sins in general, and for thy daily excesses and offences have sighings and sorrowings more special. And if the time will suffer it, confess unto God in secret of thine heart the miseries of all thy passions.

Weep and sorrow that thou art yet so carnal and worldly, so unmortified from thy passions, so full of motions of concupiscence, so unwary, and so evil ordered in thy outward wits; so oft wrapped in vain phantasies, so much inclined to outward and worldly

[1] hinder.

things, so negligent to inward things, so ready to laughing and dissoluteness, so hard to weeping and compunction, so ready to easy things and to that which is liking to the flesh; so slow to penance and fervour of spirit, so curious to hear new things and to see fair things, so loth to meek and abject things, so covetous to have much, so scarce to give, so glad to hold, so unadvised in speaking, so incontinent to be still, so evil ordered in manners, so importune in deeds, so greedy upon meat, so deaf to the word of God, so quick to rest, so slow to labour, so attentive to fables, so sleepy to holy vigils, so hasty to the end, so unstable to take heed to the way that leads to the end; so negligent in the service of God, so dull and undevout to go to Mass, so dry in thy housel; so soon fallen at large to outward things, so seldom gathered together to inward things; so soon moved to anger and wrath, so lightly stirred to the displeasure of other; so ready to judge, so rigorous to reprove; so glad in prosperity, so feeble in adversity; so oft purposing many good things, and so seldom bringing them to effect.

And when thou hast thus confessed and bewept all these defaults, and such other like in thee with great sorrow and displeasure of thine own frailness, set thee then in a full purpose to amend thy life and to profit always from better to better. Then, with a full resigning and a whole will, offer thyself unto the honour of My Name on the altar of thy heart, as a sacrifice to Me; that is to say, faithfully committing to Me both thy body and soul, so that thou mayest be worthy to offer to Me this high Sacrifice, and to receive healthfully the Sacrament of My holy Body.

For there is no oblation more worthy, nor satisfaction greater to put away sin, than for a man to offer himself purely and wholly to God, with the offering of the Body of Christ in Mass and in Holy Communion. If a man do that which is in him, and is truly penitent, as oft as he cometh to Me for grace and forgiveness, I am the Lord that saith : *'Have I any pleasure at all that the wicked should die? saith the Lord God: and not that he should return from his ways, and live?'*[1] Because I will no more remember his sins, but they shall all be forgiven unto him.

The Eighth Chapter: Of the oblation of Christ on the cross, and of a full forsaking of ourselves. ¶ Our Lord Jesus saith to His servant thus: As I hanging all naked, with Mine arms spread abroad upon the cross, offered Myself to God the Father for thy sins, so that nothing remained in Me, but all went in sacrifice to please My Father and to appease His wrath against mankind ; so thou oughtest daily in the Mass to offer thyself freely to God, as much as thou mayest, in a pure and holy oblation, with all thy power and affection. What require I more of thee, than that thou shouldst study wholly to resign thyself unto Me? Whatsoever thou givest beside thyself I regard it not; for I look not for thy gifts, but for thee.

As it would not suffice to thee to have all things

[1] Ezek. xviii. 23.

beside Me, so it may not please Me, whatsoever thou give beside thyself. Offer thyself to Me, and give thyself all to God, and thy oblation shall be acceptable.

Lo, I offered Myself wholly to My Father for thee, and I gave My Body and Blood to thy meat, that I might be wholly thine and thou Mine. But if thou have a trust in thyself, and dost not freely offer thyself to My Will, thy oblation is not pleasant, and there shall be between us no perfect union. Hence a free offering of thyself into the hands of God must go before all thy works, if thou wilt obtain grace and the true liberty. Therefore it is that so few be inwardly illuminate and free, because they cannot wholly forsake themselves. For My words are true: '*Whosoever doth not bear his cross, and come after me, cannot be my disciple.*'[1] Offer thyself therefore fully to Me with all thine affection and love. *Amen.*

The Ninth Chapter : That we ought to offer ourselves and all ours to God, and to pray for all people.
¶ Lord! all things be Thine that are in heaven and earth. I desire to offer myself to Thee in a free and perpetual oblation, so that I may perpetually be with Thee. Lord! in simpleness of heart I offer me to Thee this day, to be Thy servant in the service and sacrifice of laud perpetual. Accept me with this oblation of Thy precious Body, which I this day offer to Thee in the presence of Thy holy Angels, that are here present invisible, that it may be to my health and to the health of all the people.

[1] Luke xiv. 27.

And, Lord, I offer to Thee all my sins and offences
that I have committed before Thee and Thy holy
Angels, from the day that I first could offend unto
this day; that Thou vouchsafe through Thy great
charity to put away all my sins, and to cleanse my
conscience of all mine offences, and to restore to me
again the grace that I through sin have lost; that
Thou forgive me all things past, and receive me
mercifully unto a blessed kissing of peace and forgiveness.

What then may I do, but meekly confess and bewail my sins, and continually ask mercy of Thee?
Forgive me, merciful Lord, I beseech Thee; for all
my sins displease me much, and I will never commit
them again, but sorrow for them, ready to do penance
and satisfaction after my power. Forgive me, Lord,
forgive me my sins, for Thy holy Name ; save my
soul that Thou hast redeemed with Thy precious
Blood. I commit myself wholly unto Thy mercy, I
resign myself wholly into Thy hands; do with me
after Thy goodness, and not after my malice and
wretchedness

I offer also to Thee all my good deeds, though they
be very few and imperfect, that Thou amend them
and sanctify them, and make them liking and acceptable to Thee, and always make them better and better,
and that Thou bring me, though I be a slow and unprofitable person, to a blessed and laudable end.

I offer also to Thee all the desires of devout persons,
the necessity of mine ancestors, friends, brothers,

sisters, and of all my lovers ; and of all them that for
Thy love have done good to me or to any other ; of
them also that have desired and asked me to pray or
to do sacrifice for them or for their friends, whether
they be alive or dead ; that they may the rather feel
the help of Thy grace, the gift of Thy heavenly consolation, protection from all peril, deliverance from
all pain; and that they being so delivered from all
evils, may in spiritual gladness yield to Thee high
laud and praisings.

I offer also to Thee my prayer and my peaceable
offering for all them that have in anything hindered
me or made me heavy, or that have done me any
hurt or grief : and for all them also whom I have at
any time made heavy, troubled, grieved, or slandered
in word or deed, wittingly or ignorantly ; that Thou
forgive us altogether our sins and offences against
Thee, and of each of us against other. Take from
our hearts, Lord, all suspicion, indignation, wrath,
variance, and whatsoever may let charity or diminish
the fraternal love that each of us should have to other.
Have mercy, Lord, have mercy on all them that ask
Thee mercy, and give grace to them that have need ;
make us to stand in such case that we be worthy to
have Thy grace, and finally to come to the life everlasting. *Amen.*

The Tenth Chapter : That the Holy Communion is not lightly to be forborne. ¶ It behoveth
thee to run oft to the fountain of grace and mercy, to
the fountain of all goodness and purity, that thou

mayest be healed from thy passions and vices, and be made more strong against all the temptations and deceitful craft of our enemy. The fiend, knowing the greatest fruit and highest remedy to be in receiving of this blessed Sacrament, enforceth him by all the ways that he can, to let and withdraw all faithful and devout people from it as much as he can; and therefore some men, when they dispose themselves to it, have greater temptations than they had before. For, as it is written in Job,[1] the wicked spirit cometh among the children of God, that he may by his old malice and wickedness trouble them, or make them overmuch fearful and perplexed ; so that he may diminish their affection, or take away their faith, if haply he may thereby make them either utterly to cease from being houseled, or else that they go to it with little devotion. But we are not to care anything for all his crafts and fantasies, how vile and ugly soever they be; but all fantasies are to be thrown again at his own head, and he is so far to be despised that, for all the assaults and commotions that he can stir up, the Holy Communion be not omitted.

Sometimes overmuch curiousness to have devotion, or over-great doubt of making confession, letteth much this holy purpose. Do therefore after the counsel of wise men, and put away all doubtfulness and scrupulousness, for they let the grace of God and destroy wholly the devotion of the mind. Also it is not good that for any little trouble or grief thou

[1] 1. 6 *et seqq*

leave this holy work, but go quickly and be confessed, and forgive gladly all that have offended thee. And if thou have offended any other, meekly ask of them forgiveness, and God shall right mercifully forgive thee.

What profiteth it long to tarry from confession, or to defer this Holy Communion? Purge thee first from sin, quickly cast out thy venom, haste thee after to take the medicine, and thou shalt feel more profit thereby than if thou tarriedst longer for it. If thou defer it to-day for this thing or that, to-morrow may happen to come a greater; and so thou mayest long be let from thy good purpose, and be made afterwards more unapt for it. Therefore, as soon as thou canst, discharge thyself from such heaviness and dulness of mind, and from all sloth; for it nothing profiteth long to be anguished, long to go on in trouble, and for such daily obstacles to sequester thyself from the divine mysteries: but it doth great hurt, and commonly bringeth on great sloth and lack of devotion. Alas for sorrow! some slothful and dissolute persons gladly seek causes to tarry from confession, and so defer the longer this Holy Communion; and that they do to the intent that they should not be bound to give themselves to any surer keeping of themselves in time to come than they have done before.

But alas, how little charity and slender devotion have they, that so lightly leave off so holy a thing! How happy is he, and how acceptable to God, that so

Thomas à Kempis

liveth and keepeth his conscience in such cleanness, that he is ready and hath good affection to be houseled every day, if it were lawful unto him, and he might do it without note or slander. He that sometimes abstaineth of meekness, or for any other lawful impediment, is to be praised for his reverence ; but if it be through slothfulness, he ought to quicken himself, and to do that in him is, and our Lord will strengthen his desire because of his good will ; for to a good will our Lord hath always a special respect.

But when he is lawfully let, he will always have a good will and a meek intent to be houseled, and so shall not want the fruit of the Sacrament. And verily every devout man may every day and every hour go healthfully, and without prohibition, unto the spiritual communion of Christ ; that is to say, in remembering His Passion. And nevertheless on certain days and at certain times he is bound to receive sacramentally the Body of his Redeemer with a great reverence ; and rather to pretend[1] therein the laud and honour of God than his own consolation. For so oft a man is houseled mystically and invisibly as he remembereth devoutly the mystery of the Incarnation of Christ and His Passion, and is thereby kindled into His love.

He that doth prepare himself for none other cause, but because a Feast is coming, or custom compelleth him thereto, he shall commonly be unready to it. Blessed is he, therefore, that as oft as he saith Mass or

[1] aim at.

is houseled offereth himself to our Lord in holy sacrifice. Be not in saying Mass over-long or over-short, but keep the good common way, as they do with whom thou livest; for thou oughtest not to do that which would grieve others, or make them tedious, but to keep the common way after the ordinance of the holy Fathers; and rather to conform thyself to that which shall be profitable to other, than to follow thine own devotion or private pleasure.

The Eleventh Chapter: That the Body of Christ and Holy Scripture are most necessary for the health of man's soul. ¶ O sweetest Jesu! how great sweetness is it to a devout soul, when he is fed with Thee at Thy heavenly feast, where there is none other meat brought forth to eat but Thou, his only beloved, that art most desirable to him above all the desires of his heart. And verily it would be sweet and pleasant to me by an inward and meek affection to weep before Thee, and with the blessed woman Mary Magdalene to wash Thy feet with the tears of mine eyes. But where is that devotion? Where is that plenteous shedding of holy tears? Certainly all my heart ought to brenn and to weep for joy in the sight of Thee and of Thy holy Angels; for I have Thee verily present with me, though Thou be hid under another likeness.

For to behold Thee in Thy proper and divine clearness mine eyes might not bear it; neither could all the world sustain to see Thee in the clearness and glory of Thy Majesty. Therefore Thou greatly helpest my weakness, in that Thou hidest Thyself under this blessed Sacrament. I have Him verily and worship Him, Whom Angels worship in heaven, but I as yet in faith, they in open sight and in Thine own likeness without any coverture. It behoveth me to be content in the light of true faith, and therein to walk till the day of everlasting clearness shall appear and the shadow of figures shall go away. When that which is perfect shall come, all use of Sacraments shall cease, for they that be blessed in heavenly glory have no need of this sacramental medicine, for they joy without end in the presence of God, beholding His glory face to face; and transformed from clearness to clearness of the Godhead, they taste the glory of the Son of God made Man, as He was in His Godhead from the beginning, and shall be everlastingly.

When I remember all these marvellous comforts, whatsoever solace I have in this world, though it be spiritual, it is grievous and tedious unto me; for as long as I see not my Lord openly in His glory, I set at nought all that I see and hear in this world. Lord, Thou art my witness that nothing may comfort me, nor any creature quiet me, but Thou, my Lord God, Whom I desire to see and behold eternally. But that is not possible for me to do, as long as I shall be in this mortal life. Wherefore it behoveth me to keep myself in great patience, and to submit myself to Thee in everything that I desire. For Thy holy Saints, that now joy with Thee, abode in good faith and patience, whiles they lived here, the coming of Thy glory. That they believed, I believe; that they hoped to have,

Of the Imitation of Christ

I hope to have; and thither as they by Thy grace are come, I trust to come. Till then I will walk in faith, and take comfort of the examples of the said holy Saints. I have also holy books for my solace, as a spiritual glass to look upon, and above all these I have for a singular remedy Thy holy Body.

I perceive well that two things be right necessary unto me in this world, without which this miserable life would be to me as importable. For as long as I shall be in this body, I confess myself to have need of two things, that is to say, of meat and light. Therefore Thou hast given unto me, who am poor and sick, Thy holy Body to the refreshing of my body and soul; and Thou hast set '*Thy word*' as '*a lamp unto my feet*'[1] to shew me the way that I should go. Without these two I may not well live, for the word of God is the light of my soul, and this Sacrament is the bread of my life. These two may also be called the two tables set on either side in the spiritual treasury of Holy Church. The one is the table of the holy altar having this holy Bread, that is the precious Body of Christ. The other is the table of the laws of God, containing the holy doctrine, instructing man in the right faith, and leading him into the inward secrecies, that are called *Sancta Sanctorum*, where the inward secrets of Scripture be hid and contained.

I yield thankings to Thee, my Lord Jesu, the brightness of eternal light, for this table of holy doctrine, which Thou hast ministered to us by Thy

[1] Ps. cxix. 105.

servants, Prophets, Apostles, and other Doctors. Thankings also be to Thee, the Creator and Redeemer of mankind, Who to shew unto all the world the greatness of Thy charity hast prepared a great supper, in which Thou settest not forth the Lamb figured in the Old Law, but Thy most holy Body and Blood to be eaten ; gladding in that holy feast all faithful people, and giving them to drink of Thy chalice of health, in which are contained all the delights of paradise, where Angels eat with us, but with much more plenteous sweetness.

O how great and honourable is the office of priests, to whom is given power to consecrate with the holy words of consecration the Lord of all Majesty, to bless Him with their lips, to hold Him in their hands, to receive Him into their mouths, and to minister Him to other! O how clean should be the hands, how pure the mouth, how holy the body, and how undefiled the heart of a priest, unto whom so oft entereth the Author of all cleanness! Truly there ought to proceed from the mouth of a priest, who so oft receiveth the Sacrament of Christ's Body, no word but that is holy, honest, and profitable.

His eyes should be full-simple and chaste, that use to behold the Body of Christ. His hands should be full-pure and lift up unto heaven, which use to touch the Creator of heaven and earth. Therefore it is specially said in the Law to priests: *'Ye shall be holy: for I the Lord your God am holy.'*[1]

[1] Lev xix. 2.

Of the Imitation of Christ

O God Almighty, Thy grace be with us and help us that have received the office of priesthood, that we may serve Thee worthily and devoutly in all purity and in a good conscience. And though we may not live in so great innocency as we ought to do, yet give us grace at the least that we may weep and sorrow the evils that we have done ; so that in spiritual meekness and in full purpose of a good will we may serve Thee hereafter. *Amen.*

The Twelfth Chapter: That he that shall be houseled ought to prepare himself thereto with great diligence.

¶ I am the lover of all purity and the liberal giver of all holiness. I seek a clean heart, and there is My resting-place. Make ready for Me a great chamber strawed—that is, thine heart—and I with My disciples will keep Mine Easter with thee.[1] If thou wilt that I come to thee and dwell with thee, cleanse thee of all the old filth of sin, and cleanse also the habitation of thine heart, making it pleasant and fair. Exclude the world and all the clamorous noise of sin ; sit solitary as '*a sparrow alone upon the housetop*,'[2] and think upon all thy offences with great bitterness of heart ; for a true lover will prepare for his beloved friend the best and the fairest place that he can, for in that is known the love and affection of him that receiveth his friend.

Nevertheless, know that thou mayest not of thyself suffice fully to make this preparing, as it ought to be in every point, though thou went about it a whole year

[1] See Mark xiv. 14.　　　　[2] Ps cii. 7

together, and hadst no other thing in thy mind to think upon. But of My mercy and grace only art thou suffered to go unto My table; as if a poor man were called to the dinner of a rich man, and he had no other thing to give him again, but only to humble himself and thank him for it. Do that in thee is with thy best diligence; and do it not only of custom, nor only of necessity for that thou art bound to it, but with dread, and reverence, and great affection take the Body of thy beloved Lord God, Who so lovingly vouchsafeth to come unto thee. I am He that hath called thee, I have commanded that this thing should be done, I will supply that which wanteth in thee.

Come therefore and receive Me; and when I give thee the grace of devotion yield thanks to Me, not for that thou art worthy to have it, but for that I have shewed My mercy lovingly to thee. And if thou have not the grace of devotion through receiving of this Sacrament, but feelest thyself more dry and indevout than thou wert before, yet continue still in prayer, wail, weep, call for grace, and cease not till thou receive some little drop of this healthful grace of devotion. Thou hast need of Me, not I of thee; neither comest thou to sanctify Me, but to make thyself better than thou wast before. Thou comest to be sanctified, and to be united unto Me; that thou mayest receive new grace, and be kindled anew to amendment. Do not forget this grace, but always with all thy diligence prepare thine heart, and bring thy Beloved unto thee.

But it behoveth not only to prepare thyself unto devotion before thou shalt be houseled, but also diligently to keep thyself therein after the receiving of the Sacrament. No less keeping is requisite after, than a devout preparation is needful before ; for a good keeping afterward is the best preparation to receive new grace hereafter, and a man shall be the more indisposed thereto if, after he hath received the holy Sacrament, he anon give himself to outward solace. Beware of much speaking : abide in some secret place, and keep thee with thy Lord God, for thou hast Him Whom all the world may not take from thee. I am He to Whom thou must give all, so that from henceforth thou live not in thyself, but only in Me.

The Thirteenth Chapter: That a devout soul should greatly desire with all his heart to be united to Christ in this blessed Sacrament. ¶ Who shall give unto me, Lord, that I may find Thee alone, and open all mine heart to Thee, and have Thee, as mine heart desireth ; so that no man may deceive me, nor any creature move me, nor draw me back, but that Thou alone speak to me and I to Thee, as a lover is wont to speak to his beloved, and a friend with his beloved friend? This it is that I pray for, this it is that I desire, that I may be wholly united to Thee, and that I may withdraw my heart from all things create, and through the Holy Communion and oft saying Mass to savour and taste eternal things. Ah! Lord God, when shall I be united to Thee, and wholly be molten into Thy love, so that I wholly forget myself? Be Thou in me and I in Thee; and grant that we may always so abide together in one.

Verily Thou art my beloved, elect and chosen before all other, in Whom my soul coveteth to abide all days of her life. Thou art the Lord of Peace, in Whom is the sovereign peace and true rest, without Whom is labour and sorrow and infinite misery. Verily Thou art the hidden God, and Thy counsel is not with wicked people, but with meek men and the simple in heart. '*O how secret and how benign is Thy Holy Spirit, Who, to the intent Thou mightest shew Thy sweetness to Thy chosen people, hast vouchsafed to refresh them with the most sweet bread that descendeth from heaven!*'[1] Verily there is none other nation so great, that hath their gods so nigh unto them as Thou, Lord God, art to all Thy faithful people,[2] to whom for their daily solace, and to raise their hearts into the love of heavenly things, Thou givest Thyself as meat and drink.

O what people is there that is so noble as the Christian people? Or what creature under heaven is so much beloved as the devout Christian soul, into whom God entereth, and feedeth her with His own glorious Flesh and Blood? O inestimable grace! O marvellous worthiness! O Love without measure, singularly shewed unto man! But what shall I yield again to God for all this grace and high charity? Truly, there is nothing more acceptable to Him than

1 Antiphon of the First Vespers of Corpus Christi.
2 See Deut. iv. 7.

that I wholly give mine heart and inwardly join my-self unto Him. Then shall all my inward parts joy in Him, when my soul is perfectly united unto Him. Then shall He say to me: *If thou wilt be with Me, I will be with thee.* And I shall answer Him again and say: *Vouchsafe, Lord, to abide with me, and I will gladly abide with Thee, for this is all my desire, that mine heart may be fast knit unto Thee without departing. Amen.*

The Fourteenth Chapter: Of the brenning desire that some devout persons have had to the Body of Christ. ¶ '*Oh how great is thy goodness, which thou hast laid up for them that fear thee.*'[1] But what is it, then, for them that love Thee? Verily, when I re-member many devout persons that have come to this holy Sacrament with so great fervour of devo-tion, I am then many times astonished and confounded in myself, that I go unto Thy altar and to the table of the Holy Communion so coldly and with so little fervour; that I abide still so dry and without any affection of heart; and that I am not so wholly kindled before Thee, my Lord God, nor so strongly drawn thereby in affection to Thee as have been many de-vout persons, who, from the great desire they have had to this Holy Communion and for a feelable love of heart that they have had thereto, could not refrain themselves from weeping: but with the mouth of their heart and body together, they affectuously open-ed their mouths to Thee, Lord, that art the living

[1] Ps. xxxi. 19.

fountain; because they could not otherwise assuage nor temper their hunger, unless they took Thy holy Body as they did, with great joy and spiritual gladness.

Truly their great brenning faith is a probable argument of Thy holy Presence; for they know verily their Lord in the breaking of bread, whose heart brenneth so strongly in them by the presence of their Lord Jesus, then sacramentally walking with them.[1] But verily, such affection and devotion, so strong fervour and love, be ofttimes far from me. Be Thou therefore, most sweet and benign Lord Jesu, merciful and meek unto me, and grant unto me, Thy poor servant, that I may feel sometimes some little part of the hearty affection of Thy love in this Holy Communion, that my faith may the more recover and amend, mine hope through Thy goodness be the more perfect, and my charity being once perfectly kindled and having experience of the heavenly manna, never fail.

Thy mercy, Lord, is strong enough to grant me this grace that I so much desire, and, when the time of Thy pleasure shall come, to visit me benignly with the spirit of a brenning fervour to Thee. And though I do not brenn with so great a desire as such specially devout persons have done, yet nevertheless I have desired the grace to be inflamed with that brenning desire, praying and desiring that I may be made partaker with all such Thy fervent lovers; and be numbered in their holy company.

[1] See Luke xxiv. 30.

Of the Imitation of Christ

The Fifteenth Chapter: That the grace of devotion is gotten through meekness and forsaking of ourselves.

¶ It behoveth thee abidingly to seek the grace of devotion, without ceasing to ask it, patiently and faithfully to abide it, thankfully to receive it, meekly to keep it, studiously to work with it, and wholly to commit to God the time and manner of His heavenly visitation, till His pleasure shall be to come unto thee. Thou oughtest principally to meek thyself when thou feelest but little inward devotion. But be not therefore overmuch cast down, nor inordinately heavy in spirit; for our Lord giveth many times in a short moment that which He denied long time before; He giveth also sometimes in the end that which in the beginning of the prayer He deferred to grant.

If grace were always to be anon granted, and were anon to be present after the will of the asker, it could not be well borne by a weak and feeble person. Therefore in a good hope and meek patience the grace of devotion is to be tarried for; and thou oughtest to impute it to thyself and to thine own sins, when grace is not given thee, or is secretly taken from thee. Sometimes it is but a little thing that letteth or hideth it away, if that may be called little and not rather great that letteth and prohibiteth so good a thing; but whether it be little or great, if thou remove it and perfectly overcome it, that shall be granted unto thee which thou desirest.

Forthwith, as thou betakest thyself with all thine

heart to God, and desirest neither this thing nor that for thine own pleasure, but wholly puttest thy will to His Will, thou shalt find thyself united to Him and set in great inward peace ; for nothing will savour so well to thee, nor so much please thee, as that the will and pleasure of God be fully done in thee. Whosoever, therefore, in a pure simple heart lifteth his intent up to God, and voideth himself from all inordinate love or displeasure of any worldly thing, he shall be more apt to receive grace, and shall be best worthy to have the gift of devotion. For there our Lord giveth His blessing, where He findeth the vessels empty and void. And the more perfectly a man can renounce himself and all worldly things, and by despising of himself the more die to himself, so much the sooner grace shall come, and shall the more plenteously enter into him, and shall lift up his heart higher into God.

Then his heart shall see and abound, shall marvel and be dilated in him, for the hand of our Lord is with him, and he hath wholly put himself into His hand for ever. Lo! so shall a man be blessed that seeketh God with all his heart. Such a man, in receiving this Holy Sacrament, deserveth the great grace of the uniting in God, for he looketh not to his own devotion and consolation, but to the glory and honour of God.

The Sixteenth Chapter : That we should open all our necessities to Christ, and ask His grace. ¶ O most sweet Lord, Whom I desire devoutly to receive, Thou knowest the infirmity and necessity

hat I am in ; in how many sins and vices I lie ; how
oft I am grieved, tempted, troubled, and defiled. I
come to Thee for remedy, and I make my prayer to
Thee for comfort. I speak to Him that knoweth all
things, to Whom all my secret and inward thoughts
be manifest and open, and Who alone may perfectly
counsel me and help me. Thou knowest what I need
to have, and how poor I am in virtue.

Lo! I stand before Thee poor and naked, asking
and desiring Thy grace. Refresh me, therefore, Thy
poorest servant begging for spiritual food, kindle my
heart with the fire of Thy love, and illumine my blindness with the clearness of Thy Presence. Turn all
worldly things into bitterness to me, and all grievous
things and contrarious things into patience, and all
created things into despising and into forgetting of
hem. Lift up my heart to Thee in heaven, and suffer
me not to live vainly, nor to err in this world. Thou,
Lord, from henceforth shalt be sweet to me for ever;
for Thou alone art my meat and drink, my love, my
oy, my sweetness, and all my goodness.

O that Thou wouldst kindle me, inflame me, and
urn me wholly unto Thee ; that I may be one spirit
with Thee by grace of inward uniting and melting of
burning love! Suffer me not to depart from Thee
fasting and dry, but work in me mercifully, as Thou
hast ofttimes marvellously wrought in Thy beloved
servants in times past. What marvel were it if I were
all inflamed in Thee and failed in myself; sith Thou
art the fire always burning and never failing, the love

purifying the hearts and lightening the understanding of all creatures.

The Seventeenth Chapter: Of the burning love and great affection that we should have to receive Christ. ¶ With high devotion and burning love, with all fervour and affection of the heart, I desire to receive Thee, Lord, as many Saints and devout persons have desired Thee in their Communion, who most specially pleased Thee in the holiness of their life, and were in most burning devotion to Thee. O my Lord God, my love eternal, my whole goodness and felicity without ending, I covet to receive Thee with as great desire and as due reverence as any holy man ever did or could do.

And though I be unworthy to have such feeling in devotion as they had, yet nevertheless I offer to Thee the whole affection of my heart, as if I alone had all the burning and flaming desires that they had. And besides that, all that a meek mind may imagine and desire, I give and offer to Thee with high reverence and worship, and with inward fervour. I desire to reserve nothing to myself, but I offer myself and all mine in sacrifice to Thee freely and liberally. And also my Lord God, my Creator and Redeemer, I desire to receive Thee this day with such affection, reverence, laud, and honour, with such thanks, dignity, and love, and with such faith, hope, and purity, as Thy most holy and glorious Mother, the Virgin Mary, desired and received Thee, when she meekly and devoutly answered the Angel that shewed her the mystery of the Incarnation, and said: '*Ecce ancilla Domini, fiat mihi secundum verbum tuum*'; that is to say, '*Behold the handmaid of the Lord; be it unto me according to thy word.*'[1]

And as Thy blessed precursor, Saint John the Baptist, the most excellent of all Saints, was glad and joyed in great joy of the Holy Ghost through Thy presence, when he was yet in his mother's womb; and when after he saw Thee walking among the people, very meekly and with devout affection said: '*The friend of the bridegroom, which standeth and heareth him, rejoiceth greatly because of the bridegroom's voice*';[2] so covet I to be inflamed in great and holy desires, and to present myself to Thee with all mine heart.

Also I offer and yield Thee all the lauds, the brenning affections, ecstasies, spiritual illuminations, and heavenly visions of devout hearts, with all the virtues and praisings done or to be done by any creature in heaven or on earth, for myself and for all that be committed to my prayer; that Thou mayest be worthily lauded and glorified for ever.

Accept, O Lord God, my mind and my desires of the manifold lauds and blessings which, after the multitude of Thy greatness, are of right to Thee due, more than can be spoken. All these I yield to Thee every day and every moment; and with all my desire and affection I meekly exhort and pray all heavenly spirits and faithful people with me to yield thankings and lauds to Thee.

[1] Luke i. 38.   [2] John iii. 29

Thomas à Kempis

I beseech Thee that all people, tribes, and tongues may magnify Thy holy and most sweet Name with great joy and brenning devotion; and that all they who reverently and devoutly minister this most high Sacrament, or with full faith receive it, may thereby deserve to find before Thee Thy grace and mercy. And when they have obtained the devotion and spiritual union with Thee that they desired, and shall have departed from Thy heavenly table well comforted and marvellously refreshed, that they will have me, poor sinner, in their remembrance. *Amen.*

The Eighteenth Chapter: That a man should not be a curious searcher of this holy Sacrament, but a meek follower of Christ, subduing always his reason to faith.

¶ Thou must beware of a curious and an unprofitable searching of this most profound Sacrament, if thou wilt not be drowned in the great depth of doubtfulness; for he that is the searcher of God's Majesty shall be anon overwhelmed by its glory. God is of power to work much more than man may understand; nevertheless, a meek and humble searching of the Truth, ready always to be taught and to walk after the teachings of holy Fathers, is sufferable.

Blessed is the simplicity that leaveth the way of hard questions, and goeth in the plain and steadfast way of the commandments of God. Many have lost their devotion because they would search higher things than appertained to them. Faith and a good life are asked of thee, and not the highness of understanding, nor the deepness of the mysteries of God.

Of the Imitation of Christ

If thou may not understand nor take such things as be beneath thee, how mayest thou then comprehend those things that be above thee? Submit thyself therefore meekly to God, and submit also thy reason to Faith, and the light of knowledge and true understanding shall be given unto thee, as it shall be most profitable and necessary for thee.

Some be grievously tempted about the Faith and the holy Sacrament; but this is not to be reputed to them, but rather to the enemy. Therefore care not for him; dispute not with thy thoughts, nor answer the doubts that thine enemy shall lay before thee, but believe the words of God, and believe His Saints and Prophets, and the wicked enemy shall anon flee away from thee.

It is ofttimes much profitable that the servant of God should feel and sustain such doubts; for commonly the enemy tempteth not unfaithful people and sinners, whom he has sure possession of, but he tempteth and vexeth in divers manners faithful and devout persons.

Go therefore with a pure and undoubted Faith, and with humble reverence proceed to this Sacrament. And whatsoever thou canst not understand, commit it faithfully to God, for God will not deceive thee, but he shall be deceived that trusteth overmuch to himself. God walketh with simple persons, He openeth Himself and sheweth Himself to meek persons. He giveth understanding to them who are poor in spirit, He openeth the wit to pure and clean minds, and hideth His grace from men curious and proud. Man's reason is feeble and weak, and anon may be deceived; but Faith is stable and true, and cannot be deceived.

Therefore all reason and all natural working must follow Faith without further reasoning; for Faith and Love surmount[1] in this most holy and most excellent Sacrament, and in secret manner work high above all reason.

The eternal God and the Lord of infinite power doth great things in heaven and on earth, that may not be searched, for if the works of God could be lightly understood by man's reason, they would not be so marvellous and so inestimable as they be.

[1] Maxime præcellunt.

Here endeth the Fourth Book of the Imitation of Christ, the which Fourth Book treateth most principally of the Blessed Sacrament of the Altar.

And in the latter ende, after the Fourth Booke, is
a short morall doctrine, which is called

The Spirituall Glasse
of the Soul

And it is right good and profitable to every
person ofte tymes to looke upon it

A Spiritual Glass

Read distinctly.

Pray devoutly.

Sigh deeply.

Suffer patiently.

Meek you lowly.

Give no sentence hastily.

Speak but rathe, and that truly.

Prevent your speech discreetly.

Do your deeds in charity.

Temptations resist strongly ; break his head shortly.[1]

Weep bitterly.

Have compassion tenderly.

Do good works busily.

Love perseverantly.

Love heartily.

Love faithfully.

Love God alonely.

And all others for Him charitably.

Love in adversity.

Love in prosperity.

Think always of love, for love is none other but God Himself.

Thus to love bringeth the lover to Love without end. *Amen.*

[1] *i.e.* quickly.

Appendix I

CONTAINING

Extracts from Original Texts

OF THE

COUNTESS OF RICHMOND AND DERBY, A.D. 1503

DR. WILLIAM ATKYNSON, A.D. 1504

AND

RICHARD WHYTFORD, A.D. 1585

Appendix I

Book One: Chapter One

TEXT OF DR. WM. ATKYN-
SON'S TRANSLATION,[1]
A.D. 1504.

WHO so foloweth me sayth Crist our sauyoure walketh nat in derkness. These be the wordes of Jhesu Crist whereby we be exorted to folowe his love & doctryne if we will be lyghtened & auoyde from all blyndnes of ignorance of mynde. Let our ful affeccion be to have our study & meditacion in ye doctryne and lyfe of Jhesu Crist whiche excelleth ye (doct)ryne of all sayntes. And who so may have ye iye of theyr soule sequestrate in worldly thynges in this scrypture of our lorde may fynde swete maña spirituel fode of the soule. But there be many oftymes herynge the worde of god that hath lytell swet-

TEXT OF RICHARD WHYT-
FORD'S TRANSLATION,
EDITION OF 1585.

HE that foloweth me (sayeth Christe our Saviour) walketh not in darknes, but he shall have the light of life. These be the words of our Lorde Jesus Christ, whereby we be admonished and warned, that we shall folowe his teachinges, and his maner of lyuing, if we will truely be illumined, & be deliuered from all blindnes of hearte. Let all the study of our heart be therefore from henceforth, to have our meditation wholly fixed in the lyfe, & in the holy teachinges of Jesus Christe. for his teachinges are of more vertue, & of more ghostlye strength, than are the teachinges of all Angels and Saintes. And he that

---

[1] For the text of this translation, and that of the Fourth Book by the Countess of Richmond, the editor is indebted to Mr. Henry Brighurst Wilson, of the British Museum.

nes or deuocyon therin for theyr inwarde affeccyon and desyres be rather of bodely thynges than of gostely. Therefore if we wyll have true & perfyte vnderstandinge of ye wordes of god we muste dylygently studye to confourme our lyfe to his preceptis.

thorough grace might have the inner eye of his soule opened into the soothfast beholdinge of the Gospels of Christe, should finde in thē manna, that is to say, spirituall foode of the soule: but it is often times seene, that some persons which ofte heare the Gospelles of Christ, have little sweetenes therein, and that is, for that they have not the spirite of Christe. Wherefore, if we will have the true understanding of Christes Gospels, we must study to conforme our life to his life as nigh as we can.

Book Three: Chapter Three
WHYTFORD'S TEXT OF 1585
A Prayer to obtepne the grace of deuotion

O Lord Jesu, thou art all my riches, and all that I have, I have it of thee. But what am I (Lorde) that I dare thus speake to thee, I am thy poorest servaunt, & a worme most abiect, more poore, and more dispisable than I can or dare say. Beholde, (Lorde) that I am nought, that I have nought, and of my selfe I am nought worth: thou art only good, righteous and holy, thou orderest all things, thou givest all things, & thou fulfillest all things with thy goodnes, leauing only the wretched sinner barrain and voyde of heavēly comfort.

Thomas à Kempis

Book Four: Chapter Eleven (*end*)

TEXT OF COUNTESS OF RICH-
MOND AND DERBY,
A.D. 1503.

O God ōipotent; thy grace
be unto us helpynge so that
we whyche have taken the
office of presthode may re-
uerently & deuoutly serue
the wyth all purite & gode
cōscience & if we may nat
lyue in so great innocēcy of
lyfe as we ought to do: gyve
vs grace at the leest that
we may wepe & sorowe the
euylles that we have com̄-
ytted and done: so that ī
spūal mekenes & purpose
of gode will we may from
hensforth strongly serue the
with feruent corage.

TEXT OF RICHARD
WHYTFORD,
A.D. 1585.

O God almightie, thy grace
be with us, and helpe us that
have receiued the office of
priesthood that we may
serue thee worthely and
deuoutly in all puritie, and
in a good conscience. And
though we maye not live in
so great innocēcie as we
ought to do, yet geve us
grace at the least, that we
maye weepe and sorowe the
euils that we have done, so
that in spirituall meeknes,
and in full purpose of a good
will we may serue thee
hereafter.   Amen.

Book Four: Chapter Seventeen

TEXT OF COUNTESS OF RICH-
MOND AND DERBY,
A.D. 1503.

O Lorde god ī souerayne
deuoōon brennynge loue,
and all faruent affeōon of
herte. I desyre as many

TEXT OF RICHARD
WHYTFORD,
A.D. 1585.

V[1] WITH high deuotiō and
burninge loue, and with
all feruour and affection of
the hart, I desire to receiue

---

[1] Ornamental capital V instead of W, which last letter is inserted
in the text in the usual small type of black letter

Appendix I

other holy & deuout p̄sones hath desyred to receyue. which hathe ben greatly pleasaūt vnto the holynes of their lyfe by greate deuocyon. O my god and eternall loue & my eternall felycite. I bye right great desire wysshe to receyue the as worthely and as reueretly as ever dyd any of thy holy seruānts.

thee Lord, as many Saintes and deuout persōs have desired thee in their communiō, & that most speciallie pleased thee in the holines of their life, & were in most burninge deuotion to thee. O my Lorde God, my loue eternall, all my goodnes and felicitie without endinge: I couet to receyue thee with as great desire, & as due reuerēce as any holie man euer did or might do.

Note

In a list of English Pilgrims who visited Rome, and were entertained at the Hospitale Anglorum, in the year 1504, we find the following entry. (*Collect. Topograph.*, vol. v. p. 64.)

Itm̄ D. Nicholaus Benynghm̄ Monach' ordiˢ S. Benedicti et Monast'ii Norwices'.

Itm̄ D. Willm̄' Attkynson p'sbit' Norwicēs.

Itm̄ D. Johannes Heddon p'bit' ejusdē Dioces.

Itm̄ D. Richard' Fox de Myddilsam ejusd Dioces.

Itm̄ D. Jhonnes Hayward de Hokold ejud. Dioces.

Venerunt om̄es isti 14 Februarii.

In all probability the first of the four Priests of the Diocese of Norwich mentioned above is the Dr. Wm. Atkynson whose version of the *De Imitatione Christi* has been compared above.

274

Appendix II
The Rules of a Christian Lyfe

MADE BY

John Picus the elder
Erle of Mirandula

AND FIRST TRANSLATED INTO ENGLISH

BY

Sir Thomas More

FOR HIS OWN SPIRITUAL GUIDANCE

IN THE MARRIED STATE

Appendix II

The Rules of a Christian Lyfe

FIRST, if to man or woman the way of virtue doth seem hard or painful, because we must needs fight against the flesh, the devil, and the world, let him or her call to remembrance that whatsoever life they will choose according to the world, many adversities and incommodities, much heaviness and labour are to be suffered.

2. Moreover, let them have in remembrance, that in wealth and worldly possessions is much and long contention, laborious also and unfruitful, wherein travail is the end of labour, and finally pain everlasting, if those things be not well ordered and charitably disposed.

3. Remember, also, that it is very foolishness to think to come unto heaven by any other mean than by the said battle, considering that our Head and Master Christ did not ascend unto heaven but by His Passion; and the servant ought not to be in better estate or condition than his master or sovereign.

4. Furthermore, consider that this battle ought not to be grudged at, but to be desired and wished for, although thereof no price or reward might ensue or happen, but only that thereby we might be conformed or joined to Christ our God and Master. Wherefore, as often as in resisting any temptation thou dost withstand any of thy senses or wits, think unto what part of Christ's Passion thou mayest apply thyself or make thyself like. As resisting gluttony, whiles thou dost punish thy taste or appetite, remember that Christ received in His drink vinegar[1]

[1] Orig. text, aysell

277

mixed with the gall of a beast, a drink most unsavoury and loathsome.

When thou withdrawest thy hand from unlawful taking or keeping of anything which liketh thy appetite, remember Christ's hands as they were fast nailed unto the tree of the cross. And resisting of pride, think on Him Who, being very God Almighty, for thy sake received the form of a subject, and humbled Himself unto the most vile and reproachful death of the cross. And when thou art tempted to wrath, remember that He, Who was God, and of all men the most just or righteous, when He beheld Himself mocked, spit on, scourged, and punished with all despites and rebukes, and set on the cross among arrant thieves as if He Himself were a false evil-doer, He notwithstanding shewed never token of indignation, or that He were grieved, but, suffering all things with wonderful patience, answered all men gently. In this wise, if thou wilt peruse all things one after another, thou mayest find that there is no passion or trouble that shall not make thee in some part conformable or like unto Christ.

5. Also, put not thy trust in man's help, but only in the virtue of Christ Jesu, Who sayed. *'Be of good cheer; I have overcome the world.'* [1] And in another place He saith : *'Now shall the prince of this world be cast out.'* [2] Wherefore let us trust, by His virtue alone, to vanquish the world and to subdue the devil. And therefore ought we to ask His help, by our own prayers, and by the prayers of His blessed Saints.

6. Remember, also, that as soon as thou hast vanquished one temptation, another is always to be looked for. The *'devil, as a roaring lion, walketh about, seeking whom he may devour.'* [3] Wherefore we ought to serve diligently, and

[1] John xvi. 33   [2] John xii 31.   [3] 1 Peter v. 8

be ever in fear, and to say with the Prophet. '*O my strength, haste thee to help me.*'[1]

7. Take heed, moreover, that not only thou be not vanquished of the devil that tempteth thee, but also that thou vanquish and overcome him. And that not only when thou dost not sin, but also when of that thing wherein he tempted thee, thou takest occasion to do good. As, if he offereth thee some good act to be done, to the intent that thereby thou mayest fall into vain-glory, forthwith thou thinking it not to be thy deed or work, but the benefit or reward of God, humble thou thyself, and judge thee to be unkind unto God in respect of His manifold benefits.

8. As often as thou dost fight, fight as in hope to vanquish, and to have at the last perpetual peace. For peradventure God shall give unto thee of His abundant grace, and the devil being confused of thy victory, shall return again no more. Yet when thou hast vanquished, bear thyself so as if thou shouldst fight again shortly. Thus always in battle thou must think on victory, and after victory thou must prepare thee to battle immediately again.

9. Although thou feelest thyself well-armed and ready, yet flee notwithstanding all occasions to sin. For, as the wise man saith: '*He that loveth danger shall perish therein.*'[2]

10. In all temptations resist the beginning, and beat the children of Babylon against the stone, which stone is Christ, and the children be evil thoughts and imaginations. For in long continuing of sin seldom worketh any medicine or remedy.

11. Remember that, although in the said conflict of temptation the battle seemeth to be very dangerous, yet consider how much sweeter it is to vanquish temptation

[1] Ps xxii 19   [2] Ecclus. iii 26

279

than to follow sin, whereto she inclineth thee, whereof the end is repentance. And herein many be foul-deceived, who compare not the sweetness of victory to the sweetness of sin, but only compare battle to pleasure. Notwithstanding a man or woman, who hath a thousand times known what it is to give place to temptation, should once assay what it is to vanquish temptation.

12. If thou be tempted, think thou not therefore that God hath forsaken thee, or that He setteth but little by thee, or that thou art not in the sight of God good or perfect; but remember that after Saint Paul had heard such secret mysteries as be not lawful for any man to speak or rehearse, he for all that suffered temptation of the flesh, wherewith God suffered him to be tempted, lest he should be assaulted with pride. Wherein a man ought to consider that Saint Paul, who was the pure vessel of election, and rapt into the third heaven, was notwithstanding in peril to be proud of his virtues, as he saith of himself. Wherefore above all temptations man or woman ought to arm the most strongly against the temptation to pride, since pride is the root of all mischief, against which the only remedy is to think always that God humbled Himself for us unto the cross. And moreover that death hath so humbled us, whether we will or no, that our bodies shall be the meat of worms loathsome and venomous.

CPSIA information can be obtained
at www.ICGtesting.com
Printed in the USA
LVHW050324140120
643547LV00014B/751/P